Beyond Behaviorism

Changing the Classroom Management Paradigm

Edited by H. Jerome Freiberg

Chapters by

Jere Brophy
Carolyn Evertson and Alene H. Harris
H. Jerome Freiberg
David W. Johnson and Roger T. Johnson
Barbara McEwan, Paul Gathercoal, and Virginia Nimmo
Roger Slee
Carol Weinstein

Allyn and Bacon

Boston • London • Toronto • Sydney • Tokyo • Singapore

Vice President, Social Sciences and Education: Sean W. Wakely
Series Editorial Assistant: Jill Jeffrey
Director of Education Programs: Ellen Mann Dolberg
Marketing Manager: Brad Parkins
Composition Buyer: Linda Cox
Manufacturing Buyer: Megan Cochran
Cover Administrator: Jenny Hart
Production Administrator: Rosalie Briand
Editorial-Production Service: Spectrum Publisher Services
Electronic Composition: Omegatype

Copyright © 1999 by Allyn and Bacon
A Division of Simon & Schuster, Inc.
160 Gould Street
Needham Heights, Massachusetts 02494

Library of Congress Cataloging-in-Publication Data

Beyond behaviorism : changing the classroom management paradigm /
    edited by H. Jerome Freiberg ; chapters by Jere Brophy ... [et al.].
        p.   cm.
    Includes bibliographical references and index.
    ISBN 0-205-28619-4 (cloth). — ISBN 0-205-28267-9 (pbk.)
    1. Classroom management.   2. Classroom management—Case studies.
3. School discipline.   4. Behavior modification.   I. Freiberg, H.
Jerome.   II. Brophy, Jere E.
LB3013.B42   1999
371.102'4—dc21   98-31691
                                                                      CIP

Printed in the United States of America

10   9   8   7   6   5   4   3   2   1   03   02   01   00   99

Contents

SECTION III   *The Evolution of Change   145*

Overview

Introduction

The evolution of *Beyond Behaviorism: Changing the Classroom Management Paradigm,* derived from the Classroom Management Special Interest Group (SIG) session at the American Educational Research Association (AERA). H. Jerome Freiberg was president of the Classroom Management Special Interest Group and had organized a session at the 1996 national meeting of AERA in San Francisco, California, along the title of this book. More than 300 people attended the session, and it became evident that the participants were looking for alternatives to the current paradigm of behaviorism so prevalent in the American classroom. A subsequent session the following year drew an equal number of interested participants. The authors in this book, who represent many of the leaders in the field of classroom management research and development, presented papers at these two AERA sessions on topics related to their chapters in *Beyond Behaviorism: Changing the Classroom Management Paradigm.*

The book is divided into three sections, with **Section I: Introduction; Section II: Best Practices & Promising Programs;** and **Section III: The Evolution of Change.** The book is designed to give the reader the philosophical underpinnings necessary to understand roots of behaviorism and why the change is needed. *Beyond Behaviorism* also provides four specific classroom management models and finally a context in which change needs to occur. It is our hope that you will leave this book wiser and richer for the effort.

There are three chapters in Section I: Chapter 1, "Beyond Behaviorism," by H. Jerome Freiberg; Chapter 2, "Theorizing Discipline—Practical Research Implications for Schools," by Roger Slee; and Chapter 3, "Perspectives of Classroom Management: Yesterday, Today, and Tomorrow," by Jere Brophy. These three chapters form the foundation of the book and are included to give you the larger picture of the what and why of changes in classroom management.

There are four chapters in **Section II: Best Practices & Promising Programs.** These four chapters in Section II illustrate specific classroom management programs and describe the ways in which changes can be made to move beyond behaviorism. The four models have as their central theme that the locus of control for classroom management and student discipline must include children and youth to a much greater degree if student self-discipline is to be achieved in the classroom. Chapter 4 is "Support for Managing Learning-Centered Classrooms: The Classroom Organization and Management Program (COMP)," by Carolyn M. Evertson and Alene H. Harris; Chapter 5, "Consistency Management and Cooperative Discipline: From Tourists to Citizens in the Classroom," is by H. Jerome Freiberg; Chapter 6 is "Application of Judicious Discipline: A Common Language for Classroom Management," by Barbara McEwan, Paul Gathercoal, and Virginia Nimmo; and Chapter 7 is titled "The Three Cs of School and Classroom Management," by David W. Johnson and Roger T. Johnson.

Section III, the final section of the book, includes two chapters that provide closure and look at the best practices for students and teachers and how individually and collectively we can move beyond behaviorism and create a model that is sustainable for children, youth, and teachers. Chapter 8 is titled "Reflections on Best Practices and Promising Programs: Beyond Assertive Classroom Discipline," by Carol Weinstein; and Chapter 9, the final chapter, is entitled "Sustaining the Paradigm," and is by H. Jerome Freiberg.

Chapter Previews

The following summarizes the nine chapters.

Chapter 1

Beyond Behaviorism. H. Jerome Freiberg, University of Houston

This chapter provides a history of behaviorism, an overview of the issues of classroom management, and what is meant by changing the classroom management paradigm. It discusses the differences between teacher-centered and person-centered classroom management. It presents a Three Dimensional Discipline and Instructional Continuum of instructional strategies and how they match with the role teachers and students play in creating an environment for teaching and learning. The first chapter should provide the opportunity for you to form a picture of why changes need to be made in the way students and teachers work with each other in the classroom. The ideas presented in this chapter give a rationale for why changes must be made in shifting the classroom management paradigm from one of student discipline as external control to one of student self-discipline.

Chapter 2

Theorizing Discipline—Practical Research Implications for Schools. Roger Slee, University of Western Australia

In this chapter, the author places his discussion of "discipline" within the political context of schooling, and discusses the international trend toward the politicizing of educational success–failure issues. In practical terms, this means high standardized test scores equate to successful schools. This leads to teachers seeking to teach in classes that are "teachable" without "unteachable students"—who must be removed elsewhere through suspension–exclusion—that is, special education classes, attention deficit hyperactivity disorder (ADHD), and special and referral units. In this environment, Slee examines and explores the application of discipline:

- Within a system not necessarily for the educational benefit of the students, but to remove them from the "normal teachable" classroom—a narrow understanding of discipline as external control—a behaviorist pedagogy is the result.
- Alternatively, Slee questions how democracy will form in the minds of youth when they rarely experience it in schools. Within a democratic society devoted towards creation of autonomous learners with a social conscience, discipline is an educational theory serving the needs of the learners, and incorporating many voices. The model has the capacity to be symbiotic to the pedagogical process. It pays attention to the social contexts of the learners. Slee concludes by providing evidence from two research studies that show that more careful defining of both discipline and disruption is necessary and a definition that takes into account both the complexity and specificity of the social and individual contexts for achieving student and teacher commitment to school and schooling.

The lesson to be learned from this section is the need for a strong and visible connection between curriculum aims, management methods, cultures, and contexts of the students in forming an educational theory of discipline in a democratic society by moving beyond the behaviorist paradigm.

Chapter 3

Perspectives of Classroom Management: Yesterday, Today, and Tomorrow. Jere Brophy, Michigan State University

Jere Brophy traces the evolution of research activity into classroom management styles and examines the relationship between management styles and approaches to instruction. Brophy begins with the Behaviorist approach to classroom control, indicating its applicability to a transmission model of knowledge in which the teacher is the primary source of information. He moves to Jacob Kounin's pioneering role in describing effective manager characteristics and the later replication, extension, and elaboration of research activities based on Kounin's work. This research focused on aspects of the social constructivist instructional model in which students need to explore, discover, and experience for themselves as part of the learning process. He concludes by setting out core principles that should guide the adoption and adaptation of management beliefs to achieve instructional aims that benefit the learner and teacher.

Throughout, Brophy stresses the primacy of achieving stated instructional aims and that management systems should be congruent with these aims.

Section II: Best Practices & Promising Programs takes theory to the next step to four models that have evidence that what they have developed works. Practices that have proved their value over time and promising programs implemented in classrooms from rural schools to the inner cities are presented. Each model has a different design and, in some instances, different outcomes, but each of the four models have the common thread that students should be a greater source of self-discipline.

Chapter 4

Support for Managing Learning-Centered Classrooms: The Classroom Organization and Management Program (COMP). Carolyn M. Evertson and Alene H. Harris, Peabody College, Vanderbilt University

Chapter 4 describes the philosophy, implementation process, and the research results of the Classroom Organization & Management Program (COMP) in operation. COMP guides teachers in developing a management framework that:

- Supports decisions about creating supportive learning environments
- Has students take responsibility for their own decisions, actions, and learning.

The focus of COMP is on problem prevention, integration of management and instruction, involving students in the entire process, and encouraging professional collaboration among teachers during program implementation. The process of implementation is through training workshops, classroom application, and collaborative reflection, with group processes used as much as possible. The training is module based. There are seven modules, each of which has built into it reflection time for teachers. At the end of the training modules, each participant must identify and write a specific strategy for use in the classroom and later professional discussion–reflection.

COMP has been tested in experimental studies using observation field studies, teacher self-reflection, and administrator reports on implementation results. Results have shown significant positive change in teacher and student behavior variables.

Chapter 5

*Consistency Management & Cooperative Discipline:
From Tourists to Citizens in the Classroom.
H. Jerome Freiberg, University of Houston*

Consistency Management & Cooperative Discipline (CMCD) is a comprehensive instructional discipline–management school reform model tailored to respond to individual campus needs that builds on shared responsibility for learning and classroom organization between teachers and students. Consistency Management combines instructional effectiveness through consistency in classroom organization with student self-discipline developed cooperatively. Major components of CMCD include Prevention, Caring, Cooperation, Organization, and Community.

The CMCD program works with geographic feeder systems of schools from prekindergarten through twelfth grade rather than individual classrooms or isolated schools. The CMCD program works with all faculty administration and support staff of the school—anyone who has contact with students. The CMCD program begins with the elementary schools during the first year and the secondary schools during the second year, and provides a minimum of three years of direct support to each participating school.

Research findings and reviews by external researchers show a strong statistically positive effect in the desirable outcomes of education—for example, greater achievement, attendance, classroom and school climate, and improved student discipline through reductions in discipline referrals to the office and reduced school violence. In its implementation, CMCD provides for roles for both the teacher and the student, thus creating environments that are not either totally teacher- or student-centered, but person-centered, in which both teachers and students benefit. It aims to teach students democratic practices and self-discipline by giving them a chance to act as committed citizens in the classroom, rather than as tourists passing through.

Professional development programs for teachers are timed to meet the needs of teachers and students. They are workshop-based and aimed at changing the discipline paradigm from control to cooperation.

Chapter 6

*Application of Judicious Discipline: A Common
Language for Classroom Management. Barbara McEwan,
Oregon State University; Paul Gathercoal, California
State Lutheran College; and Virginia Nimmo, Mankato
School District*

Chapter 6 presents a classroom management model—Judicious Discipline (JD)—that employs cognitive as opposed to behavioral management strategies. The authors describe the program principles, explain the operationalization in the classroom, and provide a synthesis of the research, assessing the positive effect of the program on student acquisition of attitudes and values consistent with the program intentions. The program is a comprehensive approach to democratic classroom management that provides educators with a foundation for teaching citizenship through classroom management decisions. It is based on the concept that it is an educator's professional responsibility to create an equitable environment that affords every student the opportunity to be successful. This is done through creating and using a common language based on the principles of human rights and responsibilities.

The authors' research—The Mankato, Minnesota Action Research Study—indicates the positive outcome for all students if consistent and deliberate instruction about the concepts of JD is provided. The results support the theory that a nonpunitive, citizenship approach to classroom–school management can facilitate the process of students becoming autonomous and responsible for their own actions. The program also postulates the need for organizational structures and schedules that allow for a collegial learning climate for teachers as well.

Chapter 7

The Three Cs of School and Classroom Management. David W. Johnson and Roger T. Johnson, University of Minnesota

According to the authors of Chapter 7, classroom management programs are instituted to deal with problems that cause disruptions and prevent learning from taking place. At one end of the management program continuum are programs based on behavioral theory, with external control of student behavior; at the other end are programs based on teaching self-regulation to the students. The Three Cs program is at the self-regulation end of the continuum.

The Three Cs are:

- Cooperative community: learning communities made up of all the stakeholders in positive interdependence on each other, working towards achieving mutual goals through cooperatively structured learning efforts.
- Constructive conflict resolution: if and when within a cooperatively structured environment conflicts arise, it is possible to solve them constructively. This is achieved through conflict resolution training for all members of the school community.
- Civic values: setting up cooperative communities and solving conflict constructively is only possible if the community shares common civic values. These values guide all decision making.

It is a classroom management program that involves all members of the school community—civic values "are the glue that holds the school together and defines how the members act towards each other."

Chapter 8

Reflections on Best Practices and Promising Programs: Beyond Assertive Classroom Discipline. Carol Simon Weinstein, Rutgers Graduate School of Education

In Chapter 8, the author critically examines the changes in classroom management since the 1970s popularity of the Canter "Assertive Discipline" precepts. Weinstein uses the changes in the language of Assertive Discipline since its inception in 1976 to the latest 1990s edition as a filter to evaluate the paradigm shift of classroom management practices proposed by the Three Cs, CMCD, COMP, and JD programs.

Where the Assertive Discipline paradigm's cognitive base emphasized the actions of the teachers to bring about desired changes, the new paradigm combines the cognitive and the affective bases. She traces the origins of this shift to Kounin's 1970s research into the relationship between teacher behavior and classroom management, resulting in the present programs that emphasize student needs and self-regulation opportunities. The new paradigm of classroom management must also, she stresses, lead to new thoughts on professional development requirements for teachers.

The reason for this paradigm shift, she comments, is to be found in the changed social and moral structures that impinge on the classroom. She concludes with a very strong caveat that to avoid becoming a "fad" or slipping into *laissez-faire* mode, self-regulation and caring should not mean abdication of responsibility by the teacher for what happens in the classroom.

Chapter 9

Sustaining the Paradigm. H. Jerome Freiberg, University of Houston

In the short term, it is easier to keep the status quo than to change. The history of reform in education has been more a pendulum than an upward spiral. The pendulum moves forward, then back to its original state. Whereas reform efforts in other professions—for example, medicine—have spiraled upward from primitive and ineffective to sophisticated and more effective, education seems to have followed a path that leads it back and forth rather than forward and upward.

Most past reform efforts have focused on changing the curriculum rather than the school or the classroom learning environment. The author maintains that both must occur simultaneously. Having a student-focused curriculum with a teacher-centered learning environment is counterproductive. Chapter 9 proposes a person-centered model of learning in which the needs of the teacher and the students are balanced. This enables changes in the classroom management paradigm to move beyond behaviorism, which mostly benefited the teacher, to incorporating the models described in the "Best Practices" section of the book.

Sustaining the paradigm provides three reasons for differences in why the changes could be maintained:

- Program development since the late 1950s has moved from theory building to application of management models in classrooms.
- Some of the models have been longitudinally researched for program effectiveness.
- Significant progress is being made toward development of an educational knowledge base that will support changes in the classroom management paradigm.

Sustaining the classroom management paradigm will not be easy, but it has a much higher chance to flourish, given other parallel changes in research and development and the need to respond and prepare youth for a changing world.

Acknowledgments

I am indebted to many people for their assistance in creating this book, including Ruth Silva for her able organization and proofing skills and Saundra McNeese for her administrative support.

This book would not be possible without the expertise, assistance, and support of the Allyn & Bacon editorial team: Nancy Forsyth, Editorial Director, for her encouragement to publish with Allyn & Bacon; Sean Wakely, current Editor-in-Chief for Education, for his sustaining support through two book projects; Jill Jeffrey, Editorial Assistant for Education, and Kelly Ricci for her timely editing.

This book is dedicated to the memory of Mrs. Armandina Farias, Principal of Jefferson Elementary School in Houston, Texas. She epitomized the caring educator, whose philosophy in practice mirrored the values expressed in this book.

References

Thomas, Lewis. (1979). *The medusa and the snail: more notes of a biology watcher.* New York: Viking Press.

Section I

Introduction

You may find the roots of behaviorism and its counterpart in education, behavior modification, to have germinated from some unusual sources—a salivating dog, a ringing bell, and, more recently, some chocolate covered candies. (H. Jerome Freiberg, p. 5)

Quick fix behavior management programs have short lives because they seek to bleach complexity from the colorful life of classrooms…. Simply put, my argument revolves around a belief that discipline is much more than the imposition of someone else's order. (Roger Slee, p. 38)

Also, any management system is incomplete if it relies on teachers to regulate student behavior but lacks a concomitant emphasis on developing student self-control. (Jere Brophy, p. 46)

1

Beyond Behaviorism

H. JEROME FREIBERG
University of Houston

Force and Fear Have No Place in Education
*….To me the worst thing seems to be for a school principally
to work with methods of fear, force and artificial authority.*
—ALBERT EINSTEIN

Introduction

Teaching is filled with words that reflect the range of possibilities and dualities of learning in the classroom: organization, disorganization; discipline, chaos; reward, punishment; indifference, caring; control, lack of control; respect, disrespect; defiance, compliance; and citizen, tourist. The words represent the dilemma and questions faced by all teachers, whether a thirty-year veteran or first-year neophyte—How do I create a positive environment for teaching and learning? What is the best way to gain control in the classroom? Which approach is best for me and the students? The answers to these questions form the basis of this book: *Beyond Behaviorism: Changing the Classroom Management Paradigm.*

The issues of classroom management, discipline and order have been an overriding concern for educators and citizens in America since the late 1800s.

"Discipline" in a school is a natural, to-be-expected, and ever-present problem. The discipline of a school may, and should, under ordinary conditions, improve from year to year; but as the work of the school means

3

continuous *process of admitting to the school register hundreds of pupils in their infancy and discharging them in their youth, just so will the problem of discipline be a* continuous *one. (p. 243)*

This quote is from Arthur Perry, a principal of School #85 in Brooklyn, New York, and was written in 1908.

Modern times see a continuation of public and educator concerns for safe and orderly learning environments (Rogers & Freiberg, 1994). Since the late 1960s, public opinion polls, conducted by Gallup and reported by *Phi Delta Kappan,* show that in 1971, discipline ranked third in leading school concerns. In 1982, a lack of discipline ranked first in public concerns. In 1992, it ranked third behind school finance and drugs, and for 1994 and 1998, "lack of discipline" in schools has been joined by "fighting/violence/gangs" as the number one concern of public opinion (Elam, Rose, & Gallup, 1994). The trend continues and there seems to be little hope that these concerns will change any time soon as we enter and begin a new millennium.

Although public concerns about classroom management, school discipline, and school violence have remained high, studies of school discipline and classroom management programs have diminished since the 1980s (Doyle, 1990). One noted exception is the work of Emmer and Aussiker (1990), who reviewed research findings of four widely used school and classroom management programs, including Teacher Effectiveness Training (TET), Reality Therapy, Assertive Discipline, and Adlerian/ Dreikurs' approaches. The review was designed to determine which programs had the greatest impact on student behavior or attitudes and perceptions about school. Emmer and Aussiker indicate the four programs were useful only in supplementing a more comprehensive approach to classroom management. They also indicate teacher attention to planning, preparation, and development of systematic activities at the beginning of the year, and "...conducting activities in efficient, interesting, and comprehensible ways throughout the year" (p. 22) would be more effective in preventing "...minor problems from becoming major ones." They found the four models lacked the more comprehensive elements of prevention and relied more on disciplining students. Emmer and Aussiker also criticized the lack of documented links between program mediation and outcome measures in the 42 studies they reported.

The National Institute of Education (NIE) 1978 report to Congress, "Violent Schools—Safe Schools: The Safe School Study Report to Congress," reported that public fears concerning lack of discipline and violence in schools are well founded. These fears are especially appropriate in the middle grades where, according to Lipsitz (1984) and Freiberg, Stein, and Parker (1995), schools appear to have the greatest difficulty becoming disciplined communities. In the Freiberg et al. (1995) study of a middle school located just beyond the city limits, a total of 388 of 1283 students in the school were referred to the office in the month of October. However, referrals for both one-time and repeated actions totaled 894 referrals for the month of October.

Management policies and practices have a significant influence on the learning outcomes of students. There is accumulating evidence from meta-analyses (a summary of the findings of multiple research studies) of variables that influence school learning and that **classroom management** has one of the greatest influences on school learning. A meta-analysis of learning factors conducted by Wang, Haertel, and Walberg (1993) identified classroom management as being first in a list of five important factors that influence school learning. Weade and Evertson (1988) and Evertson and Weade (1989) found similar connections between classroom management and student achievement using microanalyses of class lessons in language arts, reading, and mathematics. The need for order in schools and its implications for teacher education and student learning have been documented consistently in the research literature (see, e.g., Pittman, 1985; Doyle, 1986; Emmer, 1987; Rosenholtz, 1989; and Carter, 1990).

What has not been explored is the relationship between particular types of management approaches and the long-term influence beyond the initial year of implementation on student learning and well-being. The adage, "We teach the way we have been taught," is a truism unless we experience other ways.

The most common approach to classroom management in most schools is some form of behavior modification. Rules, consequences, and rewards seem to be the mainstay of most teacher repertoires for student discipline. What is the source of this approach? How useful is it in an era of active learning curriculum and an emphasis on higher level thinking skills? You may find the roots of behaviorism and its counterpart in education, behavior modification, to have germinated from some unusual sources—a salivating dog, a ringing bell, and chocolate covered candies.

Behaviorism and Behavior Modification

The movie projector clanked along as the 16-mm film was shown on a six-foot-wide screen standing near the front of the college classroom. The year was 1970 and the film was about classroom management. The narrator described a new method for teachers to motivate students and get them to behave. The movie showed a fifth-grade teacher reach into her pocket as she walked between the rows of students completing worksheets at their desks. She deposited candies at the corner of the students' desks. A student quickly looked up at the teacher, smiled and grabbed the candies and gobbled them down. This scene was repeated throughout the film. The narrator explained that the teacher was demonstrating "operant conditioning," which was part of a new approach to classroom management called "behavior modification."

The 16-mm film was an example of one of three types of behaviorist learning theories—Operant Conditioning, developed by Thorndike in 1919 and expanded by B. F. Skinner in 1938. Classical Conditioning (Pavlov) and social learning (Bandura) form the other two theories, known as **Behaviorism.** Figure 1-1 shows the roots of behaviorism from the time of Aristotle to the present. In Aristotle's essay entitled *Memory,* he spoke of "associations," in which we relate similar events or mental pictures to each other. For example, a sword and combat would be associated with each other. Other philosophers and researchers, particularly psychologists, tried to observe

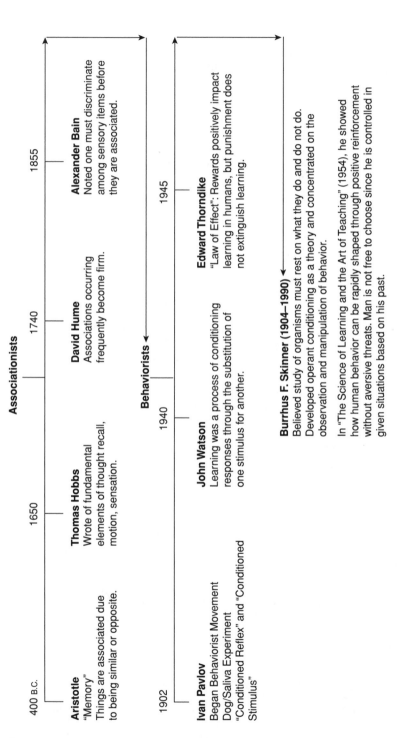

Associationists

400 B.C.   1650   1740   1855

Aristotle
"Memory"
Things are associated due to being similar or opposite.

Thomas Hobbs
Wrote of fundamental elements of thought recall, motion, sensation.

David Hume
Associations occurring frequently become firm.

Alexander Bain
Noted one must discriminate among sensory items before they are associated.

Behaviorists

1902   1940   1945

Ivan Pavlov
Began Behaviorist Movement
Dog/Saliva Experiment
"Conditioned Reflex" and "Conditioned Stimulus"

John Watson
Learning was a process of conditioning responses through the substitution of one stimulus for another.

Edward Thorndike
"Law of Effect": Rewards positively impact learning in humans, but punishment does not extinguish learning.

Burrhus F. Skinner (1904–1990)
Believed study of organisms must rest on what they do and do not do. Developed operant conditioning as a theory and concentrated on the observation and manipulation of behavior.

In "The Science of Learning and the Art of Teaching" (1954), he showed how human behavior can be rapidly shaped through positive reinforcement without aversive threats. Man is not free to choose since he is controlled in given situations based on his past.

FIGURE 1-1 Behaviorism Timeline. (Figure prepared by Lawrence Kohn, 1998.)

humankind and to develop theories and models to explain, predict, and, at times, change or modify human behavior. Prior to Skinner's work, a Russian scientist, Ivan Pavlov, who won the Nobel Prize in 1904 for his research in digestion, completed a series of experiments with dogs and their physiological responses to food, which led to a new theory of psychology for humans. **Classical Conditioning** is a theory derived by Pavlov who measured a dog's reactions to receiving food by the level of salivation. Dogs repeatedly salivated when presented with food, which was an unconditional (natural) response to the food. Pavlov sounded a bell each time the dog was presented with food and after a period of time, the dog would salivate with only the sound of the bell. The bell became a "conditioned" (unnatural-external) response. Pavlov understood that the bell reinforced the salivating response. When the food was withdrawn, the reinforcement was not provided, the dog's response would begin to disappear or become "extinguished." These experiments with animals led to further work on conditioning animal behavior and subsequently that of people to achieve certain responses.

Operant Conditioning, described by B. F. Skinner, is the reinforcing of behavior and its relationship to specific consequences. In the case of the film, the students completing worksheets quietly at their desks followed by a positive or pleasurable consequence (the giving of candies by the teacher) will more likely engage in the quiet worksheet behavior more frequently.

Conditioning is a term developed by B. F. Skinner to explain his observations of so-called contingencies of reinforcement under which learning takes place (Skinner, 1968). A "contingency" is an action—in this case, by the teacher—that is repeated to reinforce and shape a particular response by the student. However, in order to produce "efficient mathematical behavior" in students "something in the order of 25,000 contingencies" would be needed (Smith, 1996). Psychological lessons learned in the laboratory with rats and pigeons may not transfer well to the human condition or to the classroom. The teacher is not the only "reinforcing agent" in the classroom and Skinner realized that the classroom was a very complex place with only one teacher and many students.

> *Skinner argues that in the typical classroom situation, a teacher cannot supply reinforcement quickly enough or often enough. Accordingly, he recommends the use of teaching machines, which he maintains possess certain advantages (Biehler & Snowman, 1982; p. 153).*

Although behaviorist learning theory was being replaced in the 1970s with other learning theories that focused much less on controlling the individual and finding out why people behave and think in certain ways (e.g., see Cognitive Learning Theory), Behaviorism was finding a new home in the American classroom.

Since the early 1960s, many teachers have relied on behavior modification programs derived from operant conditioning to shape student behavior in the classroom. Commercial programs like Assertive Discipline (Canter, 1976) have systematized the principles of Operant Conditioning and behavior modification. Assertive Discipline asks teachers to use rules consequences (punishment) and rewards to control student behaviors. Operant Conditioning focuses on reinforcement of desired behaviors and extinction of undesirable behaviors. However, it may be easily abused or misused. One management program tells its readers to write the names of the students on the board as a warning when they misbehave. Ironically, this may produce the opposite results by "reinforcing" inappropriate student behavior. The students with names on the board may be soliciting attention and their name on the board reinforces this attention-getting behavior. Research on behaviorism and its application to schools through behavior modification has significant limitations.

Emmer and Aussiker (1987) reported in their review of classroom management studies that in one study (Bauer, 1982), "student attitude toward school was *lower* in the AD (Assertive Discipline) school" (p. 37). Discipline management programs that are highly behavioristic and focus on controlling student behaviors through punishment can diminish student attitudes toward school rather than build student self-discipline.

In a multiyear multischool study on managing adolescent behavior, Gottfredson, Gottfredson, and Hybl (1993) concluded that, "Targeted programs that use behavioral and cognitive approaches that teach students how to manage their own behavior appear highly effective for replacing inappropriate behavior with appropriate" (p. 210). The research literature on classroom management tends to show that programs that emphasize student self-discipline over external controlling factors including an emphasis on punitive responses to misbehaviors show greater promise in improving achievement and learning environments. Hoy, Tarter, and Kottkamp (1991) conclude in their study on organizational climate of schools that, "Long-term improvements in academic achievement...are more likely linked to a school with strong academic emphasis within the context of a healthy and open environment" (p. 151). Classroom management systems that ignore the potential of students and teachers as cooperative participants in creating healthy and open learning environments are missing opportunities to improve education in the inner cities. A study by Parker (1994) with 608 middle-school students in 47 classrooms: 18 using Assertive Discipline (Canter & Canter, 1992) and 29 non-Assertive Discipline found that students in non-Assertive Discipline classrooms perceived their learning environments to be significantly higher in involvement, affiliation, teacher support, and innovation than students in Assertive Discipline classrooms. Parker also found that less emphasis was placed on teacher control in non-Assertive Discipline classrooms. How does one resolve disruptive behavior when it becomes a barrier to teaching and learning?

Disruptive behaviors may be symptomatic of other classroom, school, and societal problems that influence teachers and students. Brantlinger (1993) found family income levels of students resulted in differential treatments by teachers and administrators when students from high- and low-income families broke class and school rules. The differential treatments resulted in more aggressive behaviors from students from lower income families. Moreover, Kounin (1970) demonstrated the relationship between teachers' management and instructional actions and students' behaviors. Classroom management practices were found to interfere with policy initiatives. McCaslin and Good (1992) determined that educational reform efforts are stifled by "classroom management policies that encourage, if not demand simple obedience" (p. 4).

Behaviorism assumes a paradigm or perspective in which the control is with the teacher and compliance is with the students. This leaves little flexibility for student opportunity to learn the skills necessary to function in a world where they need to work independently, making decisions and preventing and solving problems while maintaining strong interpersonal networks with others. There is another downside to behaviorism—the reliance on punishment for reducing undesirable behaviors. Given the legal and ethical implications, most school settings limit the use of punishment to actions that may have little lasting effect. Biehler and Snowman (1990) found significant limitations to its use.

Limits to Punishment

1. Mild punishment (the kind usually applied) does not eliminate undesirable behaviors permanently. At best, it suppresses them temporarily.

2. Punished behaviors may continue to occur when the punisher is not present.

3. Punishment may actually increase the strength of undesirable behavior. Many teachers assume that a public reprimand is aversive. But for some students, teacher and peer attention, regardless of the form it takes, is a positive reinforcer and thus serves to increase behaviors the teacher seeks to eliminate.

4. Punishment may produce undesirable emotional side effects. Just as a shocked rat comes to fear a Skinner box, punished children perceive the teacher and the school as objects to fear and avoid. The result is truancy, tardiness, and high levels of anxiety, all of which impair ability to learn.

5. Punishers model a type of behavior (physical aggression) that they do not want students to exhibit.

6. To be effective, punishment must often be severe and must occur immediately after an undesirable response. Legal and ethical restrictions do not allow severe punishment. (Biehler & Snowman, 1990; p. 344).

If behaviorism has outlived its usefulness in the classroom, what remains to replace it? Change requires more than substituting one set of classroom management strategies for another. Change necessitates a new way of seeing the world of classrooms and schools and a new way to see the role of the learner (both our students and ourselves). It requires a change in our paradigm from one in which "I am in control" to one in which "We are in control." The movement from "I" to "We" requires some interval to occur and the opportunity for educators to see other examples and models of ways to create learning environments that are responsive to the needs of both teachers and students.

The Paradigm

The term *paradigm* comes from the Greek, meaning "para," beside; and "deigma," example. In modern times, the term has been defined as a *model, theory, perspective, or reference point.* It relates to how we view the world from our continuous life experiences. If our eyes are lenses that mechanically enable us to see, then our *paradigm* interrupts what we see—it is a psychological process. The printing press and the computer are two technological tools that have changed how we see and interpret the events of the world.

Look at the picture in Figure 1-2. What do you see? Some of you will see a young woman in her 20s, whereas others will see a much older woman, perhaps in her 70s or 80s. How can this be? How can the same picture elicit dramatically different responses? I was introduced to this picture in my first college psychology class. The professor placed the picture on the overhead projector and we were asked to raise our hands if we saw the young woman. About half the class raised their hands. I was among that group. I was amazed that the person sitting next to me was unable to see the young woman.

I pointed to the picture and said, "Can't you see her?" He responded, "Sure, but she's really old." I took my finger and traced the outline of the young woman. Her face is looking away from us. Her noise is a slight profile with an eyelash above her nose. Even then he could not see her. He was equally amused that I could not see the old woman. He also traced the outline of the old woman. Her chin and mouth are at the bottom with the black coat on either side of her chin and mouth. Her eye is the ear of the young woman in my interpretation of the picture. I suddenly saw "his" picture of the old woman as well as "my" picture of the young woman.

FIGURE 1-2   Two women.

The picture of the two women and the vase with the two faces (see Fig. 1-3) reflect our views of the world. Those views or perceptions are driven by collective experiences. In the early 1960s, IQ tests had the word "cow" and three animal pictures: a cow, a dog, and a mouse. The students needed to match the correct picture with the word. Many inner-city students selected the dog because they had never seen a cow. We each come to the table of schooling with different life and educational experiences.

Changing Paradigms

The history of humankind is a series of paradigm shifts. In 1492, most of the known world thought the earth was flat and any ship that sailed over the horizon would fall off the earth. As I leave for my next trip abroad I am pleased that the "flat world" paradigm in no longer the prevailing paradigm. Galileo had to recant to the church his paradigm that the earth revolved around the sun to keep his life. However, we know today that he was correct. Paradigms change as new knowledge enters the social consciousnesses. The list of paradigm changes is endless. If you were born after 1970 then you are born into the world of computers. If you were born before 1945, then most of the technology and medicine we take as a given (public television, computers, video and computer software, CDs, cellular phones, antibiotics, and transplants) did not exist. This same perspective is true in the classroom. If, for example, we view children as basically good, then how we view their actions will be intrepreted from this perspective. We will allow them responsibility, provide

FIGURE 1-3   Two faces.

opportunities for self-discipline to occur and allow students to learn from their mistakes. Mistakes provide opportunities for learning and reflect growth rather than defects in the individual. The classroom management system used reflects a basic respect for the learner. If we view children as basically destructive, then our system of classroom management will reflect this perspective. We will create a system where our actions tell students they are not trusted to be alone, they need other students to monitor their actions and report to the teacher misbehavior. Rewards are needed to get students to comply without question to what may be unpleasant or mundane. Compliance rather than initiative is valued, and students as passive learners are valued over students as active learners. "Well, if you take away what I know—behaviorism and how I was educated—then what will be in its place? Good question—one usually asked by teachers, parents, administrators, and future teachers who have not experienced or seen alternatives to managing classrooms in other ways. Behaviorism requires external controls over the learner. The goal of most teachers is to encourage self-discipline, but the path many teachers take to this goal is misdirected. Too often the cooperation teachers seek from students in order to teach does not allow for real engagement in the learning process. Teachers find themselves imposing their requirements for order without relating these to the student requirements to learn. Discipline becomes mandated rather than developed. The differences between building the conditions for self-discipline cooperatively and imposing discipline is the balance point between the traditional classroom and a person-centered classroom. In a person-centered learning environment there is discipline—*self-discipline*. In the broader context of life, self-discipline is knowledge about one's self and the actions needed to grow and develop as a person. A person-centered classroom has a balance between the needs and responsibilities of teacher and students. In a teacher-centered classroom, the teacher "is in control" most if not all of the time. Students sit and wait for instructions and rarely take initiative. Teachers have control but they report being exhausted at the end of the day. "I never realized how much energy and effort it takes to control the students. I leave school each day with a headache" reported a fourth grade inner-city teacher who is known for her classroom discipline. However, in a student-centered classroom, the total focus is on the student. In many instances the teacher is unable to maintain the level of responsiveness and becomes overwhelmed with interacting one to one with thirty students every forty-five minutes in secondary schools, or all day with elementary age students. A seventh-grade algebra teacher stated, "I was burning out from trying to do everything for the students. I realized it was not possible to do it alone. I began to enlist the students to form study groups, peer tutoring, and cooperative lessons. I had a more facilitative role—it had some balance." A person-centered classroom has balance between the needs of the learner and that of the teacher. There are ample opportunities for students and teachers to work together and build an orderly environment for learning that encourages student self-discipline.

Person-Centered Classroom Management[1]

Person-centered classroom management provides the balance needed to advance active participation in cooperative learning environments. Classroom management has several meanings, including *caring, guidance,* and *cooperation,* as well as administration and oversight. Person-centered classrooms emphasize caring, guidance, cooperation, and the building of self-discipline. Person-centered classrooms encourage students to think for themselves and to help each other. Table 1-1 provides a reference point for the differences between teacher- and person-centered classrooms. Perhaps most importantly, in person-centered classrooms both the teacher and students benefit. Most classrooms are not totally on one side or the other, but there are clear differences between the two approaches.

Self-discipline is built over time and encompasses multiple sources of experiences. It requires a learning environment that nurtures opportunities to learn from one's own experiences, including mistakes, and to reflect on these experiences. Yet, what does self-discipline look like and how is it achieved? Perhaps the best way to describe it is through a brief vignette based on school and classroom examples.

TABLE 1-1   Discipline Compared in Teacher-Centered and Person-Centered Classrooms

Teacher-Centered Classrooms	Person-Centered Classrooms
Teacher is the sole leader.	Leadership is shared.
Management is a form of oversight.	Management is a form of guidance.
Teacher takes responsibility for all the paperwork and organization.	Students are facilitators for the operations of the classroom.
Discipline comes from the teacher.	Discipline comes from the self.
A few students are the teacher's helpers.	All students have the opportunity to become an integral part of the management of the classroom.
Teacher makes the rules and posts them for the students.	Rules are developed by the teacher and students in the form of a classroom constitution or compact.
Consequences are fixed for all students.	Consequences reflect individual differences.
Rewards are mostly extrinsic.	Rewards are mostly intrinsic.
Students are allowed limited responsibilities.	Students share in classroom responsibilities.
Few members of the community enter the classroom.	Partnerships are formed with business and community groups to enrich and broaden the learning opportunities for students.

Rogers, Carl/Freiberg, H. Jerome, FREEDOM TO LEARN, Third Edition, 1994, p. 240. Reprinted by permission of Prentice Hall, Upper Saddle River, New Jersey.

Self-Directed Active Learning

The students in this active second-grade classroom are working at four learning centers scattered around the room. At the writing center, four students are writing about butterflies they had seen earlier in the day. There are only places at the writing center for four students at one time and two additional students want to enter the center. The two students look at a board near the writing center and see all the "tickets" have been taken. They also see that two students have another ten minutes on the timer left at the center. They write their names on the small notebook size chalkboard that holds a place for them, and they go to Reading Bookshelf and begin reading books they had started the previous day.

Choice, managing one's time, setting goals and priorities, and a sense of order, are part of self-discipline. Very young children can flourish in environments that have freedom of choice and yet have structure. The limitations of space, materials, and time require some form of organization. Too often, the organization benefits a few students or the teacher, rarely both. In this example, the organization avoided unnecessary conflict between the students at the writing center and allowed them to make good choices. Students in this class had freedom to move about, to make decisions regarding what they would learn for parts of the day, and to interact with each other. The teacher provided the structure, but students had freedom of choice within that structure.

Myths about Discipline

There are many myths and misconceptions about discipline and they become very evident in the language used to describe philosophies about schools, children, and discipline.

"Spare the rod, spoil the child." "This is going to hurt me more than it hurts you." "No pain, no gain." "A quiet school is a good school." "She has good discipline." "They are out of control." Words that come to mind: compliance, control, punishment, respect, authority, and strict—all words typically used to describe discipline. There is another language that also describes discipline. "They really care about kids here." "I love this school." "We don't need to fight here." "Let's try it together." "I did it myself—it feels great!" "I needed the time to focus." Words that come to mind: sharing, helping, giving, cooperating, focusing, caring, respecting, and freeing; all words used to describe person-centered discipline. Language connotes attitudes, values, and one's philosophy.

We come to the heart of the matter—our philosophy about the nature of teaching, learning, and students determines the type of instruction and discipline included in schools and classrooms. We tend to teach the way we have been taught, thus ignoring changing conditions. We also tend to see discipline the way we have experienced it ourselves. These two experiences influence the course of events we take in facilitating a learning climate in classrooms and schools. New experiences in person-centered environments, both for teachers and students, change the way instruction and discipline influence student learning.

Is There Order In Person-Centered Classrooms?

Civilization may be viewed as humankind's need to create some order out of life's random events. In prehistoric times, hunting and gathering was less predictable than growing one's own food. As basic needs for food, shelter, and safety were met, people had more time for other more developed activities of art, music, writing and later reading. Day-to-day survival was a lesser concern, so people could turn their attention to the world around them. The concept of "school" evolved from this process of seeking to know more about one's world.

The word *school* can be traced to the Greek word "scholé," meaning *leisure.* During the time of the Greeks, a small class of people, through the labors of others, had the time or leisure to learn. In the same context, a *teacher* was a *guide* for the learner. The term *discipline* used as a noun comes from Latin meaning *teaching and learning.* As in life, the classroom needs a certain level of order for all people to learn. Some of the day-to-day events could be established so time is spent learning rather than organizing.

As humans, we have different levels of needs. These needs include the desire to belong; to be safe; to have food, clothing, and shelter; to be seen as a person, and for some form of stability and order to carry on our daily lives. These human needs do not change when the child enters the classroom. The interconnectedness of the modern world places a greater demand on us for predictable and consistent ways of doing things. Some events in our lives, called *routines* are established to minimize the need to make a new decision for each and every event. Classroom management allows for the routines to have a place in the classroom to enable other more important events to occur. Classroom Management is much like the foundation of a house—you seldom see it, but without a solid and well-constructed foundation, all else becomes shaky.

I recall reading an interview with Albert Einstein about his wardrobe. Einstein was known for having multiple sweaters, all the same color. When asked why he always wore the same clothes every day, he responded that deciding what to wear each day was not a decision he cared to make. He clearly had more important issues on his mind. Life's little distractions can become barriers to greater accomplishments. It is perhaps ironic that classroom management consumes so much of our time in schools when it should be at best a minor distraction. Perhaps we are looking at the result of the problem rather than the root causes. The way we look at the problems often determines its solutions.

Three-Dimensional Discipline and Learning

Discipline and instruction are not separate streams. They are interactive and have three dimensions: a **teacher-dimension** (knowledge and structure derived from one source), a **cooperative-dimension** (students and teacher working together), and a **self-dimension** (the individual learning independently from multiple sources).

The *teacher-dimension* of discipline is the one with which we are most familiar. Discipline and knowledge are derived from the teacher; the student's role is to be the listener and defer to the teacher. Some of the conflict, particularly at the secondary level, is a function of student resistance to teacher demands that minimize consideration for the learner.

The *cooperative-dimension* is a halfway point between external and self-directed discipline and instruction. Teachers and students work together at a rate based on the comfort levels of all persons in the classroom—in moving away from teacher as a source of knowledge and discipline. Working in cooperative groups builds an experiential dimension necessary in many classrooms to guide teachers and students along a continuum toward self-directed discipline and learning.

The *self-dimension* of discipline indicates teacher and students are working at a very different plane of interaction. Students conduct their own research projects, work on learning contracts, organize their own time, and report what they have learned in using a variety of media (from print and pictures to video). Schools that students love provided opportunities for self-directed learning and self-discipline. For example, at Clement McDonough City Magnet in Lowell, Massachusetts (grades K–8), self-discipline comes in the form of a student court system, in which students create the laws and judge cases without a discipline system being imposed from the outside.

Students and teachers in schools throughout the United States (See *Freedom to Learn,* Rogers & Freiberg, 1994, for examples) give students multiple opportunities for self-discipline through town meetings, projects, community service, and solving complex problems each day.

The Three-Dimensional Discipline and Instruction continuum presented in Figure 1-4 shows the interrelationship between instruction and discipline. Some teachers who have been teacher-focused for most of their lives would have difficulty moving from one end of the Three-Dimensional Discipline and Instruction continuum to the other in a short period of time. Lasting change takes time and support from all sectors of the community. The continuum represents an extended repertoire of options for every teacher. With support and opportunities to experience other approaches to discipline and instruction, movement over time from one end of the continuum to the other is both a realistic and an attainable goal. That movement is flexible rather than fixed. Teachers and students will have multiple opportunities to develop self-discipline. The teacher's role on the continuum changes along with the type of instruction. Likewise, the student's role changes at the same time. Teacher and student become *colearners.* Students, ultimately, are able to learn from the entire continuum. Teachers and students who have experienced this type of learning become part of a

FIGURE 1-4   Three-dimensional Discipline and Learning.

Teacher-focused	
Teacher dimension: Teacher directs and externally controls student behavior. **Teacher role is directive.** *Cooperative dimension:* Teacher/students cooperate in designing a positive classroom learning environment. **Teacher role is semidirective/ facilitative.** *Self-dimension:* Students are internally self-disciplined and need minimal direct adult supervision. **Teacher role is nondirective/ facilitative.**	• Lecture • Questioning • Drill and practice • Demonstration • Discussion • Cooperative groups • Guided discovery • Contracts • Role-play • Projects • Inquiry • Self-assessment
Student-focused	

Rogers, Carl/Freiberg, H. Jerome, FREEDOM TO LEARN, Third Edition, 1994, p. 243. Reprinted by permission of Prentice Hall, Upper Saddle River, New Jersey.

community of creative and self-disciplined learners who are able to do more than acquire information—they are able to invent for the future and improve on the past. The chapters in this book are designed to help you make this transition.

Conclusions

This book is about change: changing the way we think about our role as teachers and the way we think about learners. Finding ways to create healthy learning environments to teach and learn is the goal of every teacher. We challenge you to open your mind to proven approaches to classroom management that go beyond compliance and move into the realm of student involvement and self-discipline. **Section I: Introduction,** to *Beyond Behaviorism: Changing the Classroom Management Paradigm,* sets the context for changing the classroom management paradigm. The first chapter— which you are currently reading, and the following two chapters (Chapter 2, "Theorizing Discipline—Practical Research Implications for Schools," by Roger Slee, and Chapter 3, "Perspectives of Classroom Management: Yesterday, Today, and Tommorrow," by Jere Brophy) provide a background to behaviorism and the politics and history of classroom management. **Section II: Best Practices & Promising Programs** provides four models to assist you in making a change in or in enhancing a perspective you currently hold. Each of the chapters were reviewed in the introduction of this book. Chapter 4 is "Support for Managing Learning-Centered Classrooms: The Classroom Organization and Management Program (COMP)," by Carolyn M. Evertson and Alene H. Harris. Chapter 5 is entitled "Consistency Management & Cooperative Discipline: From Tourists to Citizens in the Classroom," by H. Jerome Freiberg. Chapter 6 is "Application of Judicious Discipline: A Common Language for Classroom Management," by Barbara McEwan, Paul Gathercoal, and Virginia Nimmo. Chapter 7, "The Three Cs of School and Classroom Management," is by David W. Johnson and Roger T. Johnson, and have been tested over time. In many instances, there is extensive research to support their findings of effectiveness. Each model looks at a different aspect of classroom management, and two of the models, Consistency Management & Cooperative Discipline (Chapter 5) and The Three Cs of School and Classroom Management (Chapter 7), can be viewed as whole-school reform models in addition to their classroom focus.

Section III: The Evolution of Change is the conclusion of the book and provides a summary of the four models presented in Section II (Chapter 8, "Reflections on Best Practices and Promising Programs: Beyond Assertive Classroom Discipline" by Carol Weinstein, and Chapter 9, "Sustaining the Paradigm" by H. Jerome Freiberg). The final chapter looks at how the new paradigm can be sustained.

The new millennium ushers in more than a changing of the clocks on timepieces and computers; it requires greater independent thinking from our learners and future citizens. It also requires an interdependence with each other. Technology is truly beginning to transform the way we work and learn. This new era requires a change in the way classrooms are managed and organized and how the social fabric is woven. A model of classroom management that requires compliance only is doomed to failure.

We trust you will find this book, *Beyond Behaviorism: Changing the Classroom Management Paradigm,* a stimulating context for your own ideas about classroom management. The book provides a concrete as well as philosophical basis for change. We also hope that the book provides a better understanding of the options available as you reflect and respond to changing paradigms that require a much greater interactive learning environment in which teachers and students work and learn.

Note

1. Adapted from *Freedom to Learn,* 3rd Edition, Carl Rogers and H. Jerome Freiberg, 1994, Allyn & Bacon.

References

Bauer, R. L. (1982). A quasi-experimental study of the effects of "Assertive Discipline" (Doctoral dissertation, Miami University, 1982). *Dissertation Abstracts International, 43,* 25A.

Biehler, R., & Snowman, J. (1982). *Psychology applied to teaching* (4th ed.). Boston: Houghton Mifflin Co.

Biehler R., & Snowman, J. (1990). *Psychology applied to teaching* (6th ed.). Boston: Houghton Mifflin Co.

Brantlinger, E. (1993). Adolescent's interpretation of social class influences on schooling. *Journal of Classroom Interaction, 28*(1), 1–12.

Canter, L., (1976). *Assertive Discipline: A take-charge approach for today's educator.* Santa Monica, CA: Canter & Associates.

Canter, L., & Canter, M. (1992). *Assertive Discipline: A take-charge approach for today's educator.* Santa Monica, CA: Canter & Associates.

Carter, K. (1990). Teacher's knowledge and learning to teach. In W. R. Houston (Ed.), *Handbook of research on teacher education* (pp. 291–310). New York: Macmillan.

Cohen, E. (1994). *Designing groupwork: Strategies for the heterogeneous classroom* (2nd ed.). New York: Teachers College Press.

Doyle, W. (1986). Classroom organization and management. In M. C. Wittrock (Ed.), *Handbook of research on teaching* (3rd ed., pp. 329–431). New York: Macmillan.

Doyle, W. (1990, April). *Whatever happened to all the research in classroom management?* Paper presented at the national meeting of the American Educational Research Association, Boston.

Einstein, A. (1950). *Force and Fear Have No Place in Education. On Education in My Later Years* (Essay, pp. 33–35). New York: Philosophical Library Inc.

Elam, S., Rose, L., & Gallup, A. (1994). Phi Delta Kappa 26th Annual Poll Gallop/PDK Poll of the Public's Attitude Towards Public Schools. *Phi Delta Kappan, 76*(1), 41–56.

Emmer, E. (1987). Classroom management and discipline. In Richardson-Koehler (Ed.), *Educators' handbook: A research perspective* (pp. 233–258). New York: Longman.

Emmer, E., & Aussiker, A. (1987, April). *School and classroom discipline programs: How well do they work?* Paper presented at the national meeting of the American Educational Research Association, Washington, D.C.

Emmer, E., & Aussiker, A. (1990). *School and classroom discipline programs: How well do they work?* In O. C. Moles (Ed.), *Student discipline strategies: Research and practice.* Albany, NY: State University of New York Press.

Evertson, C. M., & Weade, G. (1989). Classroom management and student achievement: Stability and variability in two junior high English classrooms. *Elementary School Journal, 89*(3), 379–393.

Freiberg, H. J. (1996). From tourists to citizens in the classroom. *Educational Leadership, 51*(1), 32–37.

Freiberg, H. J., Stein, T. A., & Huang, S. (1995). The effects of a classroom management intervention on student achievement in inner-city elementary schools. *Education Research and Evaluation, 1*(1), 36–66.

Freiberg, H. J., Stein, T. A., & Parker, G. (1995). An examination of discipline referrals in an urban middle school. *Education and Urban Society, 27*(4), 421–440.

Gottfredson, D., Gottfredson, G. D., & Hybl, L. G. (1993). Managing adolescent behavior: A multi-year, multischool study. *American Educational Research Journal, 30*(1), 179–215.

Hoy, W., Tarter, J. C., & Kottkamp, B. (1991). Open school/healthy schools: Measuring organizational climate. London: Sage.

Kounin, J. S. (1970). *Discipline and group management in classrooms.* New York: Holt, Reinhart and Winston.

Lipsitz, J. (1984). *Discipline and Young Adolescents. Issues in Middle-Grade Education. Research & Resources* (Report No. UD 023 987). Center for Early Adolescence, North Carolina University, Chapel Hill. (ERIC Document Reproduction Service No. ED 252 613.)

McCaslin, M., & Good, T. L. (1992). Complaint cognition: The misalliance of management and instructional goals in current educational reform. *Educational Researcher, 40,* 3.

Parker, G. (1994). *Gifted students perceptions of environments in Assertive Discipline and non-assertive discipline classrooms.* Unpublished dissertation, University of Houston, Houston, TX.

Perry, A. (1908). *The management of a city school.* New York: Macmillan.

Pittman, S. I. (1985). A cognitive ethnography and quantification of a first-grade teachers' selection routines for classroom management. *Elementary School Journal, 85,* 541–557.

Rogers, C., & Freiberg, H. J. (1994). *Freedom to learn* (3rd ed.). Ohio: Merrill.

Rosenholtz, S. J. (1989). *Teacher's workplace: The social organization of schools.* New York: Longman.

Skinner, B. F. (1968). *The technology of teaching.* New York: Appleton-Century Crofts Division of Meredith Corporation.

Smith, L. D., & Woodard, W. P. (1996). *B. F. Skinner and behaviorism in American culture.* London: Associated University Press.

Wang, M. C., Haertel, G. D., & Walberg, H. J. (1993). Toward a knowledge base for school learning. *Review of Educational Research, 63,* 249–294.

Weade, G., & Evertson, C. M. (1988). The construction of lessons in effective and less effective classrooms. *Teaching and Teacher Education, 4*(3), 1–18.

2

Theorizing Discipline— Practical Research Implications for Schools

ROGER SLEE
Graduate School of Education
University of Western Australia

The Political Economy of Classroom Management

In the British election campaign in 1995, education assumed center stage in the theater of electoral politics. Each of the three major parties attempted to convince the electorate that, under their stewardship, educational standards, by which they meant academic outcomes (test scores), would improve significantly. To secure this target, the political focus was narrowed to raising levels of literacy and numeracy, giving schools greater authority over the selection of students, intensifying the level of surveillance and inspection, and restoring discipline in the classroom and school playground. It is not surprising that school discipline and student behavior were singled out for particular political attention because the issue had occupied considerable media space. The preoccupation with behavior in schools continues in the wake of the Labour "landslide" as one of the litmus tests for "New Labour's" success in education policy.

In November 1996, Secretary of State for Education Gillian Shephard fell out with the prime minister when, in a radio interview, she expressed her preference for the reintroduction of corporal punishment. This interview occurred following the closure of the Ridings School in Yorkshire because the school was deemed to be "failing" by the Ofsted [Office for Standards in Education] inspectors. The General Secretary of the National Association of Schoolmasters and Union of Women Teachers argued that, before the school could turn itself around, at least eighty students needed to be expelled. In Nottingham, teachers withdrew their labor to have a student, who was named and nationally demonized, permanently excluded from their school. Gillian Shephard's call for the reintroduction of corporal punishment coincided with the media highlighting the serious escalation in the number of permanent exclusions (expulsions) of students from British schools. What is particularly significant about this controversy is the racial character of the exclusions (Gardiner, 1996; Parsons, 1996; Gillborn, 1997). Permanent exclusions have tripled in the United Kingdom during the early 1990s, and the figure for black Caribbean young people is almost six times the rate of exclusions for whites (Gillborn & Gipps, 1996:52). 1996 was also etched into the discipline debate as the year of the killing of a South London head-teacher, Phillip Lawrence, as he stepped in to protect a student from a "gang" outside the school gates at the end of a school day.

Consistent with media interest and political debate, teachers' calls for behavior management programs are increasing. Subscriptions to in-service education programs that deal with student behavior have risen. For example, I have received advertising concerning a series of seminars to be conducted by the "North American behavior management expert," Lee Canter, who is well-known in academic circles (Canter & Canter, 1976) and has established an offshore cell of his American behavior management parent company in Western Australia. Britain is now playing host to another of his offshore ventures. The Australian behavior management entrepreneur Bill Rogers is also involved in the rapidly growing market in the United Kingdom (1990). Besides the call for more off-site Pupil Referral Units, classroom management kits, and training videos, the United Kingdom is now moving, although more cautiously than was the case in either the United States or Australia, into the early stages of an attention deficit hyperactivity disorder (ADHD) epidemic. Classroom management and the student control industry is robust and thriving.

There has also been an international convergence of the politicization of student behavior as illustrated in this example of an Australian variation on the themes observed in the United Kingdom. Toward the end of 1995, a group of senior high school students were on a school camp on a small island off the coast of Queensland in Australia. In a set of events that reads like William Golding's novel, *Lord of the Flies,* the students entered into a frenzied slaughter of a colony of nesting sea birds. Even more frenzied was the political and media scrutiny that greeted the students and their teachers on returning to the mainland.

Media reportage was widespread and intense, spreading from the original incident to a general moral panic about the decline in standards of behavior in Australia's youth and the alleged death of family values. The incident coincided with a state election. Law and order was resurrected by the conservative opposition to embarrass the Labor government. Students in Queensland, according to the media, were out of control. The government, its eye trained nervously on the fickle electorate, sought to reassert itself as a no-nonsense administration tough on disruptive student behavior.

Reprisals were exacted swiftly and severely on the aberrant students. The offending students were tried before a tribunal convened to adjudicate their contravention of the provisions of the Wildlife Act. They were found guilty and ordered to undertake supervised community service work as restitution. This legally constituted body provided a forum for natural justice in which rights to representation were protected.

Due process was, however, an early casualty to the politics of behavior in schools. Public debate was encouraged about whether the students had been dealt with severely enough, about whether they had learned their lesson, and about whether the community's appetite for revenge had been satiated. A ceremony of public shaming followed that far exceeded the recommendations of criminologist John Braithwaite's (1989) program of "integrative shaming" for juvenile offenders. The school principal, together with younger students from the same school, disowned the students on national television. The opposition depicted the outcome as evidence of the soft liberalism of the government. The minister for education responded by announcing that these students would now be subjected to an education department inquiry. The ringleaders were excluded from school during their preparations for their final examinations and were presented with the option of attending adult evening school classes on the other side of town. In a departure from legal precedent, the students were tried and punished twice.

I do not defend the actions of the students. Clearly they had transgressed the bounds of acceptable behavior and were responsible for an ecological crime. These students were in need of an environmental education. Schools provide the ideal forum for such instruction. However, the permanent exclusion of the students from school at this juncture of their academic careers had devastating implications for their educational and social outcomes, thereby intensifying their hostility toward school and society. The potential for future cost to the state as a result of their disaffection is significant. We can choose to invest in education, which bridges the present with the future, or we can invest in the criminal justice, welfare, or health systems to make up for failings in educational opportunities.

This incident produced collateral damage. At the time, I had been engaged by the Queensland Education Department to advise on rewriting its discipline policies and strategies. Pursuant to the goal of more disciplined schooling, I placed greater emphasis on looking at relationships between school processes and outcomes than upon the end-stage sanctions. This was lost on a government that, following the "mutton bird incident," wanted to reassure the community that:

- schools and teachers were not going to tolerate disruptive students
- suspensions would be more frequent and longer
- teachers would be instructed in behavior management skills
- more counselors would be deployed in schools

- additional behavior units would be established for excluded students
- greater resources would be provided for the "adopt-a-cop" scheme (the placement of a policeman in the school).

The political parties debated whether it should be "three strikes and they're out" or "one strike and they're out." The most troubling aspect of this political debate was that the government was moved by populist calls for more punitive approaches to student disruption. Politicians and educators alike collapsed into the reductionist trap of seeking quick fixes for complex social and educational problems.

It has become increasingly evident that school discipline and behavior management represents an area of considerable contest and struggle in educational policy making. I argue that educational researchers, therefore, have a greater burden of responsibility to engage in more rigorous theorizing as a first step toward more useful research. Research and literature in the field of school discipline are often reductionist. This discussion offers clear distinctions between *discipline* as a discourse of management and control (e.g., Canter & Canter, 1976; Glasser, 1986) and educational theories of school discipline and student behavior (Wilson, 1973; Smith, 1985; Crittenden, 1991; Slee, 1995). By exploring and contrasting the epistemological foundations for classroom management with an educational theory of discipline, there is considerable room for a greater range of interventions that frees us from both neo-Skinnerian behavioral straitjackets and from what Basil Bernstein (1996:11) has referred to as "spurious biology" or "sets of biological metaphors" that proceed from an acceptance that disruption in schools represents a problem of dysfunctional individual pathologies.

What's in a Word? Theorizing Discipline

Discipline or Control?

Educational terminology simultaneously reveals and conceals meaning (Skrtic, 1991:124). Rorty (1989:77) refers to "local final vocabularies" that are deployed to reduce complexity and dissuade their authors and readers from pursuing precise definition. Roland Barthes (1972) earlier described this as the "discourse of concealment." This applies to discussions about school discipline primarily because of a frequent failure to establish conceptual distinctions between *discipline* and *control*. The result of this failure is theoretical flabbiness; that is, conceptual slippage and reductionism (Slee, 1988). In its most frequent usage, discipline becomes a synonym for control or punishment.

This reductionist tendency was identified by Berger (1979), who advised caution when approaching the "mindless technology" of classroom management techniques. For Berger, the technology of behavior management paid too little attention to issues of context. Rich (1979:25) swam against the tide in accusing Glasser of "glibly" underscoring the complexity of school life. Simplification and reduction have been endemic to behaviorist models of classroom management. The language used by Charles is indicative of the conceptual slippage from *discipline* as an educational process to the pragmatics of *behavioral control.* "Teachers' attempts to prevent, suppress, control and redirect those behaviors make up the essence of class control, or as it is commonly called, classroom discipline" (Charles, 1981:4).

School discipline and classroom management literature has been dominated by different genres within educational psychology. The principal influences have been Skinner's (1968, 1972) "science of behavior," Adler's (1930) work on the underlying meanings of behavior, and Carl Roger's (1969) humanist psychology. These intellectual traditions have proved convenient to the task of governance in schools. Education departments and schools throughout Australia and the United Kingdom tend to draw from this tradition, with an undisguised preference for the more overt control orientations of the neo-Skinnerian work, recognized as providing the rationale and the machinery for student compliance as a precondition for learning. Bagley's (1914:6) somewhat Kantian expression of the project is clear "...subservience of the individual will to the will of the teacher." For liberal educational thinkers such as Hirst and Peters (1970), Wilson (1971), or Smith (1985), the behaviorist character of classroom management is in opposition to the educational aspirations of teachers and schools. Crittenden presses for a philosophical approach to safeguard the educational aims and values of the school from the myopia of behavioral pragmatism.

> *A philosophical approach to classroom discipline, in its turn, cannot be indifferent to specific tactics and how effectively they work. However, its attention is focused primarily on underlying values that practices of classroom discipline explicitly or implicitly reflect...the major philosophical questions to be asked about styles of discipline are how they relate to educational values (and the distinctive educational role of the school) and to moral values (Crittenden, 1991:67).*

An educational theory of discipline should demonstrate consistency between the goals of the curriculum, preferred pedagogies, and the processes of school governance (Knight, 1988). Attention should be paid to the cognitive development and the social contexts of the learner (Vygotsky, 1962, 1978). If discipline is reduced to a euphemism for behavior modification, the educational value of the disciplinary regimen is compromised. The application of exclusively extrinsic methodologies obstructs the considered development of individual and group behavior in favor of submission and subversion.

There is nothing new in these observations. Locke had *Some Thoughts Concerning Education* in 1693. He reflected on the capacity of the tutor "...to create a disliking to that which it is his [sic] business to create a liking to..." through the application of control mechanisms. Dewey (1916) expanded on this theme by reflecting on the capacity of the teacher's control measures to drive aberrant behavior underground, thereby ensuring that things appeal to students "on the side of trickery and evasion." For Dewey, the capacity for discipline to be symbiotic to the pedagogical process is its true measure of success:

> *A person who is trained to consider his actions, to undertake them deliberately, is in so far forth disciplined. Add to this ability a power to endure in an intelligently chosen course in face of distraction, confusion, and difficulty, and you have the essence of discipline.... Discipline is positive. To cow the spirit, to subdue inclination, to compel obedience, to mortify the flesh, to make a subordinate perform an uncongenial task—these things are not disciplinary according to the development of power to recognize what one is about and to persistence in accomplishment (Dewey, 1916:129).*

Simply put, educational connection becomes a cornerstone for discipline in schools. **Connection between the learner, what they are doing, how they are doing it, and where it is leading them is fundamental to the development of an educational orderliness (Slee, 1995:28).** Pursuing such theoretical clarity is immensely practical for teachers in classrooms because it invites them to draw on their repertoires of professional knowledge and skills. Mr. and Ms. Chips do not have to make way for a classroom Dirty Harry. Teaching and learning can now be put at the center of the frame when focusing on the problem of discipline in schools.

The connection between the learner, the curriculum, and how it is delivered pushes educational researchers to reconsider the cultural and social backgrounds, experiences, and interests of students and to question the relevance and utility of the curriculum on offer. Stephen Ball (1994) depicts the National Curriculum in the United Kingdom as a restorationist "curriculum of the dead" that fails to engage students other than the preferred students. Accordingly, teachers are pressed to impose greater external control to compensate for the incapacity of the curriculum. In crude terms, we are simply asking too much of classroom management if we expect it to shield ineffective schooling or solve structural economic and social problems. If pedagogy and curriculum fail to encourage learning rather than reaffirm failure, we amplify disaffection and disruption. If students believe that schooling is leading them nowhere and that they have nothing to lose by being disruptive, we have very serious problems that challenge even the most assertive of behavioral management programs. Teachers are cast as Sisyphus straining against the eternal rock of student disruption.[1] My fear is that in the United Kingdom, and increasingly in a conservative-led Australia, the emphasis on narrowing the curriculum and restoring whole class instruction and rote learning places greater numbers of students at immediate risk of failure and increases the potential for trouble in schools.

---

[1] In Greek mythology, Sisyphus was a king of Corinth. His punishment in Hades was to push a large heavy rock uphill that rolled down again as soon as he reached the top. Sisyphus is a metaphor for futility.

Discipline and Democracy—the Problem of Authority

Let us acknowledge the conceptual difficulty surrounding the representation of authority in schools. This is not an academic indulgence. Our choices have practical implications for the level of engagement of the citizenry in the community (Hirschi, 1969). This can be pursued by posing a series of questions:

- Do we seek the restoration (or endurance) of authoritarian organizational and educational cultures?
- Do we prefer to educate teachers to be authoritative or authoritarian?
- What is the relationship between the democratic process and the exercise of authority?

The first point to make is based on educational principle. Authoritarianism articulates with behaviorist pedagogy, placing the learner in a state of passivity in the learning exchange (Friere, 1972). To argue for the importance of problem solving, inquiry-based education is in tension with authoritarianism. The sequential development of the autonomous learner and, in turn, the learning society (Ransom, 1994) invites a democratic education. There exists a strong intellectual tradition (Spencer, 1910; Dewey, 1916; Friere, 1972; Pearl, 1988) that suggests that education for civil society demands a "democratic apprenticeship" (Knight, 1985) in schools. In his treatise on *The Atrocity of Education*, Art Pearl (1972:147) is persuasive:

> To become expert in democratic citizenship the student must observe leadership that is consistent with democratic principles. Only when seen in action does all of the training the student receives come together. Only then is it real. Cynicism is bred when a student sees a teacher preach one thing while he practices something distinctly different.
>
> Democratic principles are confusing. A great many sins are committed in the name of democracy. As with nothing else, democracy has become a game of the name *[my emphasis]*. Educators who prate about it really do not know whereof they speak. And whatever they mean by democracy does not conform to any acceptable standard.

Pearl (1988:225) later set out the requirements of a democratic education, which can be summarized as follows:

- Equal preparation for debate of critical social issues
- Equal opportunity to participate in meaningful decision making
- Universal rights of expression and due process
- Encouragement of all to succeed

Democratic education is not *laissez faire!* Cumbersome in its observance of conventions, it is respectful of rights and demands responsibility. The teacher does not abdicate authority, but models responsible authority. Spencer (1910) made this observation in his reflections on the regenerative power of the excesses of the exercise of authority in British schools and government.

> *Instead of being an aid to human progress which all culture should be, the culture of our public schools, by accustoming our boys to a despotic form of government and an intercourse regulated by brute force, tends to fit them for a lower state of society than that which exists. And chiefly recruited as our legislature is from among those who are brought up at such schools, this barbarizing influence becomes a hindrance to national progress (p. 134).*

Given that schools lay the foundations for the future, we need to carefully consider the influence that different forms of school governance will have on shaping successive adult behavior.

Notwithstanding the growing body of research that suggests that democratic student participation in school governance and curriculum decision making increases student attachment and corresponds with diminishing levels of disruption (Holdsworth 1988; Knight, 1988; Warner, 1992), researchers in Melbourne, Australia, reveal the paradox that primary schools embrace more democratic processes than do secondary schools (Knight & Lewis, 1993). As students become older, and potentially more dangerous, we grasp at authoritarianism in schools. These are not "docile bodies" (Foucault, 1979). Less responsibility is afforded to the student for informed choice. Rule is by ultimatum. The behavior management gurus are commissioned and quick fixes are purchased by managers of stretched educational budgets.

Political Economy II: Governmentality and the Quest for Control

Failure and the Intensification and Expansion of Control

Schools have always produced failure and disaffection. Hitherto, the unskilled labor market and the segregated system of special education colluded with a narrow curriculum and restricted pedagogy to conceal the failure of schools. Failure was not a problem for schools. The underachiever, the slow child, and even the disruptive student had somewhere else to go. There was a place for them on the factory assembly line, on the shop floor, in the mill, down the mine, on the farm, or in the building industry. Transition into the paid labor market offered young people a currency with which to negotiate an independent adult life. The collapse of the unskilled youth labor market (Polk & Tait, 1990; Freeland, 1992) has exposed the absence of a link between schools and a meaningful future for an increasing number of students. Responses to the collapse in the unskilled labor market revolve around keeping students at schools longer (Marginson, 1993; Slee, 1995) and expanding the special education provision (Tomlinson, 1996). Stuck in school longer, more students appear to be underachieving and more are labeled disruptive. Students, however, remain at school not because they are excited by learning or because they see school as the bridge to a successful future, but because there is nowhere else to go. The extension of student dependency coincides with a world that screams at them to consume, to purchase, and to attach designer labels to their identity. This extended period of "youthdom" represents a confluence of tensions and uneasy transitions (Hargreaves, Earl, & Ryan, 1996). All of this makes for a powerful cocktail of discontent in our schools.

The implications of the pressure for selection and the publication of school results in the United Kingdom complicates this picture. Not only are students selected for successful academic trajectories, but we also publicly assign a growing residue of "undesirable students" (Gewirtz, Ball, & Bowe, 1995) to failure. Students in this second category are moved into a second tier of educational provision such as the merged nonselective Local Educational Authority schools; for example the aforementioned Ridings School, or the growing number of Pupil Referral Units (PRU) that had previously been called Behavior Units. Gewirtz, Ball, and Bowe's (1995) continuing research on choice and markets in education in the United Kingdom demonstrates how choice has proved a "...major factor in maintaining and reinforcing class divisions and inequalities":

> Well resourced choosers now have free reign to guarantee and reproduce, as best they can, their existing cultural, social and economic advantages in the new complex and blurred hierarchy of schools. Class selection is revalorized by the market (p. 23).

The schools that attempt to develop inclusive programs and cultures for all comers fall victim to the vicissitudes of the market. Choice is illusory as schools imitate each other in the scramble up and down the league tables. League tables or the ranking of schools according to the success of their students in the General Certificate for Secondary Education (GCSE) examinations are published by the media. This directly influences schools' success or otherwise in attracting new enrollments. This process is not benign. Social selection is crude and transparent. Gillborn (1997) and Gillborn and Gipps (1996) demonstrate the vulnerability of ethnic minorities in the United Kingdom. African Caribbean boys are most at risk of academic underachievement and exclusion from school. The Department for Education (DFE, 1992) reported that African Caribbean pupils were disproportionately overrepresented in the data on permanent exclusion from school (8.1% of the total number of exclusions, compared with their making up only 2% of the total number of students). Students with what are loosely referred to as "special educational needs" are also a liability for the upwardly mobile school (Slee, 1993; Gewirtz, Ball, & Bowe, 1995).

More Pervasive Patterns of Behavioral Control

It is apparent that structural economic change accompanied by changing community and student expectations corresponds with changing patterns of control and surveillance in schools. Foucault (1979) depicts the "spectacle of the scaffold," emanating from secret judicial processes that were "the privilege of the prosecution" alone, as meticulously choreographed affairs not simply interested in state retribution, but in the ritualized regulation of the innocent. The turning of the "disciplinary gaze" from the liturgies of punishment of the body to the control of the mind became the project of establishing new forms of governmentality—for normalizing and regulating the citizenry. Rose (1985, 1989, 1996) takes up this theme to suggest the normalizing aim of the "psy sciences" in calibrating and mapping the population was to render it governable.

> *...government is dependent upon knowledge. On the one hand, to govern a population one needs to isolate it as a sector of reality, to identify certain characteristics and processes proper to it, to make its features notable, speakable, writable, to account for them according to certain explanatory schemes. Government thus depends upon the production, circulation, organisation, and authorization of truths that incarnate what is to be governed, which make it thinkable, calculable, and practicable (p. 6).*

The deviant is not scrutinized for crude punishment. She or he is pathologized. "Scholastic identities" (Ball, 1990) are produced to distinguish between who comes into the normal clientele of the classroom teacher and who is to be administered through an expanding raft of special educational categories and provisions (Tomlinson, 1982; Lewis, 1993). Restricting our disciplinary gaze to aberrant individuals simultaneously deflects from other contributing factors. The individual or decontextualized group focus of classroom management techniques is convenient to the normalizing mission of schools. Perhaps this provides another theoretical entry for researching the emergence and contagion of ADHD?

The relatively recent Australian and American epidemics of ADHD (Kingston, 1995; Lacey, 1996) provides a useful platform for examining the changing patterns of control in schools through the enlistment of the machinery or panopticon of "special educational needs." Serfontein (1990:19) describes this *Hidden Handicap* for us:

> *In other words these children have difficulty in focusing and sustaining their attention long enough to initiate and complete any set task. They tend to be easily distracted from the task at hand by other stimuli, such as noise or movement. Significant disturbances in concentration may lead to daydreaming and "switching off."*

A biological disorder, ADHD is allegedly caused by an imbalance or deficiency of one or more neurotransmitters in the brain. Diagnosis is made by a physician or psychologist matching a child's reported behavior against a checklist from the American Psychiatric Association *Diagnostic and Statistical Manual of Mental Disorders* (1987). In Sydney, Australia, the Serfontein Clinic enlists the highly contentious neurometrics diagnostic tool. In both tests, the diagnoses are random and normative in their disregard for contextualized episodes.

> *Attention deficit disorder is not a disease, it's just part of the spectrum of children's behavior. The issue is to find the line where abnormality stops and normality begins…and the line moves according to who's drawing it (Swan, 1995).*

Movement of the line of child normality is reflected in the geographical variance in diagnostic behavior in Australia. For 1 in every 1000 students in the State of Victoria, there are 10 in every 1000 students in New South Wales and Western Australia (Swan, 1995).

Treatment typically takes the form of chemical intervention. Amphetamines are administered, the most popular of which is Ritalin. Although it is a stimulant, it acts on the central nervous system to sedate the child. Govoni and Hayes (1988:778–779) draw our attention to the side effects of the drug for a small number of users that include nausea and giddiness, growth repression, impeded cardiovascular function, and the development of twitches and tics. To my knowledge the treatment is experimental in that no long-term tests have been undertaken using placebos. Swan (1995) cites estimates that some 2.5 million children in the United States are using Ritalin.

ADHD is a beguiling syndrome and a powerful agent for a self-regulating population. It provides teachers and parents a much more respectable explanation for their children's errant behavior. The child is no longer bad—he or she is pathologically deficient. Neither parenting nor teaching is called to account. Moreover, Ritalin promises relief and possibly a cure. The pervasiveness of this disciplinary technique is most apparent in the rapid formation and spread of self-help groups in which parents offer up their children for diagnosis and treatment. Schools are finding that those children who do not lapse into a teaching-induced sedation may now be quieted by other means. The purpose of this discussion is neither to prove nor to disprove the clinical veracity of the condition. The concern is for caution so that we do not witness what C. Wright Mills (1959) referred to as the reconstruction of profound social and educational issues as the personal troubles of individual students.

The deployment of special educational categories to deal with disruptive behavior in schools is not restricted to ADHD. In Australia there is an escalating demand for integration or inclusive education resources to be allocated to the constellation of emotionally/socially disordered and disturbed children (Slee, 1996). Classroom management and student control is assuming new forms to contain the rise in disruption. In other words, schools enlist psychologists and special educators to formally diagnose difficult students so that they can be removed from the classroom because of their newfound special educational needs.

The More Traditional Technology of Control

Notwithstanding the British Secretary of State for Education's attempt in 1996 to resurrect corporal punishment, I resist the opportunity for extended debate, preferring to leave the final word to Richard Chiswell's proclamation in 1669:

But when our sufferings are of that nature as makes our schools to be not merely houses of correction, but of prostitution, in this vile way of castigation in use, wherein our secret parts, which are by nature shameful, and not be uncovered, must be the anvil exposed to the immodest eyes, and the filthy blows of the smiter... (Chiswell, **A Modest Remonstrance of that Intolerable Grievance Our Youth Lie Under, in the Accustomed Severities of the School Discipline of this Nation,** *in Freeman, 1966:217*).

Before considering schools that have responded in educational ways to disruptive behavior, let us consider two traditional forms of control and the lessons we may draw from existing research.

Suspension and Exclusion

Suspensions and exclusion[2] have escalated dramatically, both in Australia (Slee, 1995; Edwards, 1996) and in the United Kingdom (Slee, 1995; Gardiner, 1996; Parsons, 1996). Existing research into suspension contends that unless applied as a measure of last resort, it is a largely ineffective measure (Dettman, 1972). Frequent usage leads to greater levels of disruption (Neilsen, 1979; Wu et al., 1982; Hyde & Robson, 1984). As a reformative measure, suspension is found wanting according to data on rates of recidivism (Edwards, 1996). Once suspended, students are more likely to be suspended again. Add to this Edwards' finding that students who are suspended more than once are unlikely to complete their schooling, and there exists cause to reconsider our use of this measure. The need for reconsideration also should be driven by recognition of the racial and cultural character of suspensions (Vickers, 1993; Gillborn, 1996).

Following Hyde and Robson's (1984) work in Western Australia, my own research in Victoria and Queensland heightened my interest in the varying rates of suspensions between schools, problems in advocacy for suspended students, and the stages of a child's schooling when suspension occurs (Slee, 1995). A major change in the volume and rate of suspension across Victoria, Australia, public schools occurred when students transferred from primary to secondary schools. What this suggested was that although individual children might have idiosyncratic problems and issues that generate trouble, a constant across the student body was the institutional change. Consequently, a more practical line of inquiry was found in analyzing the educational, organizational, and experiential differences between primary and secondary schooling. In doing so, possibilities emerged for ameliorating stressors within the curriculum, teaching and learning methods, and organizational process and culture.

---

[2]In the United Kingdom and Australia, *suspension* refers to the legal suspension of a student for a specified time (even if it is specified as an "indefinite suspension" in some parts of Australia to trigger an official investigation into the case). *Exclusions* in the United Kingdom and Australia, also referred to as "expulsions" in Australia, represent a more serious measure to move the pupil out of the school.

Research into varying rates of suspension among schools has long suggested the potential value in attempting to determine the "school effect" in suspensions and exclusions (Reynolds, 1976, 1985; Grunsell, 1980; Wu et al., 1980; Galloway, 1982; Lawrence et al., 1984). It is important to quickly add that this is not a *de facto* endorsement of the problematic school effectiveness research and recipe approach to school improvement (Hamilton, 1996; Ball, 1995). This chapter does not join the very political enterprise of blaming schools and teachers for the very complex problem of disruption. The lesson from the research is that ameliorative policy must be multidimensional and dynamic.

Pupil Referral Units

Simply put, *Pupil Referral Units* (PRUs), formerly called *Behavior Units* in the United Kingdom and *Teaching Units* in Victoria, Australia, are a place, usually off the school campus, where difficult students are referred to pursue an alternative education program in smaller, more intensive groups. Typically, the focus of the curriculum is on training students in basic academic and social skills. There has been substantial research into problems with this type of off-site provision for "disruptive students" in the United Kingdom (for example: HMI, 1978; Newell, 1980; Topping, 1983; Mongon, 1988). They can be summarized as follows:

- Whereas unit referral processes are typically smooth, reintegration into regular schools is equally as unsuccessful. In other words, it is easier to get a student out of school and into a unit, but it is far more difficult to encourage a school to take a student back into the regular classroom after they have attended a PRU.
- Minority group and working-class male students are at greater risk of referral.
- Units beget their own need—having referred one student out of the classroom, we tend to find others who represent our renewed source of irritation and frustration.
- Provision, therefore, grows exponentially and represents a major financial drain on the regular school system. Because PRUs have a smaller ratio of students to teachers, they are a much more expensive type of educational provision.
- Because there are fewer teachers in each of the units, the offered curriculum is far narrower than in the schools from where the students are referred. This is problematic as these would seem to be students whose need for a broad education is greatest.
- Teachers, inside and outside the PRUs, narrow their view on who is suited to receive their education in the regular classroom.

Because the evidence exists to suggest that units fail in their basic purpose of reforming disruptive students and returning them to the regular classroom, Denis Mongon (1988) felt compelled to point out that PRUs are actually provided for those students who will never cross their entrances. Simply put, they are there for the improvement of classrooms by removing troublesome individuals. Although this debate is ongoing (Lloyd-Smith 1995; Cooper, 1995), the immediate lesson from research into off-site provision for disruptive students is that teachers, education administrators, and policy makers need to be very cautious and resist the growing temptation to establish a second tier of educational provision that constitutes little more than a holding operation for those who were never allowed to make it in traditional forms of academic schooling.

Practical Lessons from Theoretical Engagement

In this section, I refer to two research projects that draw on the epistemological foundations outlined in the first sections of the chapter that reject the utility of the behaviorist paradigm for providing the building blocks for disciplined learning environments. A more careful theorizing of disruption, it is suggested, is a requirement for the substantive changes that account for the complexity and specificity of school and student contexts. These vignettes, which constitute very partial descriptions of my research encounters in the field, are not laid out as a manifesto for school improvement. My intention is to illustrate thoughtful local responses to complex theoretical and practical dilemmas in "schooling in hard times" (Lingard, Knight, & Porter, 1993).

Struggles in "Olympia"

"Olympia" was a troubled technical school in a disadvantaged community in the northern suburbs of Melbourne, Australia. Regarded as "non-academic" with a greater emphasis on technical or manual trade subjects, it was seen as a place to send students who performed poorly at traditional schoolwork and an ideal place for students with "behavioral problems." Staff morale was low and turnover was high. Truancy, for students and teachers, was rampant. The majority of students left school before graduation. Many teachers transferred after very short periods at the school— many on "compassionate grounds." Violence was no stranger to the school, suspensions were frequent, and the caseload of guidance personnel was reportedly "unreasonable." Conversations with the school principal left little room to be sanguine.

When transferred to the school, the principal, who became the catalyst for changing the character, operation, and performance of the school, immediately declared his opposition to corporal punishment. His opposition predated the formal abolition of corporal punishment in the state of Victoria and was not well received in some quarters. His argument was simple and powerful. Diminishing violence in the student body is impossible if teachers model it as an acceptable means for the resolution of conflict. Subsequently, teachers recruited to the school were questioned on their position with regard to punishment.

As a first priority, "Olympia" devoted time to the development of a clearly articulated educational philosophy as the basis for casting the school's aims and priorities. The principal seized the initiative to engage the community in this task. Knowing that parents did not attend school meetings, he went to a local bingo game and, prior to the commencement of the game, took the stage to tell parents that he was concerned about the school and to invite them to call him if they wanted to talk about his concerns after the game the following week. The call was returned and the deliberations to write a new future for the school commenced.

The school was determined to encourage practices that included rather than marginalized failing or disruptive students. The concern for these students was linked to the school's status as a referral point by the more academic schools in the district. The so-called at-risk students represented a major section of "Olympia's" student body. Rather than refer students away from the school or label the students as "special needs students" to be administered to by outside experts, adjustments were made to the school curriculum, to teaching methods, and to the organization of classrooms and school procedures to include students and encourage success. Academics from a local university were invited to help with the task of preparing an alternative curriculum. The activity of constructing a new school program was negotiated as the basis for teachers' professional development and resulted in the university providing an inquiry-based graduate program for teachers on the school premises. A supreme opportunist, the principal used this relationship to negotiate direct entry for some of his students to the university. This was the foundation for similar negotiations at other universities and colleges.

Democratic decision-making structures were developed which established broad representation as a habit rather than a goal. All students served on the council. It was not a forum for the most popular, the most articulate, or the most respectable students. Learning how to participate in meetings and articulate dissent became an educational requirement. Dissent was legitimized and given a forum for expression. Parents were enlisted into school support activities by phone calls seeking assistance in their areas of expertise. From there they found a principal or teacher moving them into other activities that would once have been extremely daunting. During the course of our research, we had conversations with women who described the way in which they had been encouraged back into formal learning through their contact with the school.

The most remarkable aspect of the changes at "Olympia" is that the evidence supported our sense that improvement was more than cosmetic. Retention rates had increased. Staff turnover was less than it had previously been. Although this was the case for all schools because movement in the teaching force declined across the board, teachers at "Olympia" suggested, in interviews, that there was a far stronger staff commitment to the school. The numbers of students continuing their studies at the school after the legal leaving age (fifteen) increased significantly; as high as thirty-five percent more, after changes to the curriculum and the organization of the school. Reported rates of serious disruption, truancy and suspensions, which had been greater than in neighboring schools, diminished. "Olympia" was now graduating more students into higher education, training, and work than were the surrounding academic high schools that steadfastly refused to change their curricula, organization, or pedagogies and referred their dysfunctional students to "Olympia." "Dysfunctional students" were graduating and continuing their studies. This was the most dramatic impact of all. Numerous students referred to "Olympia" by educational psychologists, or who had been transferred there to avoid exclusion from school altogether were completing their secondary schooling successfully. One may speculate that their stories might have been different in schools that steadfastly refuse to change to meet the needs of all students in preference to meeting institutional custom and habit.

"Olympia" had disciplined the students according to our earlier educational theorizing of discipline rather than through recourse to monodimensional behaviorist practices. In other words, this school had been more effective in increasing the level of student and teacher commitment to the school and in producing improved academic outcomes by improving the quality of the learning environment. Such a strategy is beyond the limits of the behaviorist paradigm, which is restricted to changing dysfunctional students.

There was a sequel to our research. A change in government in the state of Victoria resulted in a dramatic downsizing of the teaching force. Some schools were merged and others were closed. "Olympia" was targeted for closure. Students, teachers, and parents occupied their school and conducted lessons as normal. Police were deployed by the state to throw these kids out of school! "Olympia" had developed a very successful Koori education program for Aboriginal students that celebrated the indigenous culture, language, knowledge, and skills of that community. Parents took the government through the Supreme Court and won the right to reopen the school by using race discrimination legislation.

Finding Voice

Some years ago, I was invited to conduct an action research project to identify the educational needs of thirteen- to fifteen-year-old students in an inner urban community. This was a part of a larger project to evaluate the work of a welfare agency and its off-site education unit for disaffected students. Believing that the world had already amassed adults' perceptions of the educational needs of these young people, I contended that enlisting the young people themselves in the establishment of the research interest, the process of gathering data and the extraction of meaning from that data might generate fresh accounts of educational needs and of life in schools. There was nothing new in this approach (Knight, 1982; Coventry et al., 1984; Holdsworth, 1988; Rogers & Freiberg, 1994); however, this was not typical of educational research (Walford, 1991) or policy making. Student voices in educational policy making and research have long been muted.

Students in Year 11 (aged sixteen) from two high schools were invited to form a research team. It was agreed that one of these schools would play host to the project and that the school would give academic credit to the students' work. Students gathering data from other students seemed consistent with the aim of expressing an authentic student voice within the data. The research team was taken to Melbourne University, where they entered into intensive discussions to establish what they saw as the critical areas to be addressed by the survey instrument. The team also learned research methodology. The students constructed and piloted their survey. They conducted the survey in other schools and then collated the voluminous data and interpreted that data for reporting and dissemination.

The students presented their research findings to senior bureaucrats in the Victorian Ministry of Education and were subsequently invited to speak at teachers' professional development seminars. The remarkable fact is that the students who formed the research team were students who had been siphoned into a nonacademic track that terminated prior to the final year of school, disqualifying them for higher education. They were "nonacademic" kids and regarded as troublesome. Their application to this task, which they regarded as purposeful and challenging, was staggering. The team decided that the project should run a parallel set of interviews with kids who had dropped, or been pushed, out of schooling to get a more complete picture of life in schools.

The research findings revolved around two foci: school and work; and school climate. I invited a colleague from another university to evaluate the project. A group of teacher trainees filmed the project while following the student research team and conducted their own interviews of the team to gauge the effectiveness of the conduct and outcomes of the research. The project had a number of positive outcomes:

- Students were engaged in meaningful work that expanded their knowledge, skills, competence, and confidence.
- A range of people, including teachers, academics, students, school support personnel, and administrators were brought together to talk about schooling and young people.
- The host school incorporated the findings of the research into its own development plans.
- The students' work was celebrated outside of the classroom and has been the basis for other projects.
- The project demonstrated the centrality of meaning, utility, and recognition of different learning requirements in the production of disciplined learners.

Rather than provide a detailed list, the research findings can be summarized in four general points:

- Students emphasized the need for connections between the curriculum and postschool options to be made explicit. Teachers need to be able to explain the point of lessons in order to secure student commitment to tasks. Some subjects were seen to be less relevant by different groups of students. To overcome estrangement of students, the curriculum must speak to them and establish links with their particular cultures and contexts.
- Teachers tend not to employ a variety of teaching approaches. Instead, they tend to rely on one approach with they are most familiar and comfortable. Schools

would be better for students if they experienced a variety of approaches to teaching and learning. A recurrent finding was that students had to endure repetition as the path to mastery. Simply put, if a student did not understand something, it was repeated in exactly the same way, but slower. Students reported that they would then say that they understood, even if they did not, in order not to appear "dumb." The lack of variety also led to boredom, which results in "mucking around."

- Girls responded negatively to the question, "Do boys get a better deal out of school than girls?" It was interesting to note that despite this positive statement, girls were more negative in their overall responses. This may suggest that although gender equity is accepted as a school's policy commitment, girls' overall experience of different aspects of school life are less favorable.

- Students reported the need for greater participation in school decision-making processes. Rules, the majority of respondents suggested, would hold greater authority if the student body contributed to the formulation of the school rules and to the discussion of the rights and responsibilities of teachers, students, and parents. The research also affirmed the importance of forums for the discussion of student issues that were taken seriously by students and staff. A number of respondents called for the right to an independent hearing when disputes arose in which they felt they had been treated unfairly.

Both the research findings and the experience of the research team suggest the centrality of engaging approaches to teaching and learning in securing and sustaining student commitment and successful learning organizations. As Pearl (1972) observed, making learning relevant, interesting, and purposeful diminishes student alienation and resistance. Allowing students to find their voice on serious issues about the experience of student life in schools and enlisting them in organizational and classroom decision making is potentially more disciplining than any behavioral program of operant conditioning to enforce student compliance and passivity. The student action research affirms the need for educators to progress beyond the behaviorist paradigm in constructing disciplined schools. Motivated students who see purpose in the curriculum and feel valued by their teachers and the organizational culture are far more likely to become self-disciplining students.

Epilogue

There is no conclusion for this discussion. The task we are engaged in goes on. The discussion aims to dispel reductionist approaches to the complex task of educational discipline. Quick-fix behavior management programs have short lives because they seek to bleach complexity from the colorful life of classrooms. This is not to say that behavior management skills have no place in the classroom. Simply put, my argument revolves around a belief that discipline is much more than the imposition of someone else's order.

Improving discipline in schools requires that we carefully theorize of educational intentions and incorporate many voices in our theory making. Relationships between educational theories, education policy, social and political context, particular models of learning and teaching, and the vision for the future articulated in and through curriculum are fundamental disciplining agents. Greater effort expended on these challenges will contribute to a diminishing reliance on developing new renditions of the behaviorist classroom management score. The frustrating fact about this discussion, and "Olympia" is indicative, is that an educational theory/practice of discipline is slow and must be multidimensional, calling all of the elements of schooling (curriculum, pedagogy, school organization) into the reformative frame.

There exists a convincing body of research evidence (Slee, 1995) and documented school reform projects (Knight & Lewis, 1993) to suggest that this painstaking process of medium- to long-term change will harvest the fruits of student commitment and successful teaching and learning. The still-persuasive behaviorist paradigm is theoretically slight and fails to acknowledge the constellation of issues that contribute to disruptive events in schools and classrooms. Its prescriptions appeal to teachers' calls for a compliant student body. These prescriptions inevitably are found wanting because they fail to ask why students are disengaged from schooling. We owe our children a more robust theory of discipline that informs a teaching force that has moved beyond behaviorism.

References

Adler, A. (1930). *The education of children.* Chicago: Gateway.

Bagley, W. (1914). *School discipline.* New York: Macmillan.

Ball, S. J. (1990). Management as moral technology: A Luddite analysis. In S. J. Ball (Ed.), *Foucault and education: Disciplines and knowledge.* London: Routledge.

Ball, S. J. (1994). *Education reform. A critical and post-structural approach.* Buckingham, Open University Press.

Ball, S. J. (1995). Intellectuals or technicians? The urgent role of theory. *British Journal of Educational Studies, 43*(3), 255–271.

Barthes, R. (1972). *Mythologies.* New York: Hill & Wang.

Berger, M. (1979). Behaviour management in education and professional practice: The danger of a mindless technology. *Bulletin of the British Psychological Society, 32,* 418–419.

Bernstein, B. (1996). *Pedagogy, symbolic control and identity: Theory, research, critique.* London: Taylor & Francis.

Braithwaite, J. (1989). *Crime, shame and reintegration.* Cambridge: Cambridge University Press.

Canter, L., & Canter, M. (1976). *Assertive discipline: A take charge approach for today's educator.* Santa Monica, CA: Seals, Canter & Associates.

Charles, C. (1981). *Building classroom discipline.* New York: Longman.

Cooper, P. (1995). When segregation works: Pupils' experience of Residential Special Provision. In M. Lloyd-Smith, & D. Davies (Eds.), *On the margins: The educational experience of 'problem' pupils.* Oakhill: Trentham Books.

Coventry, G., Cornish, G., Cooke, R., & Vinall, J. (1984). *Skipping school.* Melbourne: Victorian Institute of Secondary Education.

Crittenden, B. (1991). Three approaches to classroom discipline: Philosophical perspectives. In M. N. Lovegrove, & R. Lewis (Eds.), *Classroom discipline.* Melbourne: Longman Cheshire.

Department for Education. (1992). *Exclusions: A discussion document.* London: Department for Education.

Dettman, H. W. (1972). *Discipline in secondary schools in western Australia: Report of the government secondary school discipline committee.* Perth: Education Department of Western Australia.

Dewey, J. (1916). *Democracy and Education.* New York: The Free Press.

Edwards, B. (1996). *Suspension in victorian secondary schools.* Unpublished Master of Education dissertation, Bundoora, LaTrobe University.

Foucault, M. (1979). *Discipline and punish: The birth of the prison.* Harmondsworth: Penguin.

Freeland, J. (1992). Education and training for the school to work transition. In T. Seddon, & C. Deer (Eds.), *A curriculum for the senior secondary years.* Hawthorn: Australian Council for Educational Research.

Freeman, C. B. (1966). The Children's Petition of 1669 and its sequel. *British Journal of Educational Studies, 14,* 216–223.

Friere, P. (1972). *Pedagogy of the oppressed.* New York: Herder and Herder.

Galloway, D. (1982). A study of pupils suspended from schools. *British Journal of Educational Psychology, 52,* 205–212.

Gardiner, J. (1996). Exclusions rise relentlessly. *Times Educational Supplement,* 8 November, 1.

Gewirtz, S., Ball, S. J., & Bowe, R. (1995). *Markets, choice and equity in education.* Buckingham: Open University Press.

Gillborn, D., & Gipps, C. (1996). *Recent research on the achievements of ethnic minority pupils.* London: Office for Standards in Education.

Gillborn, D. (1997). Young, black and failed by school: the market, education reform and black students. *International Journal of Inclusive Education, 1*(1), 65–87.

Glasser, W. (1986). *Control theory in the classroom.* New York: Harper and Row.

Govoni, L. E., & Hayes, J. E. (1988). *Drugs and nursing implications.* Englewood Cliffs: Prentice-Hall.

Grunsell, R. (1980). *Beyond control: Schools and suspension.* London: Readers and Writers.

Hamilton, D. (1996). Peddling feel-good fictions. *Forum, 38*(2), 54–56.

Hargreaves, A., Earl, L., & Ryan, J. (1996). *Schooling for change: Reinventing education for early adolescents.* London: Falmer Press.

Her Majesty's Inspectorate [HMI]. (1978). *Behavioural units: A survey of special units for students with behavioural problems.* London: Department for Education and Science.

Hirschi, T. (1969). *Causes of delinquency.* Berkeley: University of California Press.

Hirst, P. H., & Peters, R. S. (1970). *The logic of education.* London: Routledge and Kegan Paul.

Holdsworth, R. (1988). Student participation projects in Australia: An anecdotal history. In R. Slee (Ed.), *Discipline and schools: A curriculum perspective.* Melbourne: Macmillan.

Hyde, N., & Robson, N. (1984). *Student suspensions from school.* Perth: Education Department of Western Australia.

Kingston, P. (1995). Give peace a chance. *Guardian Education.* 31 October, 2.

Knight, T. (1982). *Youth advocacy report.* Melbourne: Vandalism Task Force.

Knight, T. (1985). An apprenticeship in democracy. *The Australian Teacher, 11,* 5–7.

Knight, T. (1988). Student discipline as a curriculum concern. In R. Slee (Ed.), *Discipline and Schools: A curriculum perspective.* Melbourne: Macmillan.

Knight, T., & Lewis, R. (1993). Resisting the vanishing moral point: Systemic solutions to school discipline. Paper presented at Kings College University of London, June.

Lacey, H. (1996). Drug him when he teases. *Independent on Sunday.* 27 October, 12–16.

Lawrence, J., Steed, D., & Young, P. (1984). *Disruptive children, disruptive schools?* London: Croom Helm.

Lewis, J. (1993). Integration in Victorian schools: Radical social policy or old wine? In R. Slee (Ed.), *Is there a desk with my name on it? The politics of integration.* London: Falmer Press.

Lingard, R., Knight, J., & Porter, P. (Eds.). (1993). *Schooling reform in hard times.* London: Falmer Press.

Locke, J. (1693). *Some thoughts concerning education* (F. W. Garforth ed., 1964). London: Heinemann.

Lloyd-Smith, M., & Davies, D. (Eds.). (1995). *On the margins: The educational experience of 'problem' pupils.* Oakhill: Trentham Books.

Marginson, S. (1993). *Education and public policy in Australia.* Cambridge: Cambridge University Press.

Mongon, D. (1988). Behavior units, 'maladjustment' and student control. In R. Slee (Ed.), *Discipline and schools: A curriculum perspective.* Melbourne: Macmillan.

Neilsen, L. (1979). Let's suspend suspensions: Consequences and alternatives. *Personnel and Guidance Journal, 57*(9), 442–445.

Newell, P. (1980). Sin bins: The integration argument. *Where, 160,* 8–11.

Parsons, C. (1996). Exclusions from schools in England in the 1990s: Trends, causes and responses. *Children and Society, 10,* 177–186.

Pearl, A. (1972). *The atrocity of education.* New York: The Free Press.

Pearl, A. (1988). The requirements of a democratic education. In R. Slee (Ed.), *Discipline and schools: A curriculum perspective.* Melbourne: Macmillan.

Polk, K., & Tait, D. (1990). Changing youth labour markets and youth lifestyles. *Youth Studies, 9*(1), 17–23.

Ranson, S. (1994). *Towards the learning society.* London: Cassell Education.

Reynolds, D. (1976). The delinquent school. In M. Hammersley, & P. Woods (Eds.), *The process of schooling.* London: Routledge and Kegan Paul.

Reynolds, D. (Ed.). (1985). *Studying School Effectiveness.* Lewes: Falmer Press.

Rich, J. M. (1979). Glasser and Kohl: How effective are their strategies to discipline? *NASSP Bulletin, 63,* 428.

Rogers, C. (1969). *Freedom to learn.* Columbus: Merrill.

Rogers, C., & Freiberg, J. (1994). *Freedom to learn* (3rd ed.). Columbus: Merrill.

Rogers, W. (1990). *'You know the fair rule,' Strategies for making the hard job of discipline in school easier.* Hawthorn: Australian Council for Educational Research.

Rorty, R. (1989). *Contingency, irony and solidarity.* Cambridge: Cambridge University Press.

Rose, N. (1985). *The psychological complex: Psychology, politics and society in England 1869–1939.* London: Routledge.

Rose, N. (1989). *Governing the soul: The shaping of the private self.* London: Routledge.

Rose, N. (1996). *Inventing our selves—Psychology, power and personhood.* Cambridge: Cambridge University Press.

Serfontein, G. (1990). *The hidden handicap.* Sydney: Simon & Schuster.

Skinner, B. F. (1968). *The technology of teaching.* New York: Appleton, Century Crofts.

Skinner, B. F. (1972). *Beyond freedom and dignity.* London: Jonathon Cape.

Skrtic, T. (1991). *Behind special education: A critical analysis of professional culture and school organization.* Denver: Love Publishing.

Slee, R. (Ed.). (1992). *Discipline in Australian public education.* Hawthorn: Australian Council for Educational Research.

Slee, R. (Ed.). (1993). *Is there a desk with my name on it? The politics of integration.* London: Falmer Press.

Slee, R. (1995). *Changing theories and practices of discipline.* London: Falmer Press.

Slee, R. (1996). Inclusive education in Australia? Not yet! *Cambridge Journal of Education, 26*(1), 19–32.

Smith, R. (1985). *Freedom and discipline.* London: George Allen & Unwin.

Spencer, H. (1910). *Education: Intellectual, moral and physical.* London: Williams and Norgate.

Swan, N. (1995). Speed for breakfast. *Four corners.* Sydney: Australian Broadcasting Commission.

Theroux, P. (1988). *Riding the iron rooster: By train through China.* London: Penguin Books.

Topping, K. (1983). *Educational systems for disruptive adolescents.* London: Croom Helm.

Tomlinson, S. (1982). *A sociology of special education.* London: Routledge and Kegan Paul.

Tomlinson, S. (1996). Conflicts and dilemmas for professionals in special education. In C. Christensen, & F. Rizvi (Eds.), *Disability and the dilemmas of education and justice.* Buckingham: Open University Press.

Vickers, I. (1993). Exclusion: Procedures and provisions in Australia with special reference to the role of Distance Education Centre in the accommodation of excluded students. Unpublished Master of Education dissertation. Perth: Edith Cowan University.

Vygotsky, L. S. (1962). *Thought and language.* Cambridge: Massachusetts Institute of Technology Press.

Vygotsky, L. S. (1978). *Mind in society: The development of higher psychological processes.* Cambridge: Harvard University Press.

Walford, G. (Ed.). (1991). *Doing educational research.* London: Routledge.

Wilson, P. S. (1973). *Interest and discipline in education.* London: Routledge and Kegan Paul.

Wright Mills, C. (1959). *The sociological imagination.* New York: Oxford University Press.

Wu, S., Pink, W. T., Crain, R. L., & Moles, O. (1982). Student suspension: A critical reappraisal. *The Urban Review, 14,* 245–303.

3

Perspectives of Classroom Management

Yesterday, Today, and Tomorrow

JERE BROPHY
Michigan State University

> *We believe that the intended modern school curriculum,*
> *which is designed to produce self-motivated active learners,*
> *is seriously undermined by classroom management policies*
> *that encourage, if not demand, simple obedience.*
> *—McCASLIN AND GOOD, 1992, p. 4*

Teachers perform various functions in their work with students in classrooms. Four major teaching functions are instruction, classroom management, disciplinary intervention, and student socialization. *Instruction* refers to actions taken to assist students in mastering the formal curriculum (presenting information, demonstrating skills, conducting lessons or activities, supervising work on assignments, assessing progress). *Classroom management* refers to actions taken to create and maintain a learning environment conducive to successful instruction (arranging the physical environment of the classroom, establishing rules and procedures, maintaining attention to lessons and engagement in academic activities). *Disciplinary interventions* are actions taken to elicit or compel changes in the behavior of students who fail to conform to expectations. These interventions are especially necessary when misbehavior is salient or sustained enough to disrupt the classroom management system. Finally, *student socialization* refers to actions taken to influence students' personal or social attitudes, beliefs, expectations, or behavior, especially those actions designed to help the students fulfill their student role responsibilities more effectively. This chapter focuses on classroom management functions needed to support various approaches to instruction. Theory and research on disciplinary interventions and student socialization are reviewed by Brophy (1996) and included in several of the subsequent chapters in this book.

To set the stage for effective instruction, teachers need to apply the management principles involved in establishing a classroom as a successful learning environment. Such a classroom has a certain look and feel. It reveals organization, planning, and scheduling. The room is divided into distinct areas equipped for specific activities. Frequently used equipment is stored where it can be accessed easily, and each item has its own place. Traffic patterns facilitate movement around the room and minimize crowding or bumping. Transitions between activities are accomplished efficiently following a brief signal or a few directions from the teacher, and students know where they are supposed to be, what they are supposed to be doing, and what equipment they will need. Students are attentive to presentations and responsive to questions. Lessons and other group activities are structured so that subparts are discernible and separated by clear transitions. When students are released to work on their own or with peers, they know what to do and settle quickly into the task. Usually, students continue the activity through to completion without difficulty and then turn to some new approved activity. If they need help, they can get it from the teacher or from some other source, and then resume working.

To an observer who did not know better, this kind of learning environment seems to work automatically, without much teacher effort devoted to management. However, classroom research has established that such well-functioning classrooms result from consistent teacher efforts to create, maintain, and (occasionally) restore conditions that foster learning. The most successful teachers approach management as a process of establishing and maintaining effective learning environments. Less successful teachers approach it with emphasis on their roles as authority figures or disciplinarians (Doyle, 1986; Emmer, 1987; Evertson, 1987; Gettinger, 1988; Good & Brophy, 1995, 1997; Jones, 1996).

Development of Knowledge about Classroom Management

Prior to the emergence of systematic research on classroom management, advice to teachers on the topic was of the "Don't smile until Christmas" variety, with emphasis on control or discipline. The suggested guidelines amounted to a "bag of tricks," rather than an integrated set of principles.

Behaviorist Formulations

As classroom management began to receive scholarly attention, advice to teachers became more systematic and theory driven. There was some emphasis on humanistic psychology notions such as supporting students' self-concepts and depth psychology notions such as interpreting the underlying reasons for students' symptomatic behavior. However, primary emphasis was given to the theoretical concepts and techniques for bringing behavior under stimulus control that had been developed by applied behavior analysts and other behaviorists who emphasized controlling behavior by manipulating its consequences (particularly by applying or withholding reinforcement). Early behavioristic formulations were overly focused on specific behaviors and emphasized rather wooden and rigid technique prescriptions ("rules, praise, and ignoring") or converting classroom reward structures to token economy systems. As behaviorism developed and began to take into account human intentions and cognitions, behavioristic advice to teachers retained its emphasis on reinforcement but became more realistic, featuring such techniques as negotiated goal setting with students formalized through behavioral contracts. Also, emphasis shifted from a focus on eliminating particular forms of misbehavior to shaping desired behavior (high-quality engagement in lessons and learning activities).

An eclectic approach based on principles developed by Kounin (1970) and subsequent classroom researchers generally has supplanted the principle of using reinforcement to bring behavior under stimulus control as the most widely recommended basic approach to classroom management. However, behavioristic approaches are still strongly emphasized in school psychology and special education, and in sources offering suggestions about dealing with students who present persistent and severe behavioral problems. Some popular approaches to regular classroom management still rely heavily on behavioristic principles. The most prominent of these is assertive discipline, an approach developed by Canter and Canter (1992) and promoted through in-service training workshops sponsored by their corporation. It stresses the rights of teachers to define and enforce standards for student behavior that allow the teachers to instruct successfully. Teachers who use this method are described as assertive teachers and are contrasted both with submissive teachers who fail to enforce standards and with hostile teachers who enforce standards but in ways that violate the best interests of students. Recommended methods focus on developing clearly specified expectations for student behavior, translating these expectations into a set of rules that specify acceptable and unacceptable behavior, and linking expectations and behavior to a system of rewards and punishments. The most widely used punishment is a penalty system, in which the names of misbehaving students are written on the board and checkmarks are added following the names for repeated offenses. These students are subject to detention or to progressively more serious punishments, including notes sent home to parents, time out from the classroom, or referral to the principal.

Assertive discipline is controversial. Canter (1988) claims that the approach is supported by research, and supporters (e.g., McCormack, 1989) cite testimonials and survey data to suggest that it is popular among practitioners who are convinced that it works. However, independent reviewers have concluded that the Canters have failed to conduct systematic research on the effectiveness of the approach they have been promoting since the late 1970s, and that the limited research available on the approach simply does not support claims for its effectiveness (Emmer & Aussiker,

1987; Render, Padilla, & Krank, 1989). Only one study (involving fifteen elementary teachers in Australia) has involved the systematic introduction of assertive discipline and monitoring of its effects (Nicholls & Houghton, 1995). It yielded significant increases in on-task behaviors and decreases in disruptions, although these improvements were observed only in a subset of the classes studied.

Several authors have voiced philosophical objections to the assertive discipline model. Curwin and Mendler (1988) characterized it as an example of an *obedience model,* in which power-based methods are used to compel students to conform to rules. They consider such obedience models less desirable than *responsibility models,* in which the goal is to develop responsibility for inner self-guidance in students, using methods that emphasize explaining the rationales for rules and allowing students to suffer the natural consequences of misbehavior rather than issuing threats and administering punishment. Similarly, McDaniel (1989) criticized assertive discipline as being "not much more than applied behavior modification and take-charge teacher firmness with rules and consequences" (p. 82). The designers of the assertive discipline program have expanded its initial focus on controlling student behavior by adding materials on beginning the school year, working with parents, and helping students with homework. Even so, the program retains its primarily behavioral character.

The assertive discipline approach has some noteworthy strengths, especially its emphasis on developing and communicating clear expectations for student behavior. This can be helpful for those teachers who are lacking in both confidence and viable strategies for dealing with problem students. However, the approach has been rightly criticized for placing too much emphasis on threat and punishment, so that it is a much less desirable alternative than the eclectic approach outlined later that is based on replicated findings obtained by several research teams working independently in different parts of the country. Also, any management system is incomplete if it relies on teachers to regulate student behavior but lacks a concomitant emphasis on developing student self-control. As McCaslin and Good (1992) noted, it is foolish to try to teach a problem-solving curriculum while at the same time undermining it by using a rigid behavior control management system.

Kounin's Research

Research by Kounin (1970) laid the foundation for what has become a research-based consensus concerning the characteristics of successful classroom managers. Kounin began his research by comparing the behaviors of effective and ineffective classroom managers. He videotaped activities in well-managed classrooms such as those described near the beginning of this chapter, and also in poorly managed classrooms in which the teachers were fighting to keep the lid on and the students were regularly inattentive and frequently disruptive. Influenced by the "discipline" orientation dominant at the time, Kounin's initial analyses focused on the teachers' handling of disruptive incidents. Surprisingly, these analyses failed to produce consistent results.

Effective managers did not differ in systematic ways from ineffective managers when they were responding to student misbehavior.

However, Kounin noticed that effective managers differed from ineffective managers in other ways. Follow-up analyses indicated that the effective managers displayed the following key behaviors:

- *Withitness.* Remaining aware of what is happening in all parts of the classroom at all times by continuously scanning the classroom, even when working with small groups or individuals, and demonstrating this "withitness" to students by intervening promptly and appropriately when their disengaged behavior threatens to become disruptive. This minimizes timing errors (failing to notice and intervene until an incident has already become disruptive) and target errors (mistakes in identifying the students responsible for the problem).
- *Overlapping.* Doing more than one thing at a time; in particular, responding to the needs of individuals while sustaining a group activity by using eye contact or physical proximity to restore inattentive students' attention to a lesson while continuing the lesson itself without interruption.
- *Signal continuity and momentum during lessons.* Teaching well-prepared and well-paced lessons that focus students' attention by providing a continuous academic signal that is more compelling than the noise of competing distractions, and by sustaining the momentum of this academic signal throughout the lesson.
- *Challenge and variety in assignments.* Encouraging students' engagement in seatwork by providing assignments at the right level of difficulty (easy enough to ensure success with reasonable effort but new or difficult enough to provide challenge), and varied enough to sustain interest.

Kounin showed that effective managers succeed not so much because they are good at handling disruption when it occurs, but because they are good at preventing disruption from occurring in the first place. These teachers do not focus on preventing disruption; instead, they focus on establishing the classroom as an effective learning environment, preparing and teaching good lessons, and monitoring students as they work on good follow-up assignments.

Related Findings

Evertson and Emmer (1982) replicated and extended Kounin's findings in studies of how teachers establish an effective management system at the beginning of the year and sustain it thereafter. These studies demonstrated the importance of showing and telling students what to do. Clarity about rules and routines is crucial, supported, if necessary, by demonstrations of desired behavior.

In the lower grades, effective managers spend a great deal of time in the early weeks of school explaining expectations and modeling classroom routines and procedures. If necessary, they provide their students with opportunities to practice and receive feedback concerning such matters as when and how to use the pencil sharpener or how to manage the transitions between reading groups. In the upper grades, there is less need to teach daily routines (the students are already familiar with most of them or can understand them sufficiently from verbal explanations), but it is just as important to be clear and detailed in describing expected behavior.

At all grade levels, teachers need to ensure that students follow the desired procedures by providing additional reminders or feedback as needed. Effective managers consistently monitor compliance with rules and demands, enforce accountability procedures and associated penalties for late or unacceptable work, and are prepared to punish students for repeated misconduct if necessary. However, their emphasis is positive and prescriptive, not threatening and punitive. Effective management primarily involves teaching students what to do before the fact, rather than applying discipline following misconduct.

Subsequent studies by other investigators have elaborated on these findings, especially as they apply to the whole-class instruction/recitation/seatwork approach that has dominated traditional kindergarten through twelfth grade teaching. Major management elements of this approach include preparing the classroom as a physical environment suited to the nature of the planned learning activities, developing and implementing a workable set of housekeeping procedures and rules of conduct, maintaining students' attention to and participation in lessons and activities, and monitoring the quality of their engagement in assignments and their progress toward intended achievement outcomes. These broader management goals are accomplished through procedures and routines concerning such aspects as:

- storing supplies and equipment
- establishing traffic patterns
- setting general expectations and rules at the beginning of the year
- starting and ending each class period smoothly
- managing transitions between activities
- keeping activities going once they are started by stimulating involvement and minimizing interruptions
- giving directions for and getting the class started on assignments
- circulating to monitor progress and meet the needs of individual students

The major findings from observational research on classroom management agree that teachers who emphasize establishing and maintaining effective learning environments are more successful than teachers who emphasize their roles as authority figures or disciplinarians. Of course, teachers *are* authority figures and must require their students to follow certain rules and procedures. However, these rules and procedures are not ends in themselves. They are the means for organizing the classroom as an environment that supports learning.

The key to successful management is the teacher's ability to maximize the time students spend actively engaged in worthwhile academic activities and to minimize the time they spend waiting for activities to get started, making transitions between activities, sitting with nothing to do, or engaging in misconduct. Good classroom management does not just imply that the teacher elicits the students' cooperation in minimizing misconduct and intervenes effectively when misconduct occurs; it also implies that worthwhile learning activities occur more or less continuously and that the management system as a whole is designed to maximize students' engagement in those activities. The learning activities are planned and implemented effectively, and the management interventions made during and between these activities support their continuity and impact, restoring student engagement in learning activities in ways that do not disrupt the flow of the activities themselves.

Looking to the Future

Most of the research that established these principles was done in rooms that featured transmission approaches to teaching. However, views on good teaching and learning have shifted from transmission views toward social construction or learning community views (see Table 3-1). When knowledge is socially constructed, classroom discourse emphasizes reflective discussion of networks of connected content. Questions are divergent, designed to stimulate and scaffold students' thinking and help them develop understanding of powerful ideas that anchor the knowledge networks. Students are expected to strive to make sense of what they are learning by relating it to their prior knowledge and by discussing it with others. Instead of working mostly alone, practicing what has been transmitted to them, they act as a learning community that constructs shared understandings.

Merely shifting from heavy emphasis on teacher talk to greater use of questioning and discussion does not automatically transform a classroom into a learning community engaged in social construction of worthwhile knowledge. To begin with, discussions should focus on knowledge that is worth learning. Note the references in Table 3-1 to networks of knowledge structured around powerful ideas and to questioning designed to develop these ideas. Also, as discussion leaders, teachers need to perform vital functions involved in structuring and scaffolding discussions so as to maintain their coherence and quality. Newmann (1990) used the term *thoughtfulness* to summarize the qualities of the discourse observed in classrooms that best exemplify the social construction of knowledge within learning communities. The thoughtful discourse observed in these classrooms featured sustained examination of a few topics rather than superficial coverage of many, so that it was characterized by substantive cohesion and continuity. The teachers gave students time to think before requiring them to answer questions, but also pressed them to clarify or justify their assertions rather than just accepting whatever was said indiscriminately. The teachers modeled interest in the students' ideas and a thoughtful approach to problem solving, and the students generated original and unconventional ideas as the discourse developed.

TABLE 3-1   Teaching and Learning as Transmission of Information Versus as Social Construction of Knowledge

Transmission View	Social Constructivist View
Knowledge consists of a fixed body of information transmitted from teacher or text to students.	Knowledge results from developing interpretations constructed through discussion.
Texts and teachers serve as authoritative sources of expert knowledge to which students defer.	Authority for constructed knowledge resides in the arguments and evidence cited in its support by students as well as by texts or teacher; everyone has expertise to contribute.
Teacher is responsible for managing students' learning by providing information and leading students through activities and assignments.	Teacher and students share responsibility for initiating and guiding learning efforts.
Teacher explains, checks for understanding, and judges correctness of students' responses.	Teacher acts as discussion leader who poses questions, seeks clarifications, promotes dialogue, helps group recognize areas of consensus and of continuing disagreement.
Students memorize or replicate what has been explained or modeled.	Discourse emphasizes reflective discussion of networks of connected knowledge; questions are more divergent but designed to develop understanding of the powerful ideas that anchor these networks; focus is on eliciting students' thinking.
Activities emphasize replication of models or applications that require following step-by-step algorithms.	Activities emphasize applications to authentic issues and problems that require higher order thinking.
Students work mostly alone, practicing what has been transmitted to them in order to prepare themselves to compete for rewards by reproducing it on demand.	Students collaborate by acting as a learning community that constructs shared understandings through sustained dialog.

Source: From *Looking in Classrooms* (7th Edition) by Thomas L. Good and Jere E. Brophy. New York: Longman, 1997.

Teachers who wish to emphasize constructivist approaches need to prepare by identifying learning activities that feature worthwhile learning goals, exposing students to content sources that are structured around powerful ideas, and planning questions designed to develop these powerful ideas as bases for structuring and scaffolding discussions. These instructional functions must be accomplished effectively to provide a basis for thoughtfulness in classroom discourse. Then, working from this basis, teachers can support the successful enactment of their plans by effectively performing management functions that prepare their students to meet the role demands embedded in the notion of a learning community.

Adapting Established Management Principles to Social Constructivist Teaching

In developing plans for socializing their students into a learning community and supporting their active collaboration in the social construction of knowledge, teachers can begin with adaptations of established classroom management principles. These principles seem just as applicable to social constructivist approaches as to transmission approaches, *if they are interpreted appropriately.* Unfortunately, management principles are often presented as techniques for eliciting students' compliance with teachers' demands. This emphasis on compliance does not fit well with current emphases on learning through the social construction of knowledge and on helping students to become more autonomous and self-regulated learners. It is now more important than ever to emphasize that the research indicates that the most successful managers focus on establishing effective learning environments, not on functioning as disciplinarians.

Thoughtful analysis is needed to determine how to apply basic principles of good management to emerging instructional innovations. To ensure that the management system supports the instructional system within constructivist or other nontraditional approaches to teaching, a teacher can begin by identifying what students must do in order to engage optimally in the desired learning format, then work backwards from this description of desired student roles to determine what forms of managerial instruction or assistance may be needed. Successful management of social constructivist learning settings requires teaching students to take on a broader range of roles than is required of them in more traditional transmission settings (see Table 3-2).

Rogers and Freiberg (1994) analyzed what is involved in shifting to social constructivist methods by considering both teachers' general orientations toward managing classrooms and students and the kinds of activities emphasized in their approaches to instruction. They suggested that such a shift requires teachers to adopt a person-centered, rather than a teacher-centered, orientation toward classroom management, which features shared leadership and community building (see Table 3-3).

Accompanying this shift in management orientation is a shift in approaches to instruction from primarily teacher-focused methods to primarily cooperative and student-focused methods (see Table 3-4). The latter methods allow students more opportunity to display initiative and function autonomously, but they also entail a broader range of roles and an increased level of responsibility that the students must be prepared to fulfill.

Leaders in research on social constructivist approaches to teaching have emphasized the importance of socializing students into learning communities that share values and follow procedures that support the social construction of knowledge. This involves instructing students not only in how to pay attention during lessons and work alone on assignments, but also in how to participate in collaborative dialogs and work together in cooperative learning activities (Anderson & Roth, 1989; Bennett & Dunne, 1992; Cohen, 1994; Johnson, Johnson, Holubec, & Roy, 1984; Lampert, 1989; Palincsar & Brown, 1989). Collaborative knowledge construction means not only taking

TABLE 3-2   Student Roles that Might Guide Classroom Management Efforts in Social Constructivist Classrooms

A. Role competencies featured in knowledge transmission classrooms that also apply in social constructivist classrooms.

  1. Be in class/seat on time
  2. Store personal belongings in their proper place
  3. Handle classroom supplies and materials carefully and return them to their proper place after use
  4. Have desk cleared and be ready to learn when lessons begin
  5. Pay attention during lessons and learning activities
  6. Participate by volunteering to answer questions
  7. Work carefully on in-school and homework assignments
  8. If you get stuck, try to work out the problem on your own before asking for help, but do ask for help if you need it
  9. Turn in assignments completed and on time
  10. Confine conversations to approved times and forms
  11. Treat others with politeness and respect

B. Additional role competencies that need to be developed in social constructivist classrooms.

  1. In whole-class settings, participate as a member of the group as we develop new understandings
  2. Recognize that everyone has something to contribute, and you are here to learn as well as to help others learn, and act accordingly
  3. Listen carefully to what others say and relate it to your own knowledge and experience (Do you agree? Why or why not?)
  4. If you are not sure what others mean, ask for clarification
  5. In putting forth your own ideas, explain your reasoning by citing relevant evidence and arguments
  6. In challenging others' ideas and responding to challenges to your ideas, focus on the issues and on trying to reach agreement; do not get personal or engage in one-upmanship
  7. When working in pairs or small groups, see that each person's ideas are included and that everyone accomplishes the goal of the activity
  8. When helping partners or fellow group members, do not just do the work for them; instead, make sure that they learn what they need to know

Adapted from Brophy, J., & Alleman, J. (1998). Applying research-based classroom management principles to the social education learning community, *Social Education, 62,* 56–58.

turns talking, listening politely, and keeping criticism constructive, but also responding thoughtfully to what others have said, making contributions that advance the discussion, and citing relevant arguments and evidence to support one's position. When students work in pairs or small groups, collaboration includes making sure that everyone in the group understands the goals of the activity, participates in carrying it out, and gets the intended learning benefits from this participation.

TABLE 3-3 Teacher-Centered and Person-Centered Orientations to Classroom Management

Teacher-Centered Classrooms	Person-Centered Classrooms
Teacher is the sole leader.	Leadership is shared.
Management is a form of oversight.	Management is a form of guidance.
Teacher takes responsibility for all the paperwork and organization.	Students are facilitators for the operations of the classroom.
Discipline comes from the teacher.	Discipline comes from the self.
A few students are the teacher's helpers.	All students have the opportunity to become an integral part of the management of the classroom.
Teacher makes the rules and posts them for the students.	Rules are developed by the teacher and students in the form of a classroom constitution or compact.
Consequences are fixed for all students.	Consequences reflect individual differences.
Rewards are mostly extrinsic.	Rewards are mostly intrinsic.
Students are allowed limited responsibilities.	Students share in classroom responsibilities.
Few members of the community enter the classroom.	Partnerships are formed with business and community groups to enrich and broaden the learning opportunities for students.

Source: Carl Rogers and H. Jerome Freiberg (1994). *Freedom to Learn,* 3rd Edition. Columbus: Merrill Publishing. Adapted by permission of Prentice-Hall, Inc., Upper Saddle River, NJ.

Ensuring that students learn to participate optimally will still require the familiar management strategies of articulating clear expectations, modeling or providing instruction in desired procedures, cueing students when these procedures are needed, and applying sufficient pressure to compel changes in behavior when students have failed to respond to more positive methods. The teacher still retains ultimate control in the classroom and when necessary exerts authority by articulating and enforcing managerial guidance. However, this guidance emphasizes thoughtful, goal-oriented learning, not mindless compliance with rules.

Constructivist teachers also encourage students to take increasing responsibility for organizing and directing their own learning. Students cannot learn self-regulation if their teacher continuously cues and directs their learning activities. If developing self-regulation is taken seriously as a goal, students must be taught the cognitive and metacognitive skills needed to function as autonomous learners—identifying goals and setting priorities, planning work strategies and managing time, monitoring the effectiveness of their strategies, responding appropriately when they encounter difficulties, and so on. At first, students may need a great deal of explanation, modeling, and cueing of self-regulated learning strategies. As they develop expertise, however,

TABLE 3-4   Teacher-Focused and Student-Focused Instructional Methods

Teacher-focused

Teacher dimension: Teacher directs and externally controls student behavior.	• Lecture
Teacher role is directive.	• Questioning
	• Drill and practice
Cooperative dimension: Teacher/students cooperate in designing a positive classroom learning environment.	• Demonstration
	• Discussion
Teacher role is semidirective/ facilitative.	• Cooperative groups
	• Guided discovery
	• Contracts
Self-dimension: Students are internally self-disciplined and need minimal direct adult supervision.	• Role play
	• Projects
	• Inquiry
Teacher role is nondirective/ facilitative.	• Self-assessment

Student-focused

Source: Carl Rogers and H. Jerome Freiberg (1994). *Freedom to Learn,* 3rd Edition. Columbus: Merrill Publishing. Adapted by permission of Prentice-Hall, Inc., Upper Saddle River, NJ.

the teacher can reduce the intensity of this scaffolding and provide increasing opportunities for students to regulate their own learning.

Conclusion

Ideas about good teaching evolve in response to the long-term accumulation of knowledge as well as to the short-term vicissitudes of scholarly debates. Any shift or elaboration in instructional approaches may require adjustments in classroom management approaches as well. Nevertheless, certain basic classroom management principles appear to apply across all potential instructional approaches. One of these is that management that emphasizes clarifying what students are expected to do and helping them learn to do it is likely to be more effective than management that focuses on misbehavior and places more emphasis on after-the-fact discipline than on before-the-fact prevention.

A second basic principle is that management systems need to support instructional systems. A management system that orients students toward passivity and compliance with rigid rules undercuts the potential effects of an instructional system that is designed to emphasize active learning, higher order thinking, and the social construction of knowledge.

A third basic principle is that managerial planning should begin by identifying the student outcomes that constitute the goals of instruction, then consider what these outcomes imply about desired learning activities and about the knowledge, skills, values, and behavioral dispositions that students must acquire in order to engage in these learning activities most profitably. This planning process should yield clear articulation of desired student roles, which then become both the goal and the rationale for the teacher's management system. The management system functions most smoothly and supports the instructional system most effectively if it features clear articulation of desired student roles, supported by whatever structuring and scaffolding may be needed to enable students to learn these roles and begin to display them on their own when appropriate.

The student roles implied by the goals of meaningful and self-regulated learning and by social constructivist models of teaching call for students to display thoughtfulness, initiative, collaboration with others, and sustained metacognitive awareness in regulating their learning efforts. Traditionally emphasized behavioristic management models, especially those designed to train students to follow unvaried routines and respond "mindlessly" to cues, are not well suited to preparing them to fulfill today's more demanding roles. If they are to flourish in social constructivist classrooms, students will need both management and instructional methods designed to support their functioning as a community of learners engaged in the social construction of knowledge.

References

Anderson, C., & Roth, K. (1989). Teaching for meaningful and self-regulated learning of science. In J. Brophy (Ed.), *Advances in research on teaching* (Vol. 1, pp. 265–309). Greenwich, CT: JAI.

Bennett, N., & Dunne, E. (1992). *Managing small groups.* New York: Simon & Schuster.

Brophy, J. (1996). *Teaching problem students.* New York: Guilford.

Brophy, J., & Alleman, J. (1998). Classroom management in a social studies learning community. *Social Education, 62,* 56–58.

Canter, L. (1988). Let the educator beware: A response to Curwin and Mendler. *Educational Leadership, 46*(2), 71–73.

Canter, L., & Canter, M., (1992). *Assertive discipline: Positive behavior management for today's classroom* (2nd ed.). Santa Monica, CA: Lee Canter & Associates.

Cohen, E. (1994). *Designing group work: Strategies for heterogeneous classrooms* (2nd ed.). New York: Teachers College Press.

Curwin, R., & Mendler, A. (1988). Packaged discipline programs: Let the buyer beware. *Educational Leadership, 46*(2), 68–71.

Doyle, W. (1986). Classroom organization and management. In M. Wittrock (Ed.), *Handbook of research on teaching* (3rd ed., pp. 392–431). New York: Macmillan.

Emmer, E. (1987). Classroom management and discipline. In V. Richardson-Koehler (Ed.), *Educators' handbook* (pp. 233–256). New York: Longman.

Emmer, E., & Aussiker, A. (1990). School and classroom discipline programs: How well do they work? In O. C. Moles (Ed.), *Student discipline strategies: Research and practice.* Albany: State University of New York Press.

Evertson, C. (1987). Managing classrooms: A framework for teachers. In D. Berliner & B. Rosenshine (Eds.), *Talks to teachers* (pp. 54–74). New York: Random House.

Gettinger, M. (1988). Methods of proactive classroom management. *School Psychology Review, 17,* 227–242.

Good, T., & Brophy, J. (1995). *Contemporary educational psychology* (5th ed.). White Plains, NY: Longman.

Good, T., & Brophy, J. (1997). *Looking in classrooms* (7th ed.). New York: Longman.

Johnson, D., Johnson, R., Holubec, E. J., & Roy, P. (1984). *Circles of learning: Cooperation in the classroom.* Alexandria, VA: Association for Supervision and Curriculum Development.

Jones, V. (1996). Classroom management. In J. Sikula, T. Buttery, & E. Guyton (Eds.), *Handbook of research on teacher education* (Vol. 2, pp. 503–521). New York: Macmillan.

Lampert, M. (1989). Choosing and using mathematical tools in classroom discourse. In J. Brophy (Ed.), *Advances in research on teaching* (Vol. 1, pp. 223–264). Greenwich, CT: JAI.

McCaslin, M., & Good, T. (1992). Compliant cognition: The misalliance of management and instructional goals in current school reform. *Educational Researcher, 21,* 4–17.

McCormack, S. (1989). Response to Render, Padilla, and Krank: But practitioners say it works! *Educational Leadership, 47*(7), 77–79.

McDaniel, T. (1989). The discipline debate: A road through the thicket. *Educational Leadership, 47*(7), 81–82.

Newmann, F. (1990). Qualities of thoughtful social studies classes: An empirical profile. *Journal of Curriculum Studies, 22,* 443–461.

Nicholls, D., & Houghton, S. (1995). The effects of Canter's Assertive Discipline Program on teacher and student behavior. *British Journal of Educational Psychology, 65,* 197–210.

Palincsar, A., & Brown, A. (1989). Classroom dialogues to promote self-regulated comprehension. In J. Brophy (Ed.), *Advances in research on teaching* (Vol. 1, pp. 105–151). Greenwich, CT: JAI.

Render, G., Padilla, J., & Krank, H. (1989). What research really shows about assertive discipline. *Educational Leadership, 47*(7), 72–75.

Rogers, C., & Freiberg, H. J. (1994). *Freedom to learn* (3rd ed.). Columbus: Merrill.

Section II

Best Practices and
Promising Programs

The central goal of COMP is to help teachers improve overall instruction and management skills through planning, implementation, and maintaining effective classroom practices. (Evertson & Harris, p. 62)

Linked together, Consistency Management & Cooperative Discipline provides a flexible plan to improve the quality of instruction and the learning environment in order to produce a cooperative, caring, and safe place for students and teachers to work and learn. (H. Jerome Freiberg, p. 79)

Judicious Discipline…is a comprehensive approach to democratic classroom management that provides educators with a foundation for teaching citizenship each day and through every student-teacher interaction. (Barbara McEwan, Paul Gathercoal, & Virginia Nimmo, p. 100)

Effective school management programs are built on the three Cs: Cooperative community, constructive conflict resolution, and civic values…. (Roger Johnson & David Johnson, p. 121)

4

Support for Managing Learning-Centered Classrooms

The Classroom Organization and Management Program

CAROLYN M. EVERTSON
Peabody College,
Vanderbilt University

ALENE H. HARRIS
Peabody College,
Vanderbilt University

Introduction

As we look to the future, there are new calls for changing classroom practices. Activities involving higher order thinking skills, cooperative group learning, and students taking more responsibility for their own learning are all based on having classrooms that work. Indeed, many researchers and educators argue that quality programs cannot succeed in classrooms in which problems of order and student cooperation exist. As teachers deal with more diverse populations of students with differing needs and modes of learning, and as classrooms incorporate more complex ways of academically engaging students, the need for effective management practices burgeons. Appropriate professional development activities help teachers engage in a process of thinking that enables them to create the supporting structures for learning to occur. Once this process becomes a part of teacher decision making, it becomes a framework for supporting and successfully orchestrating more complex instruction in their classrooms.

After establishing some definitions, this chapter describes a program that helps teachers begin the process of examining their teaching and their classrooms and of creating what Brophy (1998) calls "dependable classroom structures" in which students can be successful.

In any discussion of classroom management, it is useful to establish definitions carefully, because conceptions of classroom management are influenced by shifts in research perspectives at various points since the late 1960s. Since that time, the meaning of the term classroom management has changed from describing discipline practices and behavioral interventions to serving as a more holistic descriptor of teachers' actions in orchestrating supportive learning environments and building community.

Individual Behavioral Approaches

The field of classroom management has been and, in some cases, remains heavily behavioral in orientation, with a chief focus on modifying individual behavior. Early investigations into classroom management were prompted by an interest in fixing misbehavior, which is centrally an individual issue (Doyle, 1986). The behavioral psychological model saw the root of behavioral problems as conditioning, and therefore sought to alter existing behavior in individuals through modification, incentive, and reward systems. Thus, research in the 1960s and 1970s focused on behavior analysis and the appropriate application of rewards and deterrents, with the central focus on the individual and the individual's misbehavior. This approach to management paralleled the behaviorist, mostly individual view of learning predominant at the time.

Approaches to Managing Classroom Groups

Central to the shift from individual to group focus in research on management was the work of Kounin beginning in the late 1960s. Kounin's interest was in desists and the effect of the desist on the individuals near the student who was being reprimanded. He learned that there was little correspondence between teacher desists and effective management. Once misbehavior occurred, there was no superior strategy for intervening. Instead, the distinction between effective and ineffective managers was in their ability to prevent and identify potential misbehavior *before* it became disruptive (Kounin, 1970).

Kounin's work led to a significant body of research focusing on proactive strategies for group management. Extensive research on effective teaching since the late 1960s has yielded a set of principles based on the knowledge that the ability of teachers to organize and manage their classrooms has a direct impact on students' opportunities to learn. This work extended the concept of classroom management past a focus on reactive control of deviant behavior toward a focus on teachers' proactive strategies for creating conditions in classrooms that support learning. (These findings have been described and explored elsewhere; e.g., Evertson & Emmer, 1982; Evertson, Emmer, Sanford, & Clements, 1983; Evertson, 1985; Evertson, 1989a; readers are referred to those sources for further details.)

Contributions of Sociocultural Studies

A number of studies have examined classrooms as social and communicative settings, and the findings from these studies are central to understanding classroom management from a sociocognitive perspective. As attempts are made to rethink, restructure, and rework curriculum, and as classrooms continue to become more and more diverse with respect to ethnic origins, primary language spoken by students, and abilities and disabilities, issues of classroom management that have been dormant have once again become central.

As Evertson and Weade (1991) pointed out, since the late 1970s, research on classroom processes has revealed important insights about the structural features of well-organized classrooms, including identification of social and academic participation structures. Knowing that these structures exist, however, is an insufficient basis for understanding how they evolve in any given classroom. Sociocultural theorists contribute important insights that help in capturing and understanding the dynamic interplay among participants and among the assorted features, structures, and factors that influence what occurs in classrooms. They argue that a child's experience during a lesson involves three concurrent strands: (1) responding to curriculum content; (2) managing the classroom culture; and (3) participating in sociocultural processes (Alton-Lee, Nuthall, & Patrick, 1993). Students are thus highly active in interpreting when and how they may participate (Green & Weade, 1985).

In several studies, Evertson and colleagues (Evertson & Randolph, in press; Evertson & Weade, 1991; Randolph & Evertson, 1995; Randolph & Evertson, 1994) have argued for a view of management, informed by sociocultural research, that encompasses all that teachers do to encourage learning in their classrooms, including creating an environment that supports instruction to promote and maintain student learning and engagement. They propose a holistic definition of classroom management, one that emphasizes teachers' ongoing choices and actions rather than narrowly considering only responses to misbehavior. It is this holistic definition that we assume in the description of the following program.

This chapter describes the Classroom Organization and Management Program (COMP), which guides teachers in developing a management framework that supports decisions about creating supportive learning environments, in which students learn to take responsibility for their decisions, actions, and learning. It also presents a brief summary of the research background that led to the program's development and the results of teacher participation in this program over the past several years.

The Classroom Organization and Management Program (COMP)

As we have argued elsewhere (Evertson & Randolph, in press; Randolph & Evertson, 1995), changes in classrooms from teacher-centered to student-centered instruction imply major changes in the roles of both teachers and students, the expectations participants have of each other, and the definitions of teaching and learning that ultimately evolve in the setting. The purpose of the Classroom Organization and Management Program (COMP) is to help teachers create a positive learning environment through the development of a management framework within which a variety of academic activities take place, and where students learn to take responsibility for their decisions, actions, and learning. Teachers who participate in a COMP workshop focus on ways to create a system that prevents problems, integrates management and instruction, involves students in its creation and maintenance, and encourages professional collaboration among teachers.

Program Goals

The central goal of COMP is to help teachers improve overall instructional and management skills through planning, implementing, and maintaining effective classroom practices. Such practices provide a framework for order and organization in classrooms and provide opportunities for students to begin to manage their own learning opportunities. Additional goals are the improvement of student task engagement, reduction of student inappropriate and disruptive behavior, promotion of student responsibility for academic work and behavior, and improvement of student academic achievement.

Program Background

The program is based on a series of studies that investigated indicators of effective classroom management practices (Table 4-1). The program was originally developed from a series of studies designed to discover effective management principles and to test these principles in field experiments. The first two studies (Emmer, Evertson, & Anderson, 1980; Evertson & Emmer, 1982) identified specific components of effective classroom management practices underlying successful classrooms (e.g., teaching procedures at the beginning of the year, monitoring students), with "successful" defined as having significantly higher student academic engagement and significantly lower inappropriate and disruptive student behavior. The next four studies involved 203 teachers of grades one through nine in their classrooms in addressing these specific components (Emmer, Sanford, Clements, & Martin, 1983; Evertson, Emmer, Sanford, & Clements, 1983; Evertson, 1985, 1989a). Since initial Federal funding of the program in 1989, an additional six experimental, quasi-experimental, and evaluation studies have been conducted with 159 teachers of grades kindergarten through twelve in both regular and special education classrooms (Evertson & Harris, 1995). Based on the findings of these studies, the program received validation by the US Department of Education's National Diffusion Network for three claims of effectiveness:

1. Students of teachers who have participated in COMP realize greater gains in academic achievement as measured by standardized tests, than students of teachers who have not participated in the program.

TABLE 4-1 Summary of Studies Investigating Effective Classroom Management Practices

Study	Grade	Subject	Evaluation Studies 1978–1985				Teaching Practices (1)	Student Behaviors (2)	Student Achievements (3)	Reference
			Schools (No.)	Teachers (No.)	Classes (No.)	Students (No.)				
Descriptive/Correlational Studies										
1. Classroom Organization Study (COS)	2–4	Reading/math	8	28	28	650	X[a]	X		Emmer, Evertson & Anderson, 1980
2. Junior High Classroom, Organization Study (JHCOS)	7–8	English/math	11	51	102	2800	X	X		Evertson & Emmer, 1982
Experimental/Evaluation Studies										
3. Classroom Management Improvement Study (CMIS)	1–6	Language arts/reading	14	41	41	1066	X	X		Evertson, Emmer, Sanford, & Clements, 1983
4. Junior High Management Improvement Study (JHMIS)	7–8	English/math	10	38	76	2052	X	X		Emmer, Sanford, Clements, & Martin, 1983
5. Classroom Management Training for Elementary Teachers (CMTET)	1–6	Language arts/reading/math	3	29	29	725	X	X		Evertson, 1989a
6. Classroom Management Training for Secondary Teachers (CMTST)	7–9	English/math	2	16	16	384	X	X	X	Evertson, 1985

Continued

TABLE 4-1 *Continued*

Study	Grade	Subject	Evaluation Studies 1978–1985 Schools (No.)	Teachers (No.)	Classes (No.)	Students (No.)	1 Teaching Practices	2 Student Behaviors	3 Student Achievements	Reference
Experimental/Quasi-Experimental Studies										
7. Project UPWARD (Phase 1)	K–6/ Resource	Reading/language arts/math Ch.I	10	31	31	762	X	X		Evertson & Harris, 1995
8. Project UPWARD (Phase 2)	K–6/ Resource	Reading/language arts/math Ch.I	10	15	15	427	X	X	X	Evertson & Harris, 1995
Evaluation Studies										
9. Project MENTOR (NW9—Ohio)	2–5 (all) 2–12	Middle- high-school, math, English, science, music, art	24	28	28	642	X	X		Evertson & Harris, 1995
10. Project MENTOR (Stark County, Ohio)	K–6 (all) K–12/ Remedial	Middle- high-school math, English, science, history, music/Vocational Education	13	19	19	450	X	X		Evertson & Harris, 1995
11. COMP REVAL I	K–5/ Resource	Reading/math/language arts	3	23	23	513	X	X		Evertson & Harris, 1995
12. COMP REVAL II	6–12	English, math, science, Spanish, history	4	21	21	521	X	X		Evertson & Harris, 1995
TOTALS			112	340	429	10,992				

[a]X, evidence for this claim is provided in the study listed.

2. Teachers who have participated in COMP workshops show changed classroom practices that result in classroom environments more conducive to students' learning (Table 4-2).
3. Students of postworkshop teachers show a significant decrease in inappropriate and disruptive behavior and a significant increase in academic engagement.

Program Philosophy, Content, and Process

COMP is a comprehensive approach to developing learning environments that takes into account what adults do as teachers and children do as students in the context of the classroom. Although it incorporates research findings from more than 5,000 hours of classroom observation with summaries of current research, it also involves teachers in conversation about their own teaching and helps them draw on their own daily classroom experiences as a grounding framework. Teachers apply research-based principles to both hypothetical situations in case studies and their own classrooms.

The program reflects the belief that teachers develop the climate for learning through proactive planning at the beginning of the school year and through ongoing thoughtful decision making. Central to the teacher's classroom management task is thinking through what students need to know to be able to operate successfully in a particular classroom environment. COMP emphasizes the uniqueness of each classroom setting and seeks to promote a way of thinking through classroom management decisions, rather than presenting a "recipe" for effective management for teachers to follow. For example, COMP does not present teachers with a list of classroom rules to copy; rather, the program emphasizes that there will always be norms and expectations in the classroom, and encourages teachers to make their own expectations visible, first to themselves, and then to students, through appropriate rules. Likewise, teachers participating in COMP are not handed a universal set of procedures that will make their classrooms run smoothly; instead, teachers are guided in analyzing what students need to know in order to interact with each other and with materials successfully, and in creating procedures that facilitate this successful interaction.

Program Philosophy

COMP is based on four principles that shape the workshop experience. First: *effective classroom management means preventing problems rather than handling them after the fact* (cf. Kounin, 1970). Creating positive learning environments in which students and teachers develop communication and shared social expectations sets the stage for classrooms as learning environments and serves to eliminate—or provides positive methods to handle—classroom conflicts.

Second: *management and instruction are integrally related.* Students participate in constructing both the academic tasks of what is to be learned (cf. Doyle, 1986) and the social requirements of how they are to participate in the learning (Evertson & Randolph, in press; Randolph & Evertson, 1995); and this makes teaching a complex enterprise. Management strategies must be developed to support the many types of

TABLE 4-2   Indicators of Effective Classroom Management Practices[a]

	No. of Studies in Which Variable Was Measured	No. of Studies in Which Variable Was Significant[b]	Percent of Studies in Which Variable Was Significant
1. Readying the Classroom			
Organizing classroom space and materials	10	8	80
2. Developing Rules and Procedures			
Efficient administrative routines	10	8	80
Appropriate general procedures	10	10	100
Efficient small group procedures	6	5	83
3. Student Accountability			
Checks for understanding	10	9	90
Routines for checking and giving feedback	10	10	100
Task-oriented focus	10	10	100
4. Managing Student Behavior			
Reinforces good performance	10	9	90
Consistent management of student behavior	10	9	90
5. Monitoring			
Student behavior	10	10	100
Transitions between activities	10	8	80
6. Organizing Instruction			
Attention spans	10	8	80
Good lesson pacing	10	8	80
Lessons related to student interests	6	8	75
7. Providing Clear Instruction			
Describes objectives	10	8	80
Clear directions for academic work	10	6	60
Clear explanations and presentations	10	8	80
Student Behavior Outcomes			
High task engagement	8	7	88
Low amount of inappropriate behavior	10	8	80
Students use time constructively	7	5	71
Students take care of own needs	4	4	100

	No. of Studies in Which Variable Was Measured	No. of Studies in Which Variable Was Significant[b]	Percent of Studies in Which Variable Was Significant
Student Academic Outcomes			
Achievement gain in reading	3	3	100
Achievement gain in mathematics	3	3	100

[a]Key measures from ten observational field experiments comparing teaching practices and student outcomes in classrooms of COMP participants vs. nonparticipants.

[b]The number of studies in which the variable was measured in which it was statistically significant (or showed an effect size of ≥ .0.40) in favor of the teachers who participated in the COMP workshop.

From Herbert J. Walberg and Geneva Haertal: *Psychology and Educational Practice.* Copyright 1997 by McCutcheon Publishing Corporation, Berkeley, CA 94702. Permission granted by the publisher.

learning activities, and different strategies are required for different situations. For example, effective management strategies for student participation in cooperative group work, at a computer station, and in whole-class content presentation will differ.

Third, *students are active participants in the learning environment,* and classroom management must take into account student differences. Attention spans, learning modalities, and intelligences vary (cf. Gardner, 1983), and teachers must create and manage an environment rich with variety that addresses students' individual differences (cf. Bransford, Sherwood, Vye, & Rieser, 1986; Gardner, 1993). Diverse strategies may be required for different groups of students, different students, and even the same student during different times of the school day.

Finally, *professional collaboration supports changes in teaching practice* (cf. Lieberman, 1988). Through collaborative dialog, teachers are able to reflect on and modify ongoing practices.

COMP attempts to bring together these principles in a workshop experience in which teachers can develop a framework that helps solve problems and make decisions for working with their own students. Because there is no single management plan, format, or strategy for all teachers and all classrooms, each teacher integrates research findings along with his or her own experience and knowledge of academics and students.

Program Content

The studies that form the research base for COMP identified six key components that teachers investigate in a COMP workshop. These areas include: (1) arranging the physical space; (2) planning and teaching rules and procedures; (3) managing student work; (4) maintaining good student behavior; (5) planning and conducting appropriate lessons; and (6) helping students maintain academic engagement in those lessons. In each module, a structured sharing time allows teachers to reflect on research and to share ideas gleaned from their own classroom experience. A brief description of each area follows.

In the first area, teachers consider how the physical setting influences students and their learning. Teachers analyze different arrangements for consistency with their own instructional goals and consider ways of helping students analyze their own locations within the classroom to improve their learning and participation.

In the second module, teachers examine differences among *rules, procedures,* and *goals.* They consider specific guidelines for developing rules and ways to involve students in both developing and teaching rules. Teachers consider ways of teaching procedures, with an emphasis on developing rationales and providing students with cues for self-monitoring.

Third, teachers examine procedures specific to helping students engage in and complete academic activities successfully. Teachers consider a two-part system of *teacher responsibility* and *student responsibility,* with the teacher providing the procedural framework necessary for development of student responsibility (e.g., communicating clearly what to do, how to do it, and when and where to submit academic work). Teachers learn about ways to follow through with consistent procedures, appropriate assessment, and timely feedback.

Next, teachers examine influences on student behavior and focus on two aspects: consequences and intervention strategies. The term *consequence* refers to "the result of a previous event," and may be positive (a reward), negative (a sanction), or corrective (a teaching). Teachers examine and share a variety of *positive consequences* appropriate to the classroom, and also consider possible counterproductive effects of tangible rewards (e.g., what are the possible short- and long-range effects of handing out stickers?). Positive consequences include praise, and teachers work to develop praise patterns that help students develop feelings of ability and competence, and thus develop intrinsic motivation for lifelong learning. For example, the ubiquitous "I like the way Johnny is sitting in his seat" may become "Johnny, the way you are sitting facing front, looking, and listening will help you learn" or "Johnny, the effort you are making to pay attention shows you are practicing good listening skills." For *negative consequences,* teachers examine a variety of sanctions typically used in schools and consider the appropriateness and the possible counterproductive results of each. *Corrective consequences* include specific strategies for helping students monitor their own behavior—for example, teaching a student to set a goal and keep track of the times the goal has been met. *Intervention strategies* focus on redirecting budding student misbehavior in ways that take the least time and effort and maintain a pleasant class climate. Two key activities in this module engage teachers in examining two crucial questions to ask before responding to any emerging misbehavior: (1) Why is the student behaving in this way? and (2) What are my ultimate goals for myself as a teacher and for this student?

Teachers examine seven possible formats for student academic activities: (1) whole group; (2) teacher-led small group; (3) cooperative small group; (4) noncompetitive small group; (5) student pairs; (6) centers and stations; and (7) individualized instruction. Each is presented in terms of *what* it is, *why* a teacher would want to use it, and *management keys* that can prevent problems and help students and teachers experience success. Teachers participate in a variety of formats and instructional strategies within this topic area. They then discuss how these formats would play out in their own classrooms with their students and the specific skills students need to engage successfully in this way of learning.

Finally, teachers consider ways to help students maintain academic involvement. Four specific areas studied include: (1) clarity of instruction; (2) checking for understanding; (3) monitoring; and (4) transitions. Teachers engage in a variety of self-evaluation activities designed to make them aware of their own classroom practices that do and do not help students maintain interest in academic tasks.

If the workshop takes place before the beginning of the school year, a seventh topic is offered to guide teachers in planning their first week of school to set the stage for year-long teacher, student, and class success. Here teachers address the many details to be attended to before the first student steps through the door (e.g., daily schedule, teacher texts, student texts, class materials, school–home communication). They also consider student concerns on the first day and ways to meet these concerns that set the framework for a positive year-long experience.

Program Methods

The program sequence involves: (1) an initial workshop including the areas already discussed, culminating with a written action plan; (2) classroom application of the plan; and (3) a follow-up session, which occurs six to eighteen weeks after the initial workshop. During the follow-up session, teachers again collaborate as they report ideas they tried and how these ideas worked or did not work. They also continue to help each other with existing classroom challenges.

During the initial workshop session, participants examine each of the six key components listed under Program Content. Because the program values teacher collaboration, during the workshop teachers engage in multiple cooperative group processes as they explore research findings and their application to their own classrooms. Groups rotate periodically so that each participant has the opportunity to work with every participant.

1. *Rationale.* The first step in each topic area involves helping teachers understand how aspects of this particular area relate to the success of the overall classroom experience for students. For example, in Module One, teachers consider how clear aisles vs. cluttered aisles that access frequently used materials affect students' learning experiences. Rationale development begins by drawing on the participants' own experiences and concludes with a specific goal for the module.

2. *Focusing checklist.* The second step engages teachers in self-evaluation of the effectiveness of current topic area–related practices in their own classrooms. Teachers reflect on from seven to twelve statements that identify the things they do well and the things they could do better. For example, in Module Two, questions include: *Do you distinguish among rules, procedures, and goals? Are major class procedures* *being followed without prompting (e.g., student talk, use of equipment)?* Teachers are encouraged to return to the focusing checklists at several points throughout the year as a way to continue self-evaluation.

3. *Research.* The third step presents teachers with summaries of area- related research findings and their implications for classroom practices, and engages teachers in relating these to experiences within their own classrooms. For example, in Module Three, teachers discuss the balance between the nature of academic tasks for students and the criteria for successful completion. They examine Doyle's (1983) research on academic work, which illustrates how the teacher defines and follows the criteria for a given assignment determines how students accomplish it. What the teacher "actually rewards" determines what the task is, not the stated goal or assignment. Teachers consider how they have experienced this insight played out in their own classrooms.

4. *Key elements.* The fourth step draws from the research base to identify and describe key elements specific to the topic area that can be applied to the classroom. For example, in Module One, research findings on classroom arrangement can be expressed with the terms *visibility, accessibility,* and *distractibility.*

5. *Initial application.* The fifth step engages teachers in applying the key concepts from the previous steps to case studies and vignettes. In Module Two, teachers consider three case studies presenting different philosophies and ways of involving students in developing classroom rules, discussing the advantages and disadvantages of each.

6. *Personal application.* The sixth step asks teachers to apply key concepts to their own classrooms and begin to consider the things they might do to improve their classroom in the given topic area. For example, in Module One, teachers use scaled templates to replicate and critique their room arrangements; in Module Three, they create checklists for students to use to evaluate themselves on academic and behavioral habits that lead to success in their classrooms.

7. *Written commitments.* The seventh step challenges teachers to identify and write down specific strategies they plan to try in their classrooms. During the six to eighteen weeks following the initial workshop, participants implement specific management strategies with technical assistance from the workshop leader as requested. Teachers tend to list ten specific changes they wish to make, and report actually implementing seven of the ten.

In the morning of the follow-up day, participants review each of the six topic areas, report the plans implemented and results for each, and identify and engage in problem-solving strategies for existing concerns. During the afternoon, the workshop leader engages participants in additional research-based content presentations selected to address participants' indicated interests and needs. An eighth module, entitled, "Climate, Communication, and Student Self-Management Strategies," provides additional text for the afternoon session. The assumption—supported by teacher and administrative feedback (Fig. 4-1)—is that after participating in the COMP work-shop and applying ideas learned in their classrooms, teachers have improved in both management skill and personal confidence and are willing to go into more depth in examining their own classrooms and to try new ways of working with students. In this module, teachers look at ways of developing positive classroom climate, evaluate the climate of their own classrooms, and explore ways to involve their students in evaluating that climate. They study and practice one-on-one communication tech-niques to help students solve problems and consider ways to help students assume greater responsibility for managing their own behavior and learning.

Program Results

COMP is based on extensive research in classrooms. From observing and listening to teachers, we developed a program of intervention to engage teachers in addressing key issues of classroom management, and we have consistently evaluated the results of the intervention. Program results have been measured repeatedly in two ways: first, with observational field studies involving a minimum of six observations per classroom; and second, with teachers' self-evaluation reports and their administra-tors' reports of observed classroom, teacher, and student change.

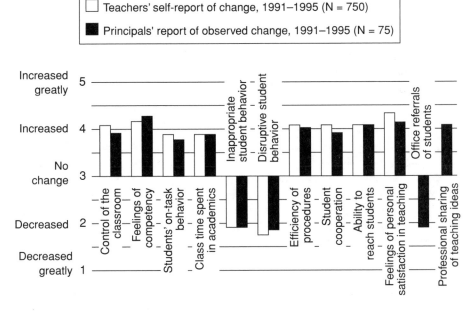

FIGURE 4-1 Perceived changes in classrooms, teachers, and student behavior as a result of teachers' participation in the COMP workshop.

Ten experimental studies comparing teaching practices and student behavior in 261 teachers' classrooms, including grades kindergarten through twelve, involving both regular and special education, span the years 1978 through 1995 (see Table 4-1). These studies consistently reveal significant change in seventeen teacher variables, four student behavior variables, and two student outcome variables (see Table 4-2). Teachers who have participated in the program do things differently in their classrooms, their students are more academically engaged and display less misbehavior, and their students have higher academic achievement. One hundred percent of the studies in which the variable was measured showed a significant increase in teachers' developing appropriate general procedures, developing routines for checking and giving feedback, maintaining a task-oriented focus, and monitoring of student transitions; and for students, 100% of the studies showed a significant increase in their taking care of their own needs, achievement gains in reading, and achievement gains in math. Ninety percent of the studies showed a significant difference in the teachers' checks for understanding, reinforcement of good student performance, and consistency in management of student behavior; and in students' high task engagement. Eighty percent of the studies indicated significant difference in teachers' developing efficient administrative routines, monitoring transition between activities, organizing instruction to address student attention span, pacing lessons appropriately, describing lesson objectives, and providing clear instruction; and in students' low amount of inappropriate behavior.

Since 1989, COMP has been implemented in more than 6,200 schools across the United States and the American territories. Schools have included urban, suburban, rural, and inner-city settings, and classrooms have included a wide range of class size, grades kindergarten through twelve, regular classrooms, regular classrooms with mainstreamed students, and self-contained resource classrooms, with varying demographic components. Workshop participants have included more than 13,800 teachers, with experience ranging from zero to thirty-eight years, and classroom management expertise ranging the full spectrum.

A random sampling of more than 11,000 Consumer Satisfaction Inventories from this wide variety of demographics, experience, and expertise indicates that teachers across the demographic spectrum and at all levels of experience and expertise value the workshop experience. Results for both novice and veteran teachers are positive.

Each year since 1991, a random sample of participant responses of perceptions of classroom, teacher, and student behavior change has been analyzed, as well as a random sample of principals' perception of changes in classrooms of teachers who participated in a workshop (see Fig. 4-1). Both teachers and their principals were asked to rate their perceptions of teacher, classroom, and student change, using a Likert scale of one to five in which the midpoint of three indicates "no change," above three indicates an increase, and below a decrease. Teachers consistently reported an increase in desired classroom activities such as students' on-task behavior, class time spent in academics, efficiency of procedures, and student cooperation, and in their own feelings of competency and feelings of personal satisfaction in teaching; and they report noticeable decrease in students' inappropriate and disruptive behaviors. Principals consistently reported observing objectively these same changes that the teachers identified subjectively, as well as a noticeable decrease in student office referrals from those teachers and an increase in professional sharing of teaching ideas among those teachers. When entire faculties of a school have participated, administrators reported school-wide positive changes, including greater academic focus, less wasted time, more positive teacher attitudes, better faculty communication, increased intrafaculty communication and professional sharing of ideas, fewer office referrals, and fewer student suspensions.

Conclusion

Learning to create conditions for learning is an evolutionary process, one for which teachers need professional development, support, and dialog. COMP shows how a holistic view of classroom management, one that incorporates all teachers do to encourage learning in their classrooms, can be developed in teachers. The program's success indicates that when such a view is put into practice, positive student behavior and learning outcomes are supported. Teaching for understanding and creating ways for students to be more involved in their own learning will not be realized unless the basic principles for creating an effective learning environment are understood.

References

Alton-Lee, A., Nuthall, G., & Patrick, J. (1993). Reframing classroom research: A lesson from the private world of children. *Harvard Educational Review, 63*(1), 50–84.

Bransford, J., Sherwood, R., Vye, N., & Rieser, J. (1986). Teaching thinking and problem solving: Research foundations. *American Psychologist, 41*(10), 1078–1089.

Brophy, J. E. (1998). *Motivating students to learn.* Boston: McGraw-Hill.

Doyle, W. (1983). Academic work. *Review of Educational Research, 53*(2), 159–199.

Doyle, W. (1986). Classroom organization and management. In M. Wittrock (Ed.), *Handbook of research on teaching* (3rd. ed., pp. 392–431). New York: Macmillan.

Emmer, E. T., Evertson, C. M., & Anderson, L. M. (1980). Effective classroom management at the beginning of the school year. *The Elementary School Journal, 80*(5), 219–231.

Emmer, E. T., Sanford, J. P., Clements, B. S., & Martin, J. (1983, March). *Improving junior high classroom management.* Paper presented at the annual meeting of the American Educational Research Association, Montreal. (ERIC Document Reproduction Service No. ED 234 021.)

Evertson, C. M., (1985). Training teachers in classroom management: An experiment in secondary classrooms. *Journal of Educational Research, 79,* 51–58.

Evertson, C. M. (1989a). Improving elementary classroom management: A school-based training program for beginning the year. *Journal of Educational Research, 83*(2), 82–90.

Evertson, C. M. (1989b, September). *Classroom organization and management program (COMP): Submission to the program effectiveness panel.* Nashville, TN: Peabody College, Vanderbilt University. (ERIC Document Reproduction Service No. ED 331 777.)

Evertson, C. M., & Emmer, E. T. (1982). Effective management at the beginning of the school year in junior high classes. *Journal of Educational Psychology, 74,* 485–498.

Evertson, C. M., Emmer, E. T., Sanford, J. P., & Clements, B. S. (1983). Improving classroom management: An experiment in elementary classrooms. *The Elementary School Journal, 84,* 173–188.

Evertson, C. M., & Harris, A. H. (1995, September). *Classroom organization and management program: Revalidation submission to the Program Effectiveness Panel (PEP), US Department of Education.* Nashville, TN: Peabody College, Vanderbilt University. (ERIC Document Reproduction Service No. ED 403 247.)

Evertson, C. M., & Randolph, C. H. (in press). Perspectives on classroom management for learning-centered classrooms. In H. Waxman, & H. J. Walberg (Eds.), *New directions for research on teaching.* Berkeley, CA: McCutchan.

Evertson, C. M., & Weade, R. (1991). The social construction of classroom lessons. In H. Waxman, & H. Walberg (Eds.), *Effective teaching: Current research.* Berkeley, CA: McCutchan.

Evertson, C. M., Weade, R., Green, J., & Crawford, J. (1985, June). *Effective classroom management and instruction: An exploration of models.* Final report. (NIE-G-83–0063) Nashville, TN: Peabody College, Vanderbilt University. (ERIC Document Reproduction Service No. ED 271 422.)

Gardner, H. (1983). *Frames of mind: The theory of multiple intelligences.* New York: Basic Books.

Gardner, H. (1993). *Multiple intelligences: The theory in practice.* New York: Basic Books.

Green, J. L., & Weade, R. (1985). Reading between the words: Social cues to lesson participation. *Theory into Practice, 24*(1), 14–21.

Kounin, J. (1970). *Discipline and group management in classrooms.* New York: Holt, Rinehart & Winston.

Lieberman, A. (Ed.). (1988). *Building a professional culture in schools.* New York: Teachers College Press.

Randolph, C. H., & Evertson, C. M. (1995). Managing for learning: Rules, roles and meanings in a writing class. *Journal of Classroom Interaction, 30*(2), 17–25.

Randolph, C. H., & Evertson, C. M. (1994). Images of management for learner-centered classrooms. *Action in Teacher Education, 16*(1), 55–64.

5

*Consistency
Management &
Cooperative Discipline*

From Tourists to Citizens in the Classrooms

H. JEROME FREIBERG
University of Houston

Introduction

One-minute student managers and classroom constitutions are two elements of Consistency Management & Cooperative Discipline, a research- and classroom-based program that builds citizenship in the classroom through experience, not just words.

Judy Kirby: It is early May. I look at my fifth-hour class and marvel at the climate of cooperation in a room full of 30 14-year-olds, hungry ones at that. They aren't disagreeing, sleeping, being insubordinate, or indifferent. They are enjoying learning and one another.

Last year, I spent all my time trying to control my students. This year, the students know they matter. The negative attention–getting has stopped—there is no longer a need for it. They belong.

Judy Kirby, a teacher for twenty-five years, is describing her English class. Within the first two minutes, students are taking role, preparing attendance records, and arranging the room for their interaction groups. Such student-centered activities, although more common in preschool and kindergarten classrooms, are less frequently found in the upper grades. Too often, classroom management systems built on trust and support in the early years are replaced with compliance and obedience systems in the latter grades, causing bright-eyed, eager first graders to become tourists in our schools by third grade. Tourists simply pass through without involvement, commitment or belonging (Rogers & Freiberg, 1994). In too many schools, a tacit agreement sometimes exists between teachers and students: "Leave me alone, and I won't give you trouble." Inner-city classrooms, in particular, rely heavily on teacher control and student compliance.[1]

Consistency Management & Cooperative Discipline (CMCD) is a research-based and classroom-tested school reform model that builds on shared responsibility between teachers and students for learning and classroom organization (Freiberg, 1983; Freiberg, Prokosch, Treister, & Stein, 1990; Freiberg, Stein, & Huang, 1995; Freiberg, 1996). The CMCD program works with geographic feeder systems of schools from Prekindergarten through twelfth grade (Fig. 5-1) that includes thousands of students, teachers, and administrators in one area of the city. Consistency Management provides sustained messages to children about what it means to be self-disciplined. Messages that are changed every year or are inconsistent for every classroom diminish discipline and achievement. CMCD also provides a sustainable message for all who work with children: administrators, teachers, specialists, aides, cafeteria workers, and bus drivers.

---

[1]Adapted from Freiberg, H. J. (1996). From tourists to citizens in the classroom. *Educational Leadership, 51*(1), 32–37.

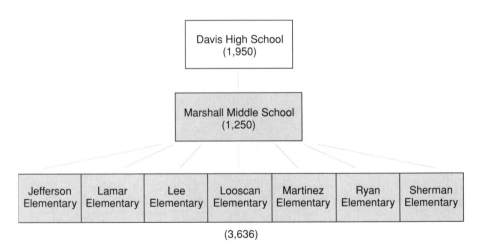

FIGURE 5-1   **Davis Feeder Pattern. Total of students: 6,836.**

As students move from one grade level to the next and from one school to the next (elementary, middle, and high schools), they continue to experience expanding opportunities for active participation in the management of their classrooms and schools. The CMCD project provides support to the educational professional and staff over a three-year period through staff development, school-based facilitators, and ongoing research (which is provided to the schools throughout the year). The teacher is able to create a consistent but flexible learning environment and joins with the students in establishing a cooperative plan for classroom rules, procedures, use of time, and academic learning that governs the classroom, all within a developing democratic structure. Classrooms and schools are usually the last place one finds democratic principles; but they should be the first.

Defining the Program

The definition for the CMCD program is evolving. It is being expanded by those most closely influenced by the program—teachers, students, administrators and parents. This evolution is also being shaped by longitudinal research studies of classroom environments, discipline, and learning.

As the name suggests, Consistency Management & Cooperative Discipline has two distinct components. *Consistency Management* focuses on classroom and instructional organization and planning by the teacher. From seating arrangements to passing out papers, sharpening pencils, attendance taking, and using time to providing equal opportunity to participate in class, the teacher as the instructional leader creates a supportive and caring environment in which all members can participate and learn.

The CMCD program moves beyond behaviorism and behavior modification techniques widely used in schools. It has become evident in our work that the need to reward students at every turn to get their cooperation is a shallow and short-term response to a long-term need of creating responsible citizens.

The following reflects representative responses of teachers who have used the CMCD program in their classrooms.

Question: What does CMCD mean to you?

Teacher 1: "Consistency Management means prevention...making sure a problem doesn't happen."

Teacher 2: "It gives all kids a chance to be in a leadership role."

Teacher 3: "It means my life in class is a whole lot easier. So much pressure has been taken off of me."

Teacher 4: "A system of managing the children that allows them to be responsible for themselves."

Teacher 5: "I've learned a lot of behavior modification, and it usually deals with a reward system...the difference is that Consistency Management builds from within."

Teacher 6: "I thought it was great! It's great because if I didn't have it, I probably would have gone nuts this year."

Teacher 7: "I think it teaches responsibility, kindness, and respect, and those are the things they need to learn."

Cooperative Discipline expands the leadership roles in the classroom from the teacher to the students. It gives *all* students the opportunity to become leaders. Given multiple chances for leadership in small and large ways, students gain the experiences necessary to become self-disciplined. Students are partners and stakeholders in the classroom, from creating a classroom constitution to establishing new job responsibilities for some fifty tasks that teachers usually take on themselves. Student responsibility includes knowing what to do when the teacher is not present, the solving of disputes, preventing problems, and working cooperatively in groups, and becomes a collaborative effort rather than the sole responsibility of the teacher.

A seventh-grade teacher in an inner-city middle school had some very serious challenges with student discipline. He decided to take the CMCD project to another level—creating a court system in his classroom to manage late students and other problems in the classroom (Ridrog, 1996). The students were the judge and jury and their teacher was the "court of appeals." Student comments were very enlightening:

Aurora: The kids are judged by what they do and not by how popular they are. The judges are fair. Mr. Rigrod makes sure that the sentences are not too stiff and that we give each person on trial a fair chance.

Julio: I enjoy asking the questions because I can learn more about the reason the kids were late.

Darvon: I like to give the sentences because it's better than receiving the sentence. I like the court because kids get to tell their side of what happened and it's handled in the classroom.

Frank: The court treats everyone fair. I decided to be good now because I know what the consequences will be if I'm not.

Martha: I like the court because the kids cooperate with the teacher to make decisions for the class. The court makes a difference in the classes and it makes people act better. I wish I had the court in all of my classes.

Bruno: I like the court because it gives you a chance to tell what happened, and many times kids never get to tell their side. I'd probably act worse if the court did not exist. I like being the judge because it's something that everyone doesn't get to do.

Repertoire of Instructional and Organizational Tools

Working with students who are self-disciplined is a personal and professional goal of almost every teacher. Achieving that goal requires a greater repertoire of instructional and organizational strategies than most teachers acquire during their first years of teaching. Planning, Instructional Design, Use of Time in the Classroom, Advancework—an information gathering strategy—and classroom management are hidden from most observers (Freiberg & Driscoll, 1996). Classroom management and instruction are different sides of the same coin and must be seen as one issue. A neophyte teacher observing a master teacher's classroom would see the outcome of effective planning—a smoothly functioning lesson—but would not be privy to the mental and visualization processes of planning that occur prior to the lesson. A student-teacher or an intern who observes after the first few days of school could miss the advancework and classroom management strategies that were developed to create a positive learning environment. Strategies utilized to save time and help design instruction may also be missed in direct observations.

Organizing strategies help create the conditions for learning and are skills that can be acquired more systematically than depending on a trial-and-error method, which could take years to establish. The CMCD program has consolidated the best organizational and instructional practices of teachers and placed them in a context that is neither totally student-centered nor totally teacher-centered, but is a person-centered environment—where students and teachers become partners in the learning process. The person-centered context is important because in a desire for teachers to create an orderly and effective learning environment, the overall climate for learning may become unhealthy for both learners and their teachers. A militaristic approach to classroom management and organization may produce quiet and orderly classrooms but at the expense of student involvement, affiliation, and teacher support and innovation. A study by Parker (1994) used 608 middle-school students in forty-seven classrooms. Eighteen classrooms used assertive discipline (Canter & Canter, 1992) and twenty-nine used non-Assertive Discipline. Parker found that students in non-Assertive Discipline classrooms perceived their learning environments to be significantly higher [as measured in Effect Size (ES) differences] in involvement (ES = +1.50), affiliation (ES = +1.28), and teacher support (ES = +0.97) and innovation (ES = +1.69) than students in Assertive Discipline classrooms. Parker also found that less emphasis was placed on teacher control in non-Assertive Discipline classrooms. The way classrooms are organized and the roles teachers and students play in developing and maintaining the learning environment has a significant influence on interpersonal and learning outcomes. Linked together, Consistency Management & Cooperative Discipline provide a flexible plan to improve the quality of instruction and the learning environment in order to produce a cooperative, caring, and safe place for students and teachers to work and learn.

The CMCD project seeks to turn tourists into citizens by helping educators create active classrooms where cooperation, participation, and support are the cornerstones. These classrooms are neither totally teacher-centered nor totally student-centered; they are person-centered (Table 5-1).

Citizenship through Experience

Although democracy is taught in schools and classrooms, it is rarely practiced. CMCD seeks to change this situation by creating caring and interactive classrooms and supportive schools that provide multiple opportunities for students to become citizens rather than tourists. In places where people respect them and care about them as individuals, students can learn to become informed and involved members of our democratic society.

The CMCD program combines instructional effectiveness through consistency of organization in the classroom, with student self- discipline developed cooperatively with teachers. The CMCD program supports teachers in creating a pro-democratic environment for both decision-making and the operations of the classroom. As Fig. 5-2 indicates, classrooms that focus on students being citizens are more democratic and create partnerships in the design of how social interactions, academic work, and learning take place. The CMCD program provides teachers with the instructional tools that allow students to develop through experience and with opportunities for self-discipline. Teachers must do more than tell students to be responsible; they need to show the trust necessary for students to take responsibility in the

TABLE 5-1 Tourist and Citizen Learning Environments

Tourist	vs.	Citizen
Students are passive learners		Students are active learners
Do low-level worksheets		Do small-group projects
Work by themselves		Work in cooperative learning groups of 2 or 4
Work on what the teacher has provided		Create new ideas and materials through projects
Seldom write		Write every day
Rarely have their work prominently displayed		Students (self-selected) work displayed
Seldom discuss the reasons for their answers		Usually, think or talk aloud about how they derived an answer
Seldom participate in class		Takes the initiative to interact with teachers and peers
It's your classroom		It's our classroom
Teacher-controlled discipline		Cooperative discipline
Have few friends in class		Have several friends in class
Usually late to class		Usually on time or early to class
Absent from school more		Have fewer absences
Neutral to hate school		Enjoy and involve themselves in school

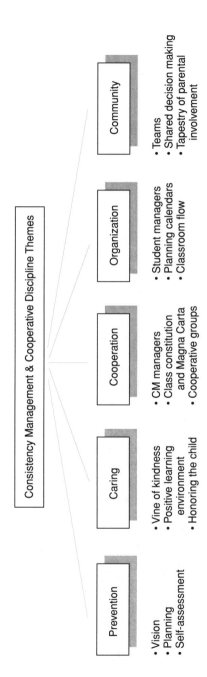

FIGURE 5-2

Written permission required for copies. © 1997 Consistency Management Associates.

classroom. Historically, teachers have provided leadership opportunities for a select few students in the classroom. Terms like *monitor* and *teacher's pet* describe these positions of opportunity. The monitor becomes an overseer or master above the other students. The teacher's pet has a privileged relationship with the teacher that is not open to all students in the classroom. These common practices perpetuate a nondemocratic environment and make the learning environment oppressive for many students.

Scope of Implementation

The CMCD model is currently being used by more than 40,000 (prekindergarten through twelfth grade) students and teachers from the inner cities to rural schools. It gives teachers and administrators a flexible framework for improving the quality of instruction and learning environments. The CMCD philosophy incorporates five themes: *Prevention, Caring, Cooperation, Organization* and *Community* (Freiberg, 1991). Each theme includes strategies and activities that allow students to become real partners in the classroom, some of which are illustrated here (Fig. 5-2).

Prevention Is 80 Percent of Classroom Management

"An ounce of prevention is worth a pound of cure"—an adage that works well in the classroom. Why spend valuable time and energy solving problems when they could be prevented in the first place? In many instances discipline problems reflect a breakdown in a prevention plan or a lack of inclusion by the pupils into the classroom organization. In some instances, student misbehavior is a healthy student response to an unhealthy learning environment.

I have observed that classroom management is *problem prevention* rather than *problem solving,* thus reducing the need for intervention. Teachers can prevent or minimize future discipline problems by spending time before the start of the school year and during the first days and weeks establishing opportunities for students to achieve high standards for behavior as well as for academics. Consistency by students and teachers throughout the year helps to create a rising tide of expectations for behavior and learning. For example, in a classroom in which CMCD is being incorporated during the start of the school year, teachers and students establish rules for learning based on mutual needs by developing classroom constitution or Magna Carta. A sample statement developed by students in a fifth-grade classroom might read as follows:

> *We the students are entitled to: learn, feel safe, complain to the grievance committee [which the class created along with the constitution], ask questions, speak freely, have friends, not be put down, be treated fairly, share our feelings, get help, understand, and be treated kindly. (Tina Smith, 1995)*

All members of the classroom, including the teacher, sign the documents, which are in effect throughout the year. A classroom constitutional convention may be held to revise the constitution. Such experiences enable students to test their own values and build important bridges to their future roles in society.

Caring Is the Heart and Soul of Teaching

Students want to know how much you care, not how much you know. Authentic caring requires listening, reflecting, trusting, and respecting the learner (Rogers & Freiberg, 1994). Honoring the child while correcting the behavior is an important first step. Being a positive role model goes a long way to communicating positive expectations. Students need positive models for caring, from both adults and one another.

One way teachers can promote awareness of caring actions and behaviors is by audiotaping their classrooms. After listening to the tone of the dialog, teachers play the tapes for their classes. A discussion follows in which everyone identifies "killer statements" by students or teachers—for example, "That's a dumb question." A killer statement is any comment made by a class member (teacher or student) that will inhibit any person from sharing their ideas.

A caring climate can be built through a variety of other ways. For example, administrators often teach classes, read stories, or share experiences with students, allowing students to see them as educators, not just disciplinarians. Students' birthdays and important events (like the birth of a brother or sister) are celebrated. As part of the celebration, the teacher may take the birthday child's picture in front of a happy birthday sign. A seventh-grade middle-school teacher who started this in her social studies class initially was discouraged by the response. Only one student was willing to have his birthday celebrated. In the past, students' birthdays were met in this inner-city school with "nuggies" (rubbing the top of the head with a knuckle) and "hits" from other students. However, once she explained the rule that no student should be hit on their birthday, every student wanted their birthday celebrated. Even students born during the summer requested that their birthdays be celebrated.

Cooperation Means Sharing and Helping Each Other Succeed

Helping, sharing, participating, planning, and working together—these are the heart of a cooperative classroom. Cooperation leads to ownership, involvement, and greater opportunities for student self-discipline. However, trust must come first.

Students learn to trust through opportunities to take ownership. Sergio, a seventh-grade student from an inner-city middle school, wrote in his journal about starting the school day when his teacher was absent and the substitute did not show.

> *I feel lucky today because the day has just started and we have already been trusted in something we have never been trusted on, being alone. It is 8:15 and everything is cool. Nothing is even wrong...*

When students become citizens of the school, they take responsibility for their actions and those of others. On the October day that Sergio wrote about, one student sent the attendance to the office while another student reviewed the homework with the class and started classroom presentations scheduled for the day. When the substitute teacher finally arrived, the students were engaged in learning. They had been taking responsibility for the classroom operations since September and, in a sense, were being prepared for this experience. The following teacher comments also reflect the need for a partnership in the classroom.

Teacher 1: "CMCD means that we're going to discipline and manage together, both teacher and student."

Teacher 2: "It means that kids can work together as a team. They cooperate with each other. They get along and they have respect not only for the teacher, but each other as well."

Teacher 3: "I thought it was not going to work with the older kids. I had to eat my words. It's wonderful. My biggest surprise was to see that the sixth graders like it. And the ones that seemed to be discipline problems, they don't seem to be any more..."

Teacher 4: "There is more time to do things and it [CMCD] motivates more children."

Teacher 5: "CMCD is helpful in getting the students really involved in the program to the point where they are actually managing the classroom.".

Organization Is the Foundation of the Classroom

Classroom organization is a mutual responsibility that adds valuable teaching and learning time and builds student ownership and self-discipline. For example, one-minute student managers are an important element of the project.

Classroom management positions, which range from passing out papers to assisting the substitute teacher, are posted in the classroom; students complete job applications for them. Teachers review the applications and select students based on stated interests. Jobs are rotated every four to six weeks so that all students hold positions in the classroom. Many teachers also conduct job interviews. Younger students discuss their jobs. In a bilingual classroom of four-year olds, the students decided that two shoelace managers were needed to save their teacher's back and to speed their exit to lunch.

At Sergio's middle school, a student attendance manager keeps the roll on the computer while their teacher talks with the other students. Next door, students decided the teacher was losing teaching time setting up printers. The printer manager describes the impact of her job on the teacher.

Well, like today, since all of us had questions about our work and one of the printers was messing up. So instead of her wasting her time in trying to fix the printer, she helped some kids and I fixed the printer. She was able to help a few kids instead of nobody.

Management positions are open to every student rather than a select few. The forty-plus one-minute jobs vary by the age of the student and needs of each classroom. During regular classroom meetings, students decide whether they need to add or delete jobs. When surveyed, teachers indicated that the one-minute jobs give them, on average, fourteen to thirty more minutes of teaching time daily.

Students do not receive external rewards for their manager jobs. The work itself and the accompanying interaction with the teacher and peers is its own reward. The decision to use behavior incentives in other parts of the program, however, is up to the teachers and administrators of each school. Some program schools use incentives; others do not.

Community Builds Resilience

The CMCD model recognizes that today's family patterns require diversified, flexible approaches to involving parents and other stakeholders. Baking cookies and watching their children in school performances has limited viability today, given the number of one-parent families and even two-parent families who both must work during the day. During the first week of school, some teachers invite parents to talk to students about how workplace rules relate to classroom rules. Many teachers send home a weekly classroom calendar of events to keep parents informed.

A tapestry of parental and community involvement activities and events are necessary to meet the needs of the changing American family. Figure 5-3 displays the variety of successful events that enable schools, parents, and communities to achieve greater connectedness. Children need to see other adults in school in addition to those who are paid to be there. They provide important positive role models for students and validate the importance of their education and your work. The five themes of CMCD *Prevention, Caring, Cooperation, Organization, and Community* form the foundation of the program.

In-Service Design: Just-In-Time Staff Development

The CMCD staff development program is timed to match the needs of teachers and students. The first session is held in the spring of the year with an all-day workshop and a follow-up in May. This is timed when the need for caring and peaceful learning environments are at a premium. A second two-day workshop is provided before school begins in August and six three-hour workshops are held approximately once every two months after school from September until March. Thirty-six contact hours of faculty and principal development are provided to each CMCD program school. The spring and August workshops also provide the time and materials for teachers to make posters and other artifacts to implement the program. However, based on teacher interviews, a much greater number of noncontact hours (three- to fourfold) were used by the participants to develop classroom materials (e.g., management posters, absent packets, positive postcards, want ads for student managers, and in and out boxes); to observe each other using on- and off-task charts; self-assessment, using audiotapes; as well as spending time in team- or grade-level planning sessions discussing instructional management and program implementation. During the second year, an all-day workshop before school starts is provided to the original cohort of teachers and a second set of six staff development sessions is presented in year two for teachers new to the schools. High-implementing teachers also become CMCD facilitators for the school, and are responsible for keeping the knowledge base of the program at the classroom and school level. Sessions for the new teachers include training on the development of classroom rules and procedures, effective use of instructional time, student motivation, teacher self-assessments and peer observations, school management, community and parental involvement, and faculty–administration team building.

Workshop Contents[2]

The introductory Consistency Management workshop conducted on a Saturday in April focuses on changing the way teachers view student discipline from one of control to one of cooperation. Specific strategies for including students at the end of the year are provided, including the use of students as managers in the classroom, rewriting rules in the form of a classroom constitution to reflect students needs and responsibilities and the relationships between positive classroom environments and learning.

The August CMCD workshop builds from the teacher experiences in April of the previous school year and focuses the faculty on the ecology of the start of the school year. Efforts are made to emphasize the interactions between learner, content, and context (Freiberg & Driscoll, 1996) and the importance of establishing a positive learning environment that prevents disruptions rather than focus on discipline interventions as a primary goal. Follow-up workshops are provided to maintain a level of support and internal consistency. The professional development sessions are provided throughout the year to provide opportunities for teachers to reflect, discuss and receive additional support during their first year of implementation.

> Workshop #1: The first follow-up session emphasizes the need for positive parental contacts at the beginning of the year, when behavior or academic problems are at a minimum. Teachers call home (when parents have telephones) to provide a portrait of the school day and strategies for parental assistance at home for their children. A telephone script is provided during the workshop for teachers who are uncertain about parental contacts. Strategies are provided for teachers to

---

[2]The description of workshop contents was adapted from Freiberg, H. J., Prokosch, N., Treister, E., and Stein, T. A. (1990). Turning around five at-risk elementary schools. *Journal of School Effectiveness and School Improvement, 1*(1), 5–25.

FIGURE 5-3 Tapestry of Parent–Community Involvement

Field Trips with business mentors	Mentor Program	Extended learning projects	Shows & Plays	PTA/PTO Classes	Parent Book Report	Reading Conference *Parent reads to student in hallway*
Parents attend class for one hour	Parent convention on Saturday	Clubs	Adopt a room/school	Certificates for citizenship and academics	Clean up *Each class has a designated area to keep clean*	Creative Book Binding
Positive Post Cards mailed home	Parents in Education	Teach For A Half Day *Parent teaches class so teacher can attend in-service*	Parents Make Center Activities *Parents supply materials.*	Help Beautify the School *Each class is responsible for an area of school*	Special Person's Day *Students invite a special person to lunch*	Parent Repairs Furniture
Big Brothers and Big Sisters	Report card night *Parents pick up report cards in evening and meet with their child's teacher*	Call home 'ET' *Teacher calls home before school begins and 3 more times during the year.*	Parent Packets *To be worked on at home over holidays and summer for their children*	Saturday Scholars Program	Parents' Grade Day	Grandparent Day
Seat time reading with parent	Parents connect work and school *Parent explains how math is used in daily work*	Parents donate books on child's birthday to the class	Lunch Theater *students provide theater for community members*	Parents donate books and work in library	Homeroom Parents	Parent Breakfast
Six-foot book cover on door *Parents help to construct cover with child*	Mother's Day tea	Shell II Science Program with parents and children on Saturday	Pinning ceremony twice a year for Good Citizenship	Community leaders discuss rules and procedures with students	Principal reads stories to students in class	College students talk with classes about careers

help students feel part of a learning community. Positive Post Cards are sent home supporting timely return of homework or being punctual to school. Teachers visit other classrooms, taking pictures of students involved in academic tasks. Pictures of students studying, presenting information, working in groups, and reading are posted on a bulletin board in the main hallway. Discussions are also held to review the ideas, plans and materials from previous workshops.

Workshop #2: This session focuses on increasing active learning while minimizing disruptions. The teachers are shown videotaped examples of other teachers using active learning strategies in the content areas of mathematics and reading. One video example showed individual student chalkboards to help in assessing student learning. The teacher in the videotape presented a math problem and the students wrote their answers on their own chalkboards. On cue from the teacher, all the students held up their answers. Only the teacher saw their responses. The teacher made a mental note of which students missed the problem and worked with them during seatwork time. If enough students missed the problem, the teacher stopped and retaught the concept. This workshop also focuses on greater parental involvement, with a workshop presented to parents at the school to assist them in helping their children be more effective learners in the classroom.

Workshop #3: The third workshop asks teachers to assess their instruction. Each teacher audiotapes a thirty-minute segment of their classroom and uses the Low Inference Self-Assessment Measure (see Freiberg, 1987; and Freiberg & Driscoll, 1996, Chapter 15, for a detailed description of the LISAM instrument) to analyze their interactions with their students. The teachers listen to the tape and then prepare written critiques to share with their peers. The principals who attend most of the sessions do not stay for the teacher self-assessment sessions.

Workshop #4: The research on cooperative grouping (Slavin, 1983) and peer tutoring (Berliner & Casanova, 1988) support these strategies as powerful learning tools, particularly for low-achieving students. This workshop provides examples of how to develop these active learning strategies. Many of the teachers have prior training in both strategies but have difficulty in managing the student-focused activities. The sessions include ways of phasing in cooperative learning groups, starting with groups of two and building slowly to groups of four over several weeks or months.

Workshop #5: This workshop focuses on learning centers and their management. It is designed as a means of moving away from teacher and student dependency on worksheets and is conducted by master teachers who have been trained in the CMCD program and have had extensive experience in learning centers. The workshop leaders bring their own classroom centers to the workshop and allow the teachers to participate in the centers and assist the teachers in building their own math or reading center. Using centers as part of reading time allows students to circulate from reading with the teacher to seatwork to center work. This flow of instructional activities reduces the amount of time a child spends on any one task to about twenty minutes, reducing boredom and, ultimately, off-task student behavior.

Workshop #6: The final workshop is held in the spring. The session includes teachers reporting on the on-task and off-task seating charts and interactive instruction observations conducted by teachers' peers during the previous week (see Stallings, Needles, & Sparks, 1987, for examples of the instruments). The teachers discuss the types of interactions they had with their students and how best to create a relaxed but productive classroom.

Findings

The CMCD program has been replicated in controlled studies over time. The findings from both qualitative and quantitative studies show a strong positive change in many of the outcomes viewed as desirable for reforming schools and transforming classrooms.

The CMCD program has undergone extensive research on its initial and long-term effectiveness. Following is a summarization of the findings of the program. Published research is referred to in each of the findings (Freiberg, Prokosch, Treister & Stein, 1990; Freiberg & Huang; 1994; Freiberg, Stein & Huang, 1995; & Freiberg, 1995). In addition, ongoing research findings are reported from a third party evaluation (Opuni, 1996), a review of CMCD as part of a national study (Olatokunbo & Slavin, 1997), and current office discipline referrals across seven elementary schools. The following documents results of instituting the CMCD model:

1. Increase in student attendance. The CMCD school gained in student attendance from ninety-four to ninety-five percent whereas the comparison school lost in attendance from ninety-five to ninety-four percent (Freiberg, Stein, & Huang, 1995).

2. Increase in teacher attendance. The CMCD school gained in teacher attendance from ninety-four to ninety-eight percent, whereas the comparison school lost in attendance from ninety-five to ninety-four percent during the same time period (Freiberg, Stein, & Huang, 1995).

3. Significant increases in student achievement. Statistically significant improvement was found in achievement scores on TAAS, TEAMS (state tests), and MAT-6 (standardized tests) with students who had teachers implementing the CMCD program over matched students who had teachers not using the program (Freiberg, Prokosch, Treister, & Stein, 1990; Freiberg & Huang, 1994; Freiberg, Stein, & Huang, 1995; & Freiberg, 1995).

4. Significant increase in long-term student achievement. Statistically significant sustaining improvement after CMCD had concluded on achievement scores on TAAS, TEAMS, and MAT-6 with students who had teachers implementing the CMCD program over matched students who had teachers not using the program. The overall effect size due to program treatment on the MAT-6 test scores was large, ranging from

0.43 (1986–1987) and 0.83 (1987–1988) during intervention to 0.73 (1988–1989) after intervention. Similar results were found in the TEAMS test associated with the program intervention with overall effect size of 1.02 (1987–1988) and 0.78 (1988–1989) in mathematics, 0.68 and 0.77 in reading, and 0.59 and 0.77 in writing for the respective years (Freiberg, Prokosch, Treister, & Stein, 1990; Freiberg & Huang, 1994; Freiberg, Stein, & Huang, 1995; and Freiberg, 1995).

5. Statistically significant reductions in discipline referrals. Statistically significant reduction (pre–post) in discipline referrals to the office from fifty to seventy percent (Freiberg, Prokosch, Treister, & Stein, 1990; Freiberg, Stein, & Huang, 1995; Opuni, 1996).

6. Statistically significant improvement in classroom climate reported by students. Statistically significant improvement in classroom learning environments as reported by students (Freiberg & Huang, 1994; Freiberg, Stein, & Huang, 1995).

7. Statistically significant improvement in school climate. Statistically significant improved school climate as measured by teachers (Freiberg & Huang, 1994; Freiberg, Stein & Huang, 1995; Lorentz, 1997).

8. Improvement in school climate from principals perspective. Improved school climate as measured by principals (Freiberg & Huang, 1994; Freiberg, Stein, & Huang, 1995).

9. Time to learn—time to teach. On average, teachers report fourteen to twenty additional minutes of teaching time each day. For a 180-day school year, with six hours each day, this would be the equivalent of seven to ten and a half additional teaching days without lengthening the school day or year (Opuni, 1996).

A third-party evaluation conducted as part of a larger study of Project GRAD, in which the CMCD was a component (Opuni, 1996) found that discipline referrals dropped from baseline data by seventy-eight and seventy-two percent ($p < .001$) in two CMCD elementary schools, respectively. Opuni (1996) reported after the first year of the project in the feeder pattern middle school the following changes at the school:

The disciplinary problems that experienced the most reductions were Assaults on Students/Teachers by Students (76%), Defiance/Disrespect of School Personnel (52%), and Disturbance of Educational Process, School Activity, or Cafeteria (47%), a remarkable achievement in the initial year of CMCD. (p. 48)

Fighting dropped twenty-four percent and skipping class dropped thirty-five percent in the first year. In addition to discipline reductions, pre–post student achievement improved significantly in all grade levels (sixth, seventh, and eighth) in mathematics and reading. Also, student achievement of a cohort of sixth-grade students beginning in 1994–1995 showed significant improvements by eighth grade (1996–1997) in mathematics and reading. Teacher, student, parent and administrator interviews provided a context for these changes.

Question: How would you describe the student behavior in the school and in your classroom before and after CMCD?

Answer (ten-year teacher at the middle school, May 1997): You can't even begin to compare, really. The student behavior was so, so bad we dreaded the end of the year because they would destroy the school, they would tear up the school...especially the third floor, you would have holes all over the wall. By this time of the year, before we had CM, there wasn't a place where you could write anything else in the bathrooms. [Before]...You would see more students out in the hall than you would see inside the classroom, because everybody was just tired and nobody wanted to deal with the kids. The kids didn't want to learn anymore. They didn't want to be with us anymore. And, now...we're looking forward to the end of school along with the kids. But, you know, we're looking forward to it because of the celebrations, because of the things coming up and we're working together. They're excited. We're excited. We're both tired but it's in a different way. You know, we both realized, "Hey guys, you're tired, I'm tired, but you know, let's keep working and let's give it our best. And there's more working together, where before the kids ran the school.... Now I tell the kids how important it is that they continue to bring their tools for learning [at the end of the year] because we are still working, grades are still counting. Where before I would allow the kids to get by, if they didn't want to bring their binders, they didn't have to; if they didn't want to keep writing with pen, they didn't have to...you know, we pretty much let it go...the end of [this 1997] school, it's been very smooth.

The CMCD program was also included in a report from Johns Hopkins University by Olatokunbo and Slavin (1997) entitled: "Effective and replicable programs for students placed at risk in elementary and middle schools." They indicate that the CMCD program meets their evaluation criteria for achievement gains, finding that the program (CMCD) students performed significantly better academically than did the control school students, the program demonstrated replicability, had effect size differences beyond ES +0.25, and was implemented with low-income minority students.

The CMCD program seems to have an additive effect on the reform curriculum in place in project schools. Current analysis on mathematics gains in seven elementary schools shows a significant increase in mathematics achievement (Freiberg, Connell, & Lorentz, 1997). The effect size (ES +0.33) shows that a student in the Math Only group who scored at the fiftieth percentile would have scored at the sixty-third percentile when placed in the CM+Math group. The findings, which are consistent with other achievement results utilizing the CMCD program, have implications for the types of classroom organization needed for active learning mathematics curriculum to be employed in urban schools. The CMCD program was also cited as one of five promising programs by the American Association of Colleges for Teacher Education in 1996.

A study of the implementation of the CMCD program in three cities in northern Italy found that student achievement in mathematics and reading as well as school climate improved significantly in the schools with teachers using the CMCD program as compared to control schools that were not trained in the program (Chairi, 1997).

How Can a Classroom Management Program Achieve These Results?

Fewer disruptions, better teacher planning, and classroom organization allow for more teaching and learning time and greater achievement. Teachers report less stress and less need to be absent for "mental health days." Higher teacher attendance is a direct result. Inner-city parents report that their children do not want to be late or absent because they have responsibilities in the classroom. Students like school more and feel a greater responsibility for being at school. Teachers and principals also report significantly fewer student "tardies" in the morning and significantly fewer absences.

When students and teachers see each other as partners, the instructional climate (teaching and learning) improves for both teachers and students. When students become more self-disciplined and teachers have a greater management and discipline repertoire, referring students to the office becomes unnecessary or used only as the last resort. This results in significantly fewer referrals. Figure 5-4 shows the number of instances of discipline referrals for students from seven elementary schools over a four-year period from 1994–1995 until 1996–1997. There is a seventy percent decline in the overall number of discipline referrals to the principals office for the seven schools.

Time to Teach, Time to Learn

A veteran teacher at the middle school level talks about the impact on instruction:
I see a big difference at the beginning of class. Where before you had to do so many little things, you couldn't get right to teaching and now with the managers assisting you in the classroom it just gives you a lot more time. And I can really tell in the student progress because…especially my low class, because I don't think that I have ever been able to move them that far because we do have some kids that are still second- and third-grade level reading. But this year, I saw the growth, you know, for the first time, I mean, real growth. And that's because I have more time to spend with them, more time to give them individual time or move from table to table, sit down, and talk to the group. That's a big difference. And they love for you to sit with them and spend time with them. I think that's really an important factor. They respond so well when you just sit there with them and work with them and they think that you are part of the class because you're doing the work with them. They really understand it better… It's giving me at least forty minutes [more teaching time per class] because our classes are ninety minutes.

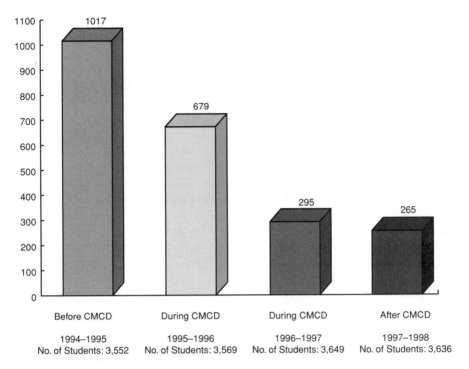

FIGURE 5-4   1994–1998 Office Discipline Referrals for Seven Elementary Schools: Davis Feeder Pattern.

The Rippling Effects of Discipline Problems

Disruptive student behaviors have a rippling effect, influencing the disruptive individual, classmates, the school learning environment, and the nearby community. The individual who is referred to the office loses learning time, and the teacher who ceases instruction to respond to disruptions destroys learning time for all the other students. Students who misbehave in school are at higher risk of dropping out of school, abusing substances, and engaging in other delinquent behaviors. Later in life they have greater problems adjusting to marital and occupational transitions (Gottfredson, Gottfredson, & Hybl, 1993). A pattern of disruptions also engulfs the school administration in noninstructional activities, with hundreds of hours spent in responding to disciplinary referrals sent to the office. In one suburban middle school with 1,283 students, 388 individual students were referred to the office for discipline in the month of October. When repeat referrals are included, the total climbs to 894 discipline referrals for the month (Freiberg, Stein, & Parker, 1995). Students who receive out-of-school suspensions are also potential problems to the community. Sustained student misbehaviors can inhibit instructional approaches by teachers who foster active learning through cooperative groupings, learning centers, or other interactive teachings (Cohen, 1994). Teachers may be less willing and able to use active instructional strategies like cooperative learning groups, which require greater student independence and self-discipline when student behavior is a barrier.

Few people go into teaching to shuffle papers, fill out forms, stop disruptions, discipline students, or feel exhausted from constantly dealing with little problems that accumulate and cascade over us by day's end. The CMCD model does not resolve every problem that students bring to the classroom, but a decade of research and practice shows that it will prevent many of today's problems that teachers encounter and help create solutions that are unique to one's own teaching context. A beginning teacher in her forties said about a teacher education class including aspects of the CMCD program: "We have not ultimately been given a model to teach like anyone else, but suggestions that will let us teach like ourselves, only better" (Kurnitz-Thurlow, 1996).

Conclusions

The centralized and mandated efforts at school reform in the past have not been directed to changing the way classrooms function (Murphy & Hallinger, 1993). The interconnectedness between classroom management, instruction, and learning has been a missing factor in discussions about school reform. McCaslin and Good (1992) address the importance of this linkage when they state:

> *We maintain that in order to reform schools significantly, we must consider the various constructions of students in the popular culture and educational community and their implication for school management policies. We believe that the intended modern school curriculum, which is designed to produce self-motivated, active learners, is seriously undermined by classroom management policies that encourage, if not demand, simple obedience. We advocate that a curriculum that seeks to promote problem solving and meaningful learning must be aligned with an authoritative management system that increasingly allows students to operate as self-regulated and risk-taking learners. (p. 4)*

The implications of classroom management in the broader picture of school reform is further highlighted by Wang, Haertel, and Walberg (1993). Their meta-analysis of learning factors from educational research experts, quantitative research synthesis, and handbook chapters, resulting in more than 11,000 statistical relationships identified classroom management as being first in a list of five factors that influence school learning.

The longitudinal data presented in this chapter may add weight to the importance of alterable variables like classroom management on student learning. Classroom management may be acting as a primer for other variables cited by Wang, Haertel, and Walberg (1993) that improve the opportunity and quality of learning. The importance of active learning environments in inner-city schools begins with the teacher's ability to create a learning environment that allows for interaction in different group settings, student talk, and student self-governing behaviors (Cohen, 1994; Freiberg, 1993; McCaslin & Good, 1992). It would be difficult to incorporate higher level learning activities without self-discipline on the part of the students. Observations of traditional inner-city classrooms have shown a preponderance of noninteraction between teacher and students and among students (see Rogers & Freiberg, 1994). Schools can build resilience in children, rather than becoming another risk factor in their lives (Freiberg, 1994).

Research findings from two longitudinal studies of large-scale school improvement interventions have significant implications for the importance of alterable classroom variables. A study by Wehlage, Smith, & Lipman (1992) described the findings after three years of an intervention to "increase the life chances of disadvantaged youth by promoting intentional change in schools and other youth-serving agencies" (p. 51). The study, as part of the New Futures effort, found the schools have not been restructured after three years and conclude the following.

> *interventions were supplemental and left the basic activities and practices of schools unaltered. Little change could be found in the relations between educators and students; curriculum and instruction left students unengaged in serious academic work; new roles for teachers and administrators largely failed to materialize and schools were unable to find ways of collaborating with other institutions both public and private, to strengthen their educational resources. (p. 51)*

A second four-year study of dropout prevention programs in the New City schools by Teachers College Office of Research, Evaluation, and Assessment (Meyer, 1990) from 1986–1990 studied the impact of interventions in thirty-nine high schools, ninety-eight middle schools, and five elementary schools for a cost of 120 million dollars. The general findings indicate that less than forty percent of the high-school students improved their attendance; program participation by middle-school students did not stem the decline of attendance from year to year; and high-school students' passing courses and promotion rates did not improve. The report proposes thirteen recommendations for improving the dropout intervention. At the heart of the recommendations is the need for the school experiences for at-risk students to be restructured by giving in part more opportunities and responsibilities for students to design and implement their academic programs and to improve the quality of data used to make decisions that focus on needs of the student.

The two studies reflect the importance of looking into the classroom for change. If interventions do not change classroom practices, then they will remain peripheral to school reform efforts. In view of limited resources, costly reinventions of the wheel minimizes the profession's credibility with the general public. If real changes are to occur in inner-city classrooms, then interaction patterns must change and orderly learning environments created cooperatively between students and teachers are a necessary prerequisite.

We need to create classrooms that are democratic and caring—few would argue with this position. How we arrive at this destination has been a source of debate for decades. There are many pathways. The CMCD program represents one such pathway. The evidence is accumulating that when implemented authentically, the model improves a range of factors that support the improvement and the lives of children and youth and their teachers and administrators.

References

Berliner, D., & Casanova, U. (1988). Peer tutoring: A new look at a popular practice. *Instructor. 97,* 14–15.

Brookover, W. B., Beady, C., Flood, P., Schweitzer, J., & Wisenbaker, J. (1979). *School social systems and student achievement: Schools can make a difference.* New York: Praeger.

Canter, L., & Canter M. (1992). *Assertive Discipline: A take-charge approach for today's educator.* Santa Monica, CA: Canter & Associates, Inc.

Chiari, G. (1997). *Climi di classe e apprendimento.* FrancoAngeli, Milano, Italy.

Cohen, E. (1994). *Designing groupwork: Strategies for the heterogeneous classroom.* New York: Teachers College Press.

Freiberg, H. J. (1983). Consistency: The key to classroom management. *Journal of Education for Teaching, 9*(1), 1–15.

Freiberg, H. J. (1989). Multidimensional view of school effectiveness. *Educational Research Quarterly, 13*(2), 35–46.

Freiberg, H. J. (1994). Understanding resilience: Implications for inner-city schools and their near and far communities. In M. C. Wang, & E. W. Gordon (Eds.), *Educational resilience in inner-city America: Challenges and prospects.* Hillsdale: Lawrence Erlbaum.

Freiberg, H. J., Prokosch, N., Treister, E. S., & Stein, T. A. (1990). Turning around five at-risk elementary schools. *Journal of School Effectiveness and School Improvement, 1*(1), 5–25.

Freiberg, H. J., & Huang, S. (1994). Study 2.4: Longitudinal study of the life-cycle of improving schools: Final report. *National Center on Education in the Inner Cities.* Philadelphia, Pennsylvania.

Freiberg, H. J. (1995). Promoting reflective practices. In G. Slick (Ed.), *Adapting field experience to future needs.* Newbury Park: Corwin Press, Inc.

Freiberg, H. J., Stein, T., & Huang, S., (1995). The effects of classroom management intervention on student achievement in inner-city elementary schools. *Educational Research and Evaluation, 1*(1), 33–66.

Freiberg, H. J., Stein, T. A., & Parker, G. (1995). An examination of discipline referrals in an urban middle school. *Education & Urban Society, 27*(4), 421–440.

Freiberg, H. J., & Driscoll, A. (1996). *Universal teaching strategies* (2nd ed.). Needham Heights, MA: Allyn & Bacon.

Freiberg, H. J. (1996). From tourists to citizens in the classroom. *Educational Leadership, 51*(1), 32–37.

Freiberg, H. J., Connell, M., & Lorentz, J. (March, 1997). *The effects of socially constructed classroom management on mathematics achievement.* Paper presented at the National Meeting of the American Education Research Association, Chicago, IL.

Gottfredson, D., Gottfredson, G. D., & Hybl, L. G. (1993). Managing adolescent behavior: A multi-year, multischool study. *American Educational Research Journal, 30*(1), 179–215.

Hoy, W., Tarter, C., & Kottkamp, R. (1991). *Open schools/healthy schools: Measuring organizational climate.* Newbury Park: Sage.

Kirby, J. (1995). Personal communication.

Kurnitz-Thurlow, A. (1996). Personal communication.

McCaslin, M., & Good, T. (1992). Compliant cognition: The misalliance of management and instructional goals in current school reform. *Educational Researcher, 40*(3), 41–50.

Meyer, C. (1990). *Dropout prevention initiatives FY 1986 to 1990: Lessons from the research.* Division of Strategic Planning/Research and Development, New York City Public Schools, n.d.

Murphy, J., & Hallinger, P. (Eds.). (1993). *Restructuring schooling: Learning from ongoing efforts.* Newbury Park: Corwin Press, Inc.

Olatokunbo, S. F., & Slavin, R. E. (1997, January). Effective and replicable programs for students placed at risk in elementary and middle schools. *Office of Educational Research and Improvement, US Department of Education.*

Opuni, K. A. (1996). Project evaluator. *Project GRAD Evaluation.*

Parker, G. (1994). *Gifted students perceptions of environments in assertive discipline and non-assertive discipline classrooms.* Unpublished dissertation, University of Houston, Houston, TX.

Rigrog, S. (1996). Personal communication.

Rogers, C., & Freiberg, H. J. (1994). *Freedom to learn* (3rd ed.). Columbus: Merrill.

Sergiovanni, T. J. (1991). *The principalship: A reflective practice perspective* (2nd ed.). Needham Heights, MA: Allyn & Bacon.

Smith, T. (1995). Personal communication.

Slavin, R. (1983). *Cooperative learning.* New York: Longman.

Stallings, J., Needles, M., & Sparks, G. (1987). Observation for the improvement of classroom learning. In D. Berliner, & B. Rosenshine (Eds.), *Talks to teachers: A Festschrift for N. L. Gage.* New York: Random House.

Wang, M. C., Haertel, G. D., & Walberg, H. J. (1993). Toward a knowledge base for school learning. *Review of Educational Research, 63,* 249–294.

Wehlage, G., Smith, G., & Lipman, P. (1992). Restructuring urban schools: The new futures experience. *American Educational Journal, 29,* 50–93.

Application of Judicious Discipline

A Common Language for Classroom Management

BARBARA McEWAN
Oregon State University

PAUL GATHERCOAL
California State
Lutheran College

VIRGINIA NIMMO
Mankato School District

Introduction

Historically, classroom management has been defined as a collection of behaviorist strategies based primarily on rewards and punishments, all of which are designed to make students behave. Such a limited perspective has contributed to the common belief that classroom management can be reduced to "a bag of tricks" applicable to all students, regardless of their individual needs and capable of solving every imaginable behavioral problem that might be presented in a classroom. The act of managing a classroom was viewed as a process of doing things to people to make them behave in preselected and preferred ways. Educators who accepted this narrowly focused definition of management became more concerned with outcomes rather than process, believing that a quiet classroom filled with acquiescent students was more important to their educational needs than engaging in practices that would contribute to the moral development of children.

In a classroom based on behaviorist management strategies, teachers determine what they want their classes to look like and sound like, then codify their visions into a limited number of "do and don't" rules. In such classrooms, teachers begin by telling students about the rules and explaining the system to be used for rule enforcement. Popcorn parties, stickers, token dollars, free time, and reduced homework assignments are just some of the rewards dangled in front of students in an attempt to secure their continued good behavior. When students break the rules, the responses they receive typically consist of a loss of privileges, public embarrassment, physical pain, isolation inside or outside of the classroom, or some other form of punishment designed to eradicate inappropriate behavior.

However, as the knowledge of brain functions, psychology, sociological factors and pedagogy has increased, classroom management has taken on a definition that moves beyond isolated student behaviors to a broad range of decision-making and problem-solving activities that are useful in maintaining safe and equitable learning environments. The arrangement of desks, bulletin board decorations, the process for developing classroom rules, the applications of due process when students feel they are not being treated fairly—all of these issues and more fall under our current understanding of what constitutes classroom management.

Educators who are employing cognitive as opposed to behavioral management strategies are, in part, motivated by the concern that our human society is suffering from a diminished sense of personal responsibility and a breakdown in civility. Behaviors that reflect a lack of moral conscience are blamed not only on a weakened family structure, but also on questionable educational practices. Politicians, religious leaders, and social workers are joining forces with educators in a common call for an increased emphasis on character education in schools.

Democratic strategies that rely on peaceful resolutions of conflict through negotiation, conferences, and a sense of comity are increasingly being advocated in pedagogical literature. Despite the availability of several successful approaches to democratic management, a number of administrators and teachers remain skeptical about the worthiness of such strategies and call them impractical in the "real world." Without ever engaging in a deliberate application of democratic management practices in their schools or classrooms, many educators believe students are too immature, troublesome, sneaky, untrustworthy or unruly to be treated in an equitable and respectful manner. However, as noted by Kohn (1996):

> *[T]o reject a sour view of human nature, one predicated on the assumption that people are inherently selfish or aggressive, is not necessarily to assume that evil is illusory and everyone means well. We do not have to cast our*

lot with Carl Rogers—or Mr. Rogers, for that matter. Rather, we might proceed from the premise that humans are as capable of generosity and empathy as they are of looking out for Number One, as inclined (all things being equal) to help as to hurt. (p. 8)

A Description of Judicious Discipline

In their book, *Hope at Last for At-Risk Youth,* Barr and Parrett (1995) stated: One program, Judicious Discipline, has been developed to help schools apply a simple set of legal principles based on [human rights] to involve students in rule formulation in schools and classrooms. Early studies of Judicious Discipline have yielded promising results as evidenced by a number of schools being able to eliminate expulsion and suspension by using this particular method. (p. 114)

Judicious Discipline (Gathercoal, 1991) is a comprehensive approach to democratic classroom management that provides educators with a foundation for teaching citizenship each day and through every student–teacher interaction. The key to this model lies in helping students learn to apply a common language of civility to their daily interactions that occur within and without the school community. The premise of Judicious Discipline is that citizenship can and should be taught through classroom management decisions that consistently model how our individual human rights are always balanced against the limitations that protect humanity's need to be safe, healthy, and undisrupted.

Judicious Discipline is unique primarily because it creates a common language based on the principles of human rights and responsibilities and it emphasizes the concept that an educator's professional responsibility is to create an equitable environment that affords every student the opportunity to be successful. Educators using Judicious Discipline become role models who practice in word and deed the values of a democratic society through the professional and ethical relationships they establish with all members of their learning community.

Certainly there are other theories of management that are based on democratic practices. Writers such as Rudolf Dreikurs (1982), William Glasser (1969), Alfie Kohn (1996), Jerome Freiberg (1996), and Thomas Lickona (1991), all discuss a variety of democratic strategies such as class meetings, problem solving, and other ideas that empower students to make their own good decisions about behavior. Judicious discipline is designed to be integrated into these other approaches by specifically framing the decision-making process of management in the language of human rights and responsibilities.

Teachers incorporating Judicious Discipline into their democratic classroom structures begin by introducing students to the rights encompassed in the concepts of freedom, justice, and equality. Students are taught that they have the freedom to express themselves in their speech, their clothing, and their writing, as well as in other aspects of their lives. However, it is also made very clear to students that a free society only functions successfully when all citizens understand and abide by the limits to those freedoms. The most commonly used example of the balance between rights and responsibilities is that citizens have freedom of speech, but the freedom to speak openly does not include yelling "Fire!" in a crowded theater. The potential danger to all of those in attendance at the theater outweighs an individual's right of expression.

Unlike behavioral management approaches, Judicious Discipline does not have a "one-size-fits-all" set of rules and regulations. Jones and Jones (1995) stated:

> *In his book* Judicious Discipline *(1993), attorney and educational psychologist Forrest Gathercoal provided educators with an excellent foundation for viewing school rules and decisions regarding student behavior.... Gathercoal's thoughtful work provides a foundation for a democratic and responsible approach to managing student behavior.*

Judicious discipline provides all members of a school community with sufficient understanding of rights, responsibilities, and equitable practices to set about building the foundation for a sustainable democratic learning environment.

A school setting using Judicious Discipline, then, becomes a microcosm of the larger free society. Students in classes using this approach to management are taught their rights and when those rights can and should be limited. If a teacher, administrator, or staff member is able to demonstrate that the actions of students pose a threat to the health and safety, property, or educational purpose of the school, then students should have restrictions placed on their freedoms.

Using the language of Judicious Discipline, students learn to monitor their own behaviors. The model empowers young people to examine their actions critically in terms of Time, Place, and Manner. As educators, we soon learn that it is difficult to apply hard-and-fast rules to specific behaviors in every imaginable setting. Judicious Discipline provides us with another option—teaching Time, Place, and Manner. What follows is a practical example of how these terms can be applied in a classroom setting.

There are many times in the average school day during which students converse with each other. Sometimes those conversations occur over lunch, sometimes in a small group work session, sometimes on a playground, and sometimes in the school library. Each class activity, or *Time,* and each setting, or *Place,* has its own expectations of what constitutes appropriate volume levels for voices. Rather than a rule that forbids any talking in a library, students would be asked to consider their voice levels when talking with another person. What level would be appropriate in the library? What would be disruptive? Would whispering on the playground be necessary? What voice level would be appropriate for a small group activity? With these guidelines, students soon learn that they are capable of monitoring the *Manner* of their own behaviors according to the Time and Place of the activity in which they are engaged.

When a problem does occur or a rule is broken, Judicious Discipline advocates approaching the situations as teachable moments. Teachers using cognitive management strategies begin by asking questions. The first question might be "What is happening?" or "Is this the appropriate Time, Place, and Manner for what you are doing?" Sometimes asking a question is enough to redirect the students and sometimes it is not.

Before educators using Judicious Discipline order a Consequence for an inappropriate act, they would first want to know what students need to learn in order to avoid repeating the inappropriate behavior next time. Brief conferences with students to ascertain the problem and to develop appropriate consequences should occur in a timely fashion. This provides the opportunity to ensure due process and demonstrate respect for students, even though their actions were not appropriate. Teachers need good information in order to understand the needs of their students and help them recover from a problem successfully.

As with other cognitive management models, Judicious Discipline advocates avoiding the use of consequences designed to humiliate or to hurt but using it rather to develop consequences that will redirect student behavior and provide genuine opportunities to learn new social skills. Conferences, community service, and restitution are among the many appropriate options available. It is most important for educators using Judicious Discipline to be flexible about the Consequence that is most appropriate for one situation or another. This flexibility helps to avoid the mistake of being locked into predetermined responses that have little application to the variety of problems that present themselves on any given school day.

Effectively Addressing a Broad Range of Needs

One positive outcome associated with the Judicious Discipline framework is that it helps to move management issues away from a struggle between student and teacher for classroom control, and towards a method by which two people can work together to resolve a conflict. However, some teachers believe troubled or emotionally disturbed students—in other words, the students who typically can create the most problems in a school environment—are not capable of responding in appropriate ways to the knowledge that they have rights or to the responsibilities expected of them by society. As a result, educators believe these students should be the recipients of a school's most punitive measures.

Those of us who have worked to develop Judicious Discipline have found that its framework is particularly well suited to serving the multifarious interests of all students. No matter how diverse the individual members of a community or how acute their needs might be, when they come together in a Judicious Discipline classroom and use the language of human rights and responsibilities for decision making, they share common understandings and values that can sustain a peaceful and equitable learning community.

The language of Judicious Discipline helps educators view their decisions from the perspective of how they might best serve the needs of everyone. Assessment, attendance, emotional outbursts, and whatever else an average day might include are all these issues that can be approached by using the language of rights and responsibilities.

A Synthesis of Research on the Effects of Judicious Discipline

The applications of Judicious Discipline have been the focus of several studies being conducted by researchers in various school districts around the United States. This chapter discusses the Mankato, Minnesota Action Research Study. The primary objective of this study was to assess the effects Judicious Discipline has on helping students acquire attitudes and values consistent with what Lawrence Kohlberg described as a Principled Level of Behavior.

Mankato, Minnesota, lies in the south central portion of this Midwestern state. The population of Mankato and its immediate neighbor, North Mankato, exceeds 42,000. The majority of residents are employed in professional jobs, and unemployment averages are lower than the statewide average. There are three colleges and one university located in Mankato–North Mankato, making this area the educational center of south central Minnesota. The public schools are attended predominantly by white students, although there is some diversity represented.

The subjects of the Mankato study were students, faculty, administration, and school support personnel who volunteered to participate. Data collection was done through surveys, meetings, and videotaped interviews. The Mankato Action Research Project proved to have both theoretical and practical significance. The results of this study support the theory that a nonpunitive, citizenship approach to classroom–school management can facilitate the process of students becoming autonomous and responsible for their own actions (Gathercoal, 1990; Sarson, 1990).

The Mankato study also provides support for a transfer effect of good citizenship at home, at work, on the sporting field, and in other social settings. Citizenship skills were found to be transferable from situation to situation, unlike behavioral models that tend to be situation specific. There is data to support the idea that students who are experiencing Judicious Discipline develop a better self-concept, achieve higher levels of moral development, demonstrate a greater sense of ethical decision making, establish better student–educator and student–student relationships, and spend more quality time in school and classrooms. As a result, it can be argued that the principles of Judicious Discipline contribute to the development of responsible citizens and help prepare students for living and learning in our democratic society.

Results in the Mankato Study

In 1995, a group of educators set about designing a study that would assess the effectiveness of Judicious Discipline as an approach to effective classroom management. The school year began with the first administration of the survey selected to assess developmental levels of students. It was agreed among the researchers that the questionnaire to be used was one that had been originally developed by The Social Development Group, Research Branch of the South Australian Department of Education, and published in the 1980s as *Developing the Classroom Group*. The questionnaire differentiates between power and affect relationships through a series of eight true–false questions and places the individual in one of four developmental groups: 1 = dependent; 2 = rebellious; 3 = cohesive; and 4 = autonomous.

Student behavior for each developmental stage is described as follows:

- **Stage 1—Dependence.** Students are generally dependent and submissive, and do what the teacher says. The students' interactions are mostly through the teacher, so there is low covert interaction among students. There is little disruptive behavior, but some "attention getting." Some students are bored. Motivation is extrinsic and based on approval, praise and encouragement from the teacher and parent–caregiver(s). There is fear of punishment.
- **Stage 2—Rebellion.** The students test, challenge, and try out the teacher. The student group separates into two camps, one in opposition to the teacher, the other seeking to maintain dependent group behavior. Some students challenge or ignore the teacher's efforts to control the class. Noise levels tend to be high. Trust levels among students are low; accordingly, aggressive interactions and put-downs are common. The rebellious subgroup is extrinsically motivated by peer group approval moderated by fear of teacher punishment. The intrinsic motivation is for autonomy, moderated by dependency needs.
- **Stage 3—Cohesion.** Students are friendly and trusting of each other and the teacher. There is little disruptive behavior. There is a good deal of social interaction, but of an orderly type. The interactions conform to group norms. There is little disagreement, as this is seen as disruptive to the harmony of the group. Extrinsic motivation comes from praise and encouragement from peer group and teacher. Breach of class norms brings strong group disapproval.
- **Stage 4—Autonomy.** Individuals are self-directed, able to seek and give support but function well without it. Students take responsibility for their own learning. There is a high level of interaction. Agreement and discussion are the norm. Feelings, positive and negative, are expressed openly. Students work the same with or without the teacher present. Disruptive behavior is virtually nonexistent. Students show flexibility and adaptability in a variety of learning situations without demanding conformity of all members. They utilize self-awareness and empathy rather than rules to choose behavior. Motivation is mainly intrinsic. Social behavior is based on respect for self and others. Learning is seen as a way of gaining personal competence and joy. (Education Department of South Australia, 1980)

Step One: The Survey Is Administered

In the Mankato study, the survey was administered to the participating Mankato students three times through the nine-month period in which the research was conducted. The questionnaire was administered and scored by the primary researchers. All students had the questions read to them (See Tables 6-1 and 6-2).

TABLE 6-1   Scoring Guide

Analysis of Questionnaire

The first four statements deal with power and the last four statements deal with affect. On each questionnaire, write the stage numbers down by each pair of questions. For example:

	True	False	
Statement 1:	☒	☐	
Statement 2:	☒	☐	1
Statement 3:	☒	☐	
Statement 4:	☐	☒	3
Statement 5:	☐	☒	
Statement 6:	☒	☐	1
Statement 7:	☐	☒	
Statement 8:	☐	☒	1

Using the data from the above results, total the scores from the class under the four stages.

S1	S2	S3	S4
3	0	1	0

The class result may look something like this:

S1	S2	S3	S4
27	14	9	10

This can be converted to a percentage by adding up the total number of responses, for example:

27 + 14 + 9 + 10 = 60

and dividing the stage totals by this number, as shown here:

$$\frac{27}{60} \qquad \frac{14}{60} \qquad \frac{9}{60} \qquad \frac{10}{60}$$

and multiplying by $\frac{100}{1}$ to get a percentage.

For example:

S1	S2	S3	S4
45%	23%	15%	17%

TABLE 6-2   Analysis of Questionnaire

Scoring the Questionnaire

1. There are eight statements in four pairs. Each pair of statements give four possible results (e.g., the first pair is questions 1 and 2, and they deal with *power* in the classroom).

		True	False	
If they marked as follows:	Statement 1:	☒	☐	
	Statement 2:	☒	☐	

This would be a Stage 1 or an Stage S1 response.

The three other possible responses follow:

Statement 1:	☒	☐	An S2 response
Statement 2:	☐	☒	

Statement 1:	☐	☒	An S3 response
Statement 2:	☒	☐	

Statement 1:	☐	☒	An S4 response
Statement 2:	☐	☒	

We can summarize these as follows:

If you read the questions and look at the scoring system, you will see how they fit into the Stages of Development model.

The overall scoring scheme is thus:

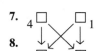

The survey used for this study consists of eight questions that are marked true or false by the subjects.

1. This teacher nearly always tells us what to do.
2. We have to do what the teacher says in this class.
3. The whole class helped to make the class rules.
4. I often decide for myself what I will do and where I will do it in this class.
5. We are all very friendly together in this class.
6. When students argue in this class, people get upset.
7. Nearly all of this class feels warm and friendly to this teacher.
8. It's okay to disagree strongly with this teacher.

The eight statements are actually four pairs of assessment items. Each pair provides four possible results. When each pair of answers is assessed, they reveal the developmental stages of the students. Before the survey items are read to the students, they are told the researchers want to know "what this class is like with [teacher's name]." They are also told not to put their names on the papers. The class is instructed to put a mark in one box for either true or false (Table 6-1). The students should mark each of the eight items. Researchers who administer the test must make it clear that what matters are the opinions of the students. Students should be reminded not to look at the answers others are recording, nor should the answers be discussed until after the whole survey has been administered.

Researchers are encouraged to speak with students after the survey has been administered to get their verbal opinions about the class and how they feel about it. Often these exchanges can yield qualitative information that enriches the study and provides some concrete goals toward which teachers and students may work.

The results of the Mankato study indicated that in September 1995, twenty-six percent of the student responses to the questionnaire at School A were at the developmental dependence stage, four percent were at the rebellion stage, forty-two percent were at the cohesion stage, and twenty-eight percent were at the autonomy stage. The results of the September survey at a sixth-grade only school (known here as School B) indicated forty percent of the student responses were at the dependent stage, thirteen percent were at the rebellion stage, twenty-five percent were at the cohesion stage, and twenty-two percent were at the autonomous stage.

Student responses to the survey were also analyzed to provide information about how they viewed four constructs: teacher power, student power, student–student relationships, and teacher–student relationships. Teacher power, or how well the teacher was able to share power with students, was measured by the students' responses to the first two questions of the survey. Student power, or how well students were able to share power among themselves, was measured by the students' responses to the third and fourth questions on the survey. Student relationships, or how well developed the students' relationships were with each other, was measured by the students' responses to the fifth and sixth questions on the survey. Teacher–student relationships, or how well developed the relationships were between students and teachers, was measured by responses to the last two questions on the survey. Survey results were quantified, averages were assigned, and scoring was based on a four-point scale, with one indicating the dependent stage and four indicating the autonomous stage.

In September 1995, schoolwide results for School A indicated teacher power averaged 1.45, student power averaged 2.95, student–student relationships averaged 3.04, and teacher–student relationships averaged 3.52. Schoolwide results for School B indicated that teacher power averaged 1.49, student power averaged 1.56, student–student relationships averaged 3.04, and teacher–student relationships averaged 3.11.

Step Two: Students Receive Instruction in Judicious Discipline

During the month of September, at both schools, students were taught about the basic principles of Judicious Discipline. Instruction began with presentations by the school principals, counselors, and other resource staff (e.g., school psychologists, police liaison officers). After these initial presentations, classroom teachers taught lessons about rights and responsibilities. Students were also taught Time, Place, and Manner, mentioned earlier in this chapter, to help them regulate their own behaviors. The participants in this study learned to make judgments about their own behaviors and determine whether they were acting appropriately according to the standards of Time, Place, and Manner. Lesson plans developed by other teachers using Judicious Discipline and presented in *Practicing Judicious Discipline* (McEwan,1994) were made available to every classroom teacher in Schools A and B. However, it was left to the classroom teacher's discretion as to the amount of time used for these lessons and the amount of follow-up that occurred after the initial presentations. Although discussed in more detail later in the chapter, this decision was later recognized as an error. Researchers found that students did not achieve any desired measure of autonomy unless their teachers followed up the initial presentations of Judicious Discipline with class meetings, additional lessons, and group discussions.

The teachers who took the time to teach about Judicious Discipline and developed the language of civility in their classrooms were the teachers whose students responded with a score of more than fifty percent at the autonomous stage during the February reapplication of the questionnaire. Although a result indicating fifty percent of the students were operating at the autonomous level might not seem significant, observations by the researchers conducting the study indicated that a classroom in which one-half the students were functioning autonomously was sufficient to sustain an equitable learning environment. The students who achieved autonomy had several opportunities every day to model behaviors during peer interactions. In class meetings, small group problem-solving activities, contributions made in whole-class discussions or while reviewing expectations for various lessons—in general during the usual give-and-take of an educational day—these students shared their understanding of autonomy through their comments and input. Therefore, even with an outcome of fifty percent, there were many occasions for other students to hear and incorporate

the views of their autonomous peers. Although the goal of judicious discipline, ide-
alistically, might be one hundred percent, there are too many variables that would
prevent that outcome. A more realistic goal is to create a critical mass of students
whose influence is felt throughout the rest of the classroom.

Step Three: Follow-Up Lessons and Assessment

From November to January, faculty, administrators, and staff in both schools were
apprised of the developmental stages represented in their student populations, as
measured by the questionnaires administered in September. (Throughout the year,
school administrators were never shown individual scores, they were only shown the
schoolwide results.) Various interventions by resource staff (e.g., psychologists,
counselors) occurred in both buildings to assist faculty and staff with their understanding of Judicious Discipline components and to help them learn more about successful strategies that were being used to implement the concepts in the classrooms
of colleagues. In addition, faculty, administration, and staff held meetings devoted
to brainstorming democratic methods and individual strategies for dealing with troublesome student behavior.

As mentioned earlier, it is critically important to provide deliberate instruction
for students about the concepts of Judicious Discipline. Of equal importance are
opportunities for teachers and administrators to participate in some professional
development workshops during which they can share strategies, air concerns, and
discuss their successes in the area of classroom management.

Given the history of classroom management, the idea of treating students as citizens is very new to many educators. The researchers in Minnesota typically offer a
series of one-week summer institutes that instruct teachers in the concepts of Judicious Discipline. They have found that teachers seem more confident and comfortable
implementing Judicious Discipline after they have worked with the strategies over the
course of a five-day workshop than when the ideas are presented in a brief after-
school or half-day session. The researchers conducting the Mankato study provided
regular opportunities for teachers to gather and discuss their work in the area of management. At School A, a judicious discipline support group met regularly to discuss
delights and concerns associated with its implementation. At School B, discussions
occurred on an "as-needed" basis to brainstorm possible judicious responses to student behaviors.

The questionnaire was administered a second time in February. When administering the questionnaire to the first- and second-grade students, it was determined
that each student should have the questionnaire read individually to ensure understanding of each item. This time the schoolwide results at School A indicated that
twenty percent of students responded to questions at the dependence stage, ten percent at the rebellion stage, thirty-four percent at the cohesive stage, and thirty-five
percent were at the autonomous stage. At School B, the results indicated that fifteen
percent of the students responded to questions at the dependence stage, twenty-one

percent at the rebellion stage, eighteen percent at the cohesion stage, and forty-six percent at the autonomous stage.

When the constructs of teacher power, student power, student–student relationships, and teacher–student relationships were measured in February, the school averages for teacher power and student power increased from the September survey averages. This suggests that, on average, both schools were moving towards more democratic environments in which teachers and students alike were beginning to share responsibility for decision making and the establishment of mutual expectations. Student responses in School A indicated the teacher power average to be 2.33, student power average to be 2.99, student–student relationships average to be 2.70, and teacher–student relationships average to be 3.35. School B student responses indicated the teacher power average to be 3.33, student power average to be 2.80, student–student relationships average to be 2.63, and teacher–student relationships average to be 3.02.

Schoolwide results of the February survey were shared with faculty, administration, and staff at meetings in both schools, and optional conferences were scheduled with faculty to discuss their individual classroom results. Faculty who chose to discuss their individual class results spoke with a school psychologist. Together they worked to determine if there were extenuating circumstances that might have effected the survey results. The teachers who met to discuss their survey results were invited to share the results of the two surveys with their students and to use the survey results as a stimulus for class discussion in order to determine how, as a class, they might better develop their community.

As a result of the discussions, strategies and ideas were developed with teachers who wanted to correct particular behaviors evident in their classrooms. Some teachers voiced concern that certain students may have effected the results of the survey. The discussion then centered on how the teachers might respond to the behavioral problems within their classroom settings in a judicious manner through the use of class meetings and private discussions with students.

Both schools were surveyed again in May in order to determine any changes that may have occurred through the year. Results indicated an increase in student responses at the autonomous stage and a continued decrease in student responses at the dependent stage. Survey results at School A indicated that seventeen percent of students responded at the dependence stage, eight percent at the rebellion stage, thirty-one percent at the cohesive stage, and forty-five percent were at the autonomous stage. At School B, the results indicated that fourteen percent of the students responded at the dependence stage, twenty-three percent were at the rebellion stage, eighteen percent were at the cohesion stage, and forty-five percent were at the autonomous stage.

The data clearly indicate an increase in Autonomous behaviors. Equally evident is a smaller increase in Rebellion behaviors. The Rebellion behaviors are tangentially associated with Judicious Discipline in that not every teacher in these site schools was using the model. The data reflect the behaviors of students in those classes practicing democratic management and those that were not. The students who were in classes relying on more behaviorist management practices were perhaps more rebellious given that they knew their peers were being treated more equitably in other rooms.

Step Four: Survey Results Are Analyzed

The survey results indicate that students thought their teachers were increasingly sharing power with them, that they were taking on more responsibility, and that they were better able to handle power relationships between themselves and their teachers.

When power and relationship constructs were analyzed, it was clear that continued growth in shared power occurred at both schools. Students indicated that teachers were sharing power, and that they were taking responsibility for decision making and were able to handle power relationships among themselves. School averages for power and affect relationships at School A were 2.67 for teacher power, student power average was 3.22, student–student relationships average was 2.81, and teacher–student relationships average was 3.38. School B student responses indicated the teacher power average to be 3.49, student power average to be 2.68, student–student relationships average to be 2.66, and teacher–student relationships average to be 2.87. It is important to note that these numbers reflect data gathered in May, and not summary data for the two time periods.

The data indicate that there were gains in student power as well as in teacher power. This outcome is one that the researchers had hoped to see. The numbers reflect the fact that students were taking more responsibility for their own behaviors and, as mentioned previously, a gain in teacher power indicates teachers were more willing to share their power with students. In classrooms practicing Judicious Discipline, an increase in both would be a positive result. Of concern to the researchers was the drop in student–student and teacher–student relations. It is uncertain what the cause of this might be and one that will be more carefully investigated in follow-up studies. On a qualitative level, researchers were able to observe many positive and supportive interactions between and among students and teachers. The drop in numbers certainly sparks curiosity, but does not negate the other positive outcomes.

Although both schools showed results that are impressive and supportive of the efforts made to implement Judicious Discipline, it is equally important to analyze and examine individual class results to determine effective strategies that can be used to further implement the Judicious Discipline philosophy in schools.

Step Five: Gathering Qualitative Data to Triangulate Survey Results

The qualitative data, collected on videotape, indicated that some educators were more comfortable with judicious concepts than were others. Interviews with students and educators support the survey results for individual teachers, adding validity to the quantitative results. For example, at School A, students in a class we will call

"AA" were interviewed about Judicious Discipline. From the interview, it was obviously that there had been very little follow-up after the initial introduction to the model by the principal and the school counselor. Correlating with the interview, students in the same AA class indicated a marked decrease in the percentage of autonomous stage responses on the social development survey throughout the year.

However, students in a class we will call "S" indicated a dramatic increase in the percentage of student responses at the autonomous stage of social development throughout the year. It was clear that the teacher in class S had been practicing Judicious Discipline in a manner that is closely aligned with the ideas in the book and had taken the time to teach students about their rights and responsibilities. Similar parallels can be drawn at School B. When analyzing the data gathered about class "I," the positive results indicate that this is an educator who took time to teach the language of Judicious Discipline to students throughout the year. In fact, the observations made by researchers support that finding. The quantitative data indicates that class I's students increased their autonomous stage responses from twenty-four percent at the beginning of the year to eighty percent at the end of the year.

The implications of the results cited here are clear. Judicious Discipline most likely will not be successful if there is no conscientious attempt to revisit the concepts often. Administrators, school counselors, and others involved in the daily life of the school must offer teachers support and encouragement for their work with the Judicious Discipline concepts. In the Mankato study, the decision was made to accept each teacher's decision to follow up on the model as they wished. Perhaps a more strategic approach is warranted. It may be that peer coaching to observe and time to discuss each other's work with Judicious Discipline should not only be encouraged by administrators, but the school's schedule should also accommodate that process.

When viewing individual classrooms at both buildings and taking into account discussions that occurred with teachers at the teacher's option, certain parallels emerge. Nineteen classrooms were surveyed at School A and twelve classrooms at School B. Out of thirty-one classrooms surveyed, twenty-one teachers chose to exercise their options for individual conferences with one of the primary researchers. In the classrooms where, by the end of the year, fifty percent or more of the students responded at the autonomous stage, discussions at the conference indicated that:

- A great deal of time was spent at the beginning of the year on issues of rights and responsibilities.
- Teachers spent at least one-half hour a day for the first two weeks discussing issues relating to student discipline, student rights and responsibilities, and concepts such as Time, Place, and Manner.
- Teachers indicated continuous follow up throughout the first six weeks of school, with daily reminders at appropriate moments when behavioral concerns arose.
- Teachers reported less need to continue those discussions after the first six weeks to two months of school.

In classrooms in which student survey responses were higher than sixty percent at the autonomous stage, teachers indicated that discussions regarding student discipline, student rights and responsibilities, and appropriateness (i.e., Time, Place, and Manner) were discussed throughout the year. Most of these teachers employed democratic class meetings when issues came up that needed to be managed by the group as a whole.

In classrooms in which student survey responses indicated less than fifty percent at the autonomous stage, teachers reported that lessons in Judicious Discipline were taught at the beginning of the year, but not a great deal of follow-up was done after the first month. Many of these teachers indicated that they felt some frustration with one or two students whom they perceived as significant behavioral problems in the class. Teachers reported that through discussions about rights and responsibilities with these particular students, there were times when behavior would be appropriate, but many times would not be. These teachers reported high levels of frustration, which complements the quantitative results gathered from their students' social development surveys. When student motivation is mainly extrinsic and students are continually testing the teacher, typical characteristics of the dependent or rebellion stage, teachers are likely to feel frustrated. These teachers also indicated that the high levels of frustration they were feeling with a few individual students led them to abandon more democratic practices and become more autocratic in their feedback to students and in the setting of expectations. As stated earlier in this chapter, teachers often say that they are reluctant to try Judicious Discipline because they are sure it cannot be used with "certain" students.

There emerges from this study a picture of two perspectives of classroom management. One is that effective democratic management is an ongoing dynamic that continually surfaces through daily interactions with students. This give-and-take is ripe with opportunity for teaching lessons about appropriate behaviors and making responsible decisions. The other view is that students should be expected to know how to behave and that classroom time is better spent on curriculum rather than revisiting concepts of management. Both views have their supporters. However, there is increasing evidence, not only from this study, but also from other research, that a failure to revisit management practices consistently leaves far too much to chance when it comes to maintaining a safe and productive learning community in the classroom.

Supporting the Findings with Data Gathered from Observations and Interviews

The results of the Mankato study have been supported through comments supplied by study participants during individual interviews and observations. The primary study to be cited in this section is the one conducted in Mankato. However, additional supporting data is supplied by other researchers who have been examining the effects of Judicious Discipline in other school districts around the United States. Their research findings combined with those of the Mankato study make up the balance of this chapter.

The Mankato study was designed with the intent of developing strategies suitable for educators in other settings who wish to employ the principles of Judicious Discipline. The researchers who contributed to this paper have all had the opportunity to analyze qualitative data that adds support to the theory that a nonpunitive citizenship model approach to classroom–school management can assist students in assuming personal responsibility for their actions.

The Language of Equity

The common finding in all the studies cited in this chapter is that the consistent language of equity and tolerance based on constitutional concepts can be documented as being a significant support for sustaining learning environments that are safe and productive. Carol Burns, a teacher in the Mankato School District, said:

> *As teachers we can deal respectfully with students, acknowledge that they have rights, acknowledge that they have responsibilities. The whole process, if there is such a thing with Judicious Discipline, allows us to model respect as we're working with those students. Also, when we ponder the question [of a discipline situation] with the student, how can we make this right again, it allows us to teach students about respect for themselves and respect for other people and how we treat each other.*

Another participant in the Mankato study shared her perspective. "What makes me feel good is that they are learning something they are going to take with them next year.… I think they see that this is something that is going to help them."

Using Judicious Discipline in Special Needs Settings

Judicious Discipline appears to promote a similarly positive outcome when educators are working with students who have been identified as having special needs.

> *Judicious Discipline is something that I use everyday and because I teach Special Education I use it with children of varying abilities and varying needs. This year, for the first time in a number of years, I have two Down Syndrome students and I have found that it even works with students with those abilities. They have been able to learn the language and to understand what rights and responsibilities mean and what their rights and responsibilities are.*

Similar evidence surfaced in a series of interviews that were reported in an earlier study conducted with educators in the Mankato area (McEwan & Nimmo, 1995). Karen Letcher, a special education teacher, had a caseload of three sixth-grade students at that time. Her population shifts depending on how special needs students are performing in their classes. When speaking about her students, Karen said, "It is beginning to dawn on them that their lack of [taking] responsibility doesn't get them anywhere…Judicious Discipline defuses [possible power struggles] because it removes the emotion."

Karen said that she still feels herself getting angry when faced with a sudden incident. However, she goes on to say that at those times, Judicious Discipline has helped her learn to collect her thoughts and "get my ducks in a row" before acting. Karen firmly believes students who are diagnosed with emotional disturbances should nevertheless be held accountable for their actions with consequences such as community service.

Robin Boeke is another special education teacher at a Mankato elementary school. She works with students who are third, fourth, and fifth graders. In an interview (McEwan & Nimmo, 1995), Robin stated that, based on her observations, teachers who "follow guidelines of Judicious Discipline can't get into power struggles." She went on to use a metaphor that compares a power struggle to a rope with one end being dangled by students. Robin and others who participated in the first Minnesota study stated that, with Judicious Discipline, educators have the choice of not picking up the other end of the rope because they have the language to state expectations clearly and walk away. If students continue to push Robin, she will say something like, "I think we need to take a break from each other." Robin feels this is a much more humane way to let the students know their behaviors will have to stop, as opposed to summarily dismissing a student from the classroom.

She has learned that a correction might not happen right away. However, she feels that backing off, waiting, and then later resolving conflicts peacefully fits well with Judicious Discipline concepts. Using language from Judicious Discipline, Robin reported that when she can finally work with a student, her first thought is, "What needs to be learned here?" Robin's goal is to teach students a process for avoiding problems. She encourages them to stop, consider their actions, and talk about responsibilities—theirs, hers, and that of the whole class.

Nancy Busse of Le Sueur–Henderson High School, in Le Sueur, Minnesota, began using Judicious Discipline in her special education classroom during the 1993–1994 school year. She stated in an interview that because the nature of students with emotional disturbances is to test, she views their testing of Judicious Discipline to be part of a normal process. She responds to their testing by consistently using language that focuses the students on being responsible learners. When they say, "You can't make me do this," her response is, "That's right." However, she goes on to say that she can help them with strategies for assuming their own responsibility for completing a task.

An Increased Sense of Professionalism

The language of Judicious Discipline provides educators with a sense of professionalism that they do not feel is offered to them by other democratic management strategies.

In his article entitled, "Judicious Discipline in the Music Classroom" (1997), Douglas Nimmo explains:

In the judicious rehearsal, the power is shared. The judicious teacher uses the four compelling state interests as a framework for teaching responsible behavior and learning. The conductor expects the students to be involved in the music making. A basic practice is to teach by asking questions. Respect is offered to the note passers, while asking them (after class) to remember what they already know: issues of time, place, and manner. There is an ongoing reference to earlier learning and, at the same time, an invitation to think of additional musical possibilities. The judicious teacher is genuinely interested in the students' musical thinking and musical imagination.

Gwen Moldan, a participant in the Mankato study, said:

I've learned a lot this year just through using [Judicious Discipline].... It will be something I'll always use, it won't be in and out. I think a lot of teachers complain, "Here's something new again." But I think this is something that will stay. You'll have to change the way you think about things and the way you talk to students, but I think that once you make that change you won't want to change back.

Concerns and Considerations

Judicious Discipline is not the answer to all of education's problems. There is no quick path to the establishment of trusting, caring human relationships. A common concern expressed by teachers who would like to settle their management situations swiftly is that Judicious Discipline takes time. Those engaged in researching Judicious Discipline have been told by numerous teachers at all levels that the time spent establishing and sustaining citizenship expectations is an investment. Teachers report that they spend more time teaching and less time managing because students are learning to monitor their own behaviors.

Another concern expressed about Judicious Discipline is that when one teacher is using it and all of his or her peers are relying on more behaviorist practices for management, students might find the disparities confusing. In an action research study conducted in Oregon by Susan Hays-Zumbaris, she reported:

As successful as the implementation [of Judicious Discipline] was, both [the teacher] and I found shortcomings. While the students worked at a very high, democratic level with us, they tended to regress when out of the classroom with specialists, or when a substitute teacher was present. [The teacher] felt that both students and teachers had a part in this; '...they're coming from this authoritarian point of view, so it's really easy for them to relate to that, they've had that [method of discipline] for most of their lives.... That's what's

so frustrating—they can't carry over. It will only work if more adult leaders/
teachers/parents start looking at [Judicious Discipline].'

The concerns that Hays-Zumbaris raised in her research have been expressed elsewhere; and, indeed, Judicious Discipline has been most successful in terms of reducing incidents of misbehavior in schools in which all personnel are using the common language of rights and responsibilities. However, it is important to repeat what was stated earlier—that Judicious Discipline can be used with other cognitive models and its framework supports them very well.

Discussion

The results of the research reported in this study suggest that when students are empowered to examine their own behaviors critically against the standards set by a free society, a noticeable rise in autonomy levels has been documented. Although the numbers did not reflect an increase above the fifty percent level, providing students with a deliberate process by which they can not only take responsibility for their own behaviors, but also make decisions with an increased sense of confidence, is not insignificant. The ability to function autonomously while at the same time respecting individual rights and group responsibilities is exceedingly important to the smooth functioning of a free society.

Students who have been trained to depend on the judgment of others to tell them whether their behaviors are appropriate have difficulty making those decisions as independent adults. Judicious Discipline can contribute to their levels of autonomy by teaching the common language used by free societies of the ways in which their personal freedoms are always balanced against group responsibilities.

There are many benefits for teachers who take the time to teach and use Judicious Discipline in their classrooms. In addition to having more students functioning autonomously, their teachers are less likely to feel frustrated about management issues or to experience high levels of work-related stress. Through interviews, researchers have found consistently that educators who practiced Judicious Discipline as it is designed to be used, respected students and were respected by students. These educators indicated that using Judicious Discipline gave them a feeling of professionalism. They felt that they were using management strategies that were legal, ethical, and educationally sound. In teaching a common language for civil discourse, educators found a mutually accessible means of discussing mediation and reconciliation of social problems that develop in any classroom.

References

Barr, R. D., & Parrett, W. H. (1995). *Hope at Last for At-Risk Youth.* Boston: Allyn & Bacon.
Dreikurs, R. (1982). *Maintaining sanity in the classroom: Classroom management techniques.* New York: Harper & Row.

Freiberg, H. J. (1996). From Tourist to Citizens in the Classroom. *Educational Leadership, 54*(1), 32–36.

Freiberg, H. J. (in press). *Consistency management & cooperative discipline: From tourist to citizen.* Columbus: Merrill.

Gathercoal, F. (1993). *Judicious Discipline* (3rd ed.). San Francisco: Caddo Gap Press.

Giroux, H. (1993). *Living dangerously: Multiculturalism and the politics of difference.* New York: Lang.

Glasser, W. (1969). *Schools without failure.* New York: Harper & Row.

Hays-Zumbaris, S. (1994). *Judicious Discipline: One educator's implementation.* Unpublished action research study.

Jones, V., & Jones, L. (1995). Comprehensive classroom management: Creating positive learning environments for all students (4th ed.). Boston: Allyn & Bacon.

Kohn, A. (1996). *Beyond Discipline: From compliance to community.* Alexandria, VA: Association for Supervision and Curriculum Development.

Lickona, T. (1991). *Educating for character: How our schools can teach respect and responsibility.* New York: Bantam.

McEwan, B. (Ed.). (1994). *Practicing Judicious Discipline: An educator's guide to a democratic classroom* (2nd ed.). San Francisco: Caddo Gap Press.

McEwan, B. (1996). Assaulting the last bastions of authoritarianism: Democratic education meets classroom discipline. In J. Burstyn (Ed.), *Educating tomorrow's valuable citizen.* Albany, NY: SUNY Press.

McEwan, B. & Nimmo, V. (1995). *Making inclusive classrooms equitable classrooms: Using judicious discipline with students diagnosed as being emotionally disturbed.* Study presented at American Educational Research Association Conference.

Nimmo, D. (1997). Judicious Discipline in the music classroom. *Music Educators Journal, 83*(4), 27–32.

Saleno, S. (1994). *Effective mainstreaming: Creative inclusive classrooms* (2nd ed.). New York: Macmillan.

Villa, R. A., Thousand, J. S., Stainback, W., & Stainback, S. (1993). *Restructuring for caring and effective education: An administrative guide to creating heterogeneous schools* (2nd ed.). Baltimore: Brooks Publishing Co.

7

The Three Cs of School and Classroom Management

DAVID W. JOHNSON
University of Minnesota

ROGER T. JOHNSON
University of Minnesota

Purposes of Management Programs

Classroom management problems are, by definition, disruptions to the overall cooperative nature of the school. In certain areas, the severity of classroom management problems reflects the problems in the community. Many inner cities have become what criminologists have described as **criminogenic communities**—places where the social forces that create predatory criminals are far more numerous and overwhelmingly stronger than the social forces that create virtuous citizens. Inner-city children too often grow up surrounded by teenagers and adults who are deviant, delinquent, or criminal and who may abuse, neglect, or criminally prey on the young. This is not just an urban problem. Many suburban and rural children and adolescents are also neglected or preyed on by members of their families and neighborhoods.

In Minnesota, students report frequent classroom management problems involving physical aggression (students report being punched and kicked, and seeing teachers slapped or hit by students), property damage (bathroom wastebaskets set on fire, lavatory sinks being beaten off the wall with baseball bats), and incivility (profanity in the hallways and classrooms) (Snow, 1997). One result of these classroom management problems is disruption of learning. Regardless of whether the school is urban, suburban, or rural and whether the school is public or private, students report that other students are interfering with their ability to learn.

To deal with these problems, schools institute management programs. The purposes of these programs are to (1) prevent disruptions of and resistance to learning and (2) restore order after a disruption has taken place. It is evident, therefore, that when more students are committed to the learning goals, are active and engaged, and have the competencies needed to act appropriately, there will be fewer management problems and it will be easier to restore student productivity after a disruption has taken place.

School and classroom management programs may be placed on a continuum (Fig. 7-1). At one end are management programs based on external rewards and punishments administrated by faculty and staff to control and manage student behavior. Faculty monitor student behavior, determine whether it is within the bounds of acceptability, and force students to terminate inappropriate actions. This requires a great deal of instructional and administrative time and works only as long as students are under surveillance. The external rewards and punishments approach is based on the behavioral theory, which assumes that individuals will repeat behavior that is rewarded and avoid behavior that is punished. Two of the problems with behavioral approaches are as follows. First, behavioral theory assumes and promotes the view that all behavior is based on self-interest and, therefore, individuals will seek to maximize their rewards and minimize their punishments. This assumption can become a self-fulfilling prophecy for schools. If schools act as if all students are selfish and self-centered, they implicitly teach students to be that way. In addition, intrinsic sources of motivation based on cooperation, caring, commitment, altruism, and community will not be utilized to ensure students behave appropriately. Requiring students to obey rules out of the fear of punishment, however, reduces student self-regulation (Berk, 1994). Second, no one reward works for all students or for the same students for very long. Grades or food may be a motivator for some students but not for others. A student may be highly motivated to get food right before lunch

FIGURE 7-1   Continuum of Classroom Management Programs.

Programs based on faculty-administrated external rewards and punishments

Programs based on teaching students the competencies they need to regulate their own and their schoolmates' behavior

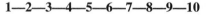

Faculty are police officers, judge, jury, and executioners; faculty monitor student behavior, judge its appropriateness, decide which consequence to administer, and give the reward or punishment

Students monitor the appropriateness of their own behavior and decide how to behave; students assist schoolmates in doing likewise but exert little effort for food immediately after lunch. There is no one extrinsic reward that works for all students or for very long with the same students and, therefore, extrinsic reward systems tend to be effective only temporarily.

At the other end of the continuum are programs aimed at teaching students the competencies and skills required to regulate their own and their schoolmates' behavior. **Self-regulation** is the ability to act in socially approved ways in the absence of external monitors by deciding how they should behave and engaging in the chosen actions. In their personal interactions, students monitor, modify, refine, and change how they behave to learn how to act appropriately and competently. Self-regulation is a central and significant hallmark of cognitive and social development. Students are empowered to solve their own problems and regulate their own and their classmates' behavior when they are involved in cooperative efforts, manage conflicts constructively, and base their actions on civic values. These three Cs are central to making the school a healthy learning community.

The Three Cs Program

Effective school and management programs are built on the three Cs: cooperative community, constructive conflict resolution, and civic values (Fig. 7-2). The school is a cooperative system in which faculty–staff, students, and parents work together to achieve mutual goals concerning quality education. Sometimes conflicts arise over how best to achieve goals and coordinate actions. These conflicts have to be resolved constructively if the community is to survive. Both a cooperative community and constructive conflict resolution are based on civic values that recognize and support the long-term benefits of working together and contributing to the welfare of others and the common good as well as working for one's own well-being.

The First C: Cooperative Community

The Nature of Community and Social Interdependence

School and classroom management begins with establishing a learning community based on cooperation (i.e., working together to achieve mutual goals). Scholarship and learning do not exist in isolation; they are products of a community and a culture characterized by mutual respect and trust. **Community** is a group of people who live in the same locality and share common goals and a common culture. The school community is made up of the faculty and staff, the students, their parents, and members of the neighborhood. Broadly, the school community includes all stakeholders including central administrators, college admission officers, and future employers.

The heart of community and culture is **social interdependence,** which exists when each individual's outcomes are affected by the actions of others (Deutsch,

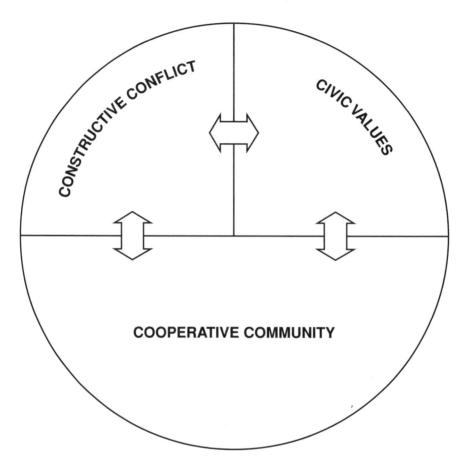

FIGURE 7-2   The Three Cs of Safe Schools.

1949; Johnson & Johnson, 1989). Social interdependence may be positive or negative. **Positive interdependence** (cooperation) exists when individuals work together to achieve mutual goals; **negative interdependence** (competition) exists when individuals work against each other to achieve a goal that only one or a few may attain. **Social independence,** where the outcomes of each person are unaffected by others' actions, is characterized by individualistic actions.

To create a learning community, positive interdependence (i.e., cooperation) must be structured at all levels of the school: learning group, classroom, interclass, school, school–parent, and school–neighborhood. Members of the community must see themselves to be partners, not adversaries. The school cannot be a learning community if students are pitted against each other in the classroom or if students are isolated with no friends in the classroom. Just as the family is the beginning of community in society, the learning group is the beginning of community in the school.

The Power of Cooperation

Since the late 1890s, more than 550 experimental and 100 correlational studies have been conducted by a wide variety of researchers in different decades with subjects different ages, in different subject areas, and in different settings [for a detailed review of the research on cooperative, competitive, and individualistic efforts, see Johnson & Johnson (1989)]. In our own research program at the Cooperative Learning Center (University of Minnesota) since the early 1970s, we have conducted more than eighty-five research studies to refine our understanding of the nature of cooperation and how it works. Research participants have varied as to economic class, age, sex, nationality, and cultural background. A wide variety of research tasks, ways of structuring cooperation, and measures of the dependent variables have been used. Many different researchers have conducted the research with markedly different orientations working in different settings, countries, and decades. The research on cooperation has a validity and a generalizability rarely found in the educational literature.

Working together to achieve mutual goals can have profound effects on the individuals involved (Hertz-Lazarowitz & Miller, 1992). The type of interdependence structured among individuals determines how they interact with each other, which in turn largely determines outcomes. Structuring situations cooperatively results in individuals promoting each other's success (individuals help, assist, support, and encourage each other's efforts). Structuring situations competitively results in individuals opposing each other's success (individuals obstruct and block each other's efforts). Structuring situations individualistically results in no interaction among individuals (individuals ignore each other and work alone) (Table 7-1). These interaction patterns affect numerous variables that may be subsumed within the three broad and interrelated outcomes of (Fig. 7-3) (Johnson & Johnson, 1989):

1. Effort exerted to achieve (higher achievement and greater productivity, more frequent use of higher level reasoning, more frequent generation of new ideas and solutions, greater intrinsic and achievement motivation, greater long-term retention, more on-task behavior, and greater transfer of what is learned within one situation to another).

2. Quality of relationships among participants (greater interpersonal attraction, liking, cohesion and esprit-de-corps, valuing of heterogeneity, and greater task-oriented and personal support).

3. Psychological adjustment (greater psychological health, greater social competencies, higher self-esteem, a shared identity, and greater ability to cope with stress and adversity).

Effective cooperation requires that five basic elements be carefully structured into the situation (Johnson & Johnson, 1989; Johnson, Johnson, & Holubec, 1998a) (Table 7-2). First, there must be a strong sense of **positive interdependence,** so individuals believe they are linked with others so they cannot succeed unless the others do

TABLE 7-1   Nature of Cooperative and Competitive Relationships

Positive Interdependence: Cooperation	Negative Interdependence: Competition
Long-term time orientation focused on achieving mutual goals and maintaining effective relationships	Short-term time orientation focused on achieving self-interests at the expense of others
Communication tends to be frequent, complete, and accurate with each person interested in informing others as well as being informed	Communication tends to be avoided or contains misleading information and threats; espionage to obtain information about others and "diversionary tactics" to delude or mislead others about oneself
Perceive accurately others' positions and motivations; any misperceptions are easy to correct and clarify	Frequent misperceptions and distortions of others' positions and motivations that are difficult to correct
Trust and like others so willing to respond helpfully to others' requests and needs	Distrust and dislike others so ignore or exploit requests and need for help
Recognize legitimacy of others' interests, needs, and feelings and search for ways to accommodate them	Deny legitimacy of others' interests, needs, and feelings; consider only own interests, needs, and feelings
Conflicts defined as mutual problems to be solved in ways that benefit everyone	Conflicts defined as "win-lose" situations in which others are to be defeated

(and vice versa). Individuals must believe that they "sink or swim" together. Positive interdependence may be structured through mutual goals, joint rewards, divided resources, complementary roles, and a shared identity. Second, each collaborator must be **individually accountable** to do his or her fair share of the work. Third, collaborators must have the opportunity to **promote each other's success** by helping, assisting, supporting, encouraging, and praising each other's efforts to achieve. Fourth, working together cooperatively requires **interpersonal and small group skills,** such as leadership, decision-making, trust-building, communication, and conflict-management skills. Finally, cooperative groups must engage in **group processing,** which exists when group members discuss how well they are achieving their goals and maintaining effective working relationships.

The heart of a learning community is carefully structuring cooperative efforts at all levels of the school, beginning with the use of cooperative learning in the classroom.

Cooperative Learning

> *"Two are better than one, because they have a good reward for toil. For if they fall, one will lift up his fellow; but woe to him who is alone when he falls and has not another to lift him up...And though a man might prevail against one who is alone, two will withstand him. A three-fold cord is not quickly broken." —ECCLESIASTES 4:9–12*

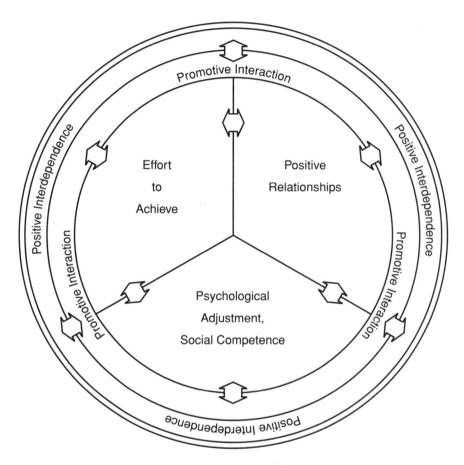

FIGURE 7-3 Outcomes of Cooperative Learning.

Taken from Johnson, D. W., & Johnson, R. (1989). *Cooperation and competition: Theory and research.* Edina, MN: Interaction Book Company.

Classroom management is enhanced by keeping students engaged constructively in learning from the moment they enter the classroom until the time they leave. The most effective way to do this is through the use of **cooperative learning,** which is the instructional use of small groups so that students work together to maximize their own and each other's learning (Johnson, Johnson, & Holubec, 1998a). Within cooperative learning groups, students discuss the material to be learned, help each other to understand it, and encourage each other to work hard. Any assignment in any curriculum for any age student can be done cooperatively. When you walk down the halls of a school you should see signs of cooperative learning in every classroom. Desks should be clustered, group name placards should designate team work stations, posters should

TABLE 7-2   Understanding Cooperative Efforts[a]

Types of Interdependence	Cooperative Learning	Essential Elements of Cooperation	Outcomes of Cooperation
Positive: cooperation	Formal cooperative learning	Positive interdependence	Effort to achieve
Negative: competition	Informal cooperative learning	Individual accountability	Positive relationships
None: individualistic	Cooperative base groups	Promotive interaction	Psychological health
		Interpersonal and small-group skills	
		Group processing	

[a]There are three types of interdependence, the most important of which is cooperation. The basic use of cooperation in schools is cooperative learning. There are three types of cooperative learning. Effective cooperation depends on five basic elements being structured into the situation. When the five elements are present, three types of outcomes tend to result.

celebrate the benefits of teamwork, bulletin boards both inside and outside classrooms should display the products of students' cooperative efforts, and students should huddle in their groups and celebrate mutual accomplishments with "high-fives," smiles, and handshakes. These signs are indicative of the use of the three types of cooperative learning (Table 7-3) (Johnson, Johnson, & Holubec, 1998a,b).

Formal cooperative learning consists of students working together, for one class period to several weeks, to achieve shared learning goals and complete specific tasks and assignments jointly (such as decision making or problem solving, completing a curriculum unit, writing a report, conducting a survey or experiment, reading a chapter or reference book, learning vocabulary, or answering questions at the end of the chapter) (Johnson, Johnson, & Holubec, 1998a). Any course requirement or assignment may be structured cooperatively. In formal cooperative learning groups, teachers perform the following functions:

1. Specify the objectives for the lesson. In every lesson there should be an academic objective specifying the concepts and strategies to be learned and a social skills objective specifying the interpersonal or small group skill to be used and mastered during the lesson.

2. Make a number of preinstructional decisions. Teachers decide on the size of groups, the method of assigning students to groups, the roles students will be assigned, the materials needed to conduct the lesson, and the way the room will be arranged.

3. Explain the task and the positive interdependence. A teacher clearly defines the assignment, teaches the required concepts and strategies, specifies the positive

TABLE 7-3   Types of Cooperative Learning

Formal Cooperative Learning	Informal Cooperative Learning	Cooperative Base Groups
Completes assignment, lesson, unit, project to maximize own and groupmates' learning	Discusses assigned questions for few minutes to focus attention, organize knowledge, set expectations, create mood, ensure cognitive processing and rehearsal, summarize, precue next session, provide closure	Permanent, lasts for one semester, one year, or several years to ensure all members make academic progress and develop cognitively and socially in healthy ways
Teacher Procedure	*Teacher Procedure*	*Teacher Procedure*
Make preinstructional decisions	Conduct introductory focused discussion	Structure opening class meeting to check homework, ensure all members understand the academic material, complete routine tasks such as attendance, and prepare members for the day
Explain task and cooperative structure	Conduct intermittent pair discussions every ten or fifteen minutes	Structure ending class meeting to ensure all members understand the academic material, know what homework to do, and are making progress on long-term assignments
Monitor learning groups and intervene to improve taskwork and teamwork	Conduct closure-focused discussion	Encourage members to help and assist each other's learning in-between classes
Assess learning and process group effectiveness		Assign semester- or year-long school or class service projects

interdependence and individual accountability, gives the criteria for success, and explains the expected social skills to be used.

4. Monitor students' learning and intervene within the groups to provide task assistance or to increase students' interpersonal and group skills. A teacher systematically observes and collects data on each group as it works. When needed, the teacher intervenes to assist students in completing the task accurately and in working together effectively.

5. Assess students' learning and help students process how well their groups functioned. Students' learning is carefully assessed and their performances evaluated. Members of the learning groups then discuss how effectively they worked together and how they can improve in the future.

Informal cooperative learning consists of having students work together to achieve a joint learning goal in temporary, ad-hoc groups that last from a few minutes to one class period (Johnson, Johnson, & Holubec, 1998b; Johnson, Johnson, & Smith, 1991). During a lecture, demonstration, or film, informal cooperative learning can be used to:

1. Focus student attention on the material to be learned.
2. Set a mood conducive to learning.
3. Help set expectations as to what will be covered in a class session.
4. Ensure that students cognitively process and rehearse the material being taught.
5. Summarize what was learned and precue the next session.
6. Provide closure to an instructional session.

During direct teaching, the instructional challenge for the teacher is to ensure that students do the intellectual work of organizing material, explaining it, summarizing it, and integrating it into existing conceptual structures. Informal cooperative learning groups are often organized so that students engage in three-to-five minute focused discussions before and after a lecture, and two-to-three minute turn-to-your-partner discussions interspersed throughout a lecture.

Cooperative base groups are long-term, heterogeneous cooperative learning groups with stable membership (Johnson, Johnson, & Holubec, 1998b; Johnson, Johnson, & Smith, 1991). Base groups give the support, help, encouragement, and assistance each member needs to make academic progress (attend class, complete all assignments, learn) and develop cognitively and socially in healthy ways. Base groups are permanent (lasting from one to several years) and provide the long-term, caring peer relationships necessary to influence members consistently to work hard in school. The use of base groups tends to improve attendance, personalize the work required and the school experience, and improve the quality and quantity of learning. School and classroom management is enhanced when base groups are given the responsibility for conducting a year-long service project to improve the school.

Benefits of Cooperative Learning
A focus on cooperative learning and persistence in its implementation in every classroom is instrumental in laying the foundation for a safe school (Johnson & Johnson, 1989). Several benefits as a result of cooperative learning are as follows:

1. Cooperative learning ensures that all students are meaningfully and actively involved in learning. Active and involved students do not tend to engage in disruptive, off-task behavior.
2. Cooperative learning ensures that students are achieving up to their potential and are experiencing psychological success so they are motivated to continue to invest energy and effort in learning. Students who experience academic failure are at risk for tuning out and acting up, which often leads to physical or verbal aggression.

3. Systematic use of cooperative learning in every classroom promotes the development of caring and committed relationships for every student. Cooperative groups help students establish and maintain friendships with peers. Students who are isolated or alienated from their peers and who do not have friends are at risk for violent and destructive behavior compared to students who experience social support and a sense of belonging.

4. Cooperative groups provide an arena in which students develop the interpersonal and small-group skills needed to work effectively with diverse schoolmates. Students learn how to communicate effectively, provide leadership, help the group make good decisions, build trust, repair hurt feelings, and understand others' perspectives. Even kindergartners can practice social skills each day.

5. The cooperative base groups and the other positive relationships promoted by working together provide the opportunity for discussions in which personal problems are shared and solved. As a result, students' resilience and ability to cope with adversity and stress tend to increase. Children who do not share their problems and who do not have caring and supportive help in solving them are at more risk for disruptive and destructive behavior.

6. Cooperative groups provide an arena in which students can feel a sense of meaning, pride, and esteem by helping and assisting each other academically and by contributing to each other's well-being and quality of life.

7. All the benefits of cooperation for students can also be found to result from the cooperation among faculty, between faculty and administrators, and among administrators.

8. The systematic use of cooperative learning promotes the development of caring relationships both within and between classes and programs. The result is a strong sense of school community, where concern for the well-being of others is prominent and individuals seek outcomes beneficial to everyone. This cooperative context affects all other aspects of school life, including the ways students resolve conflicts with schoolmates from different classes. For example, students who contribute repeatedly to each other's academic success and personal well-being in the classroom and who value one another as cooperators have an advantage when conflict occurs, because they tend to view each other as friends with mutual problems to be solved rather than as enemies to be defeated. To resolve conflicts constructively, however, everyone in school needs a common set of tools. That is why schools need to institute a schoolwide conflict resolution and peer mediation program.

Classroom Interdependence

There are numerous ways to extend the positive interdependence within the learning groups to the classroom as a whole. Class goals may be established to create positive interdependence by setting a criterion each student must reach, a goal of each student improving his or her performance level over previous scores, or a total class score as a specified criterion. Class rewards or celebrations may be created to establish positive interdependence by adding bonus points to all group members' academic scores when all class members achieve up to criterion, by giving nonacademic rewards (such as extra free time, extra recess time, stickers, food, or T-shirts), or a class party. Class positive interdependence may also be structured through class roles, such as establishing a classroom government (president, vice-president, class council, and so forth), putting teams in charge of daily class clean-up, running a class bank or business, or engaging in other activities that benefit the class as a whole. Classroom interdependence may also be structured through dividing resources, such as having the class publish a newsletter in which each cooperative group contributes one article. An example of divided resources is as follows:

One class was studying geography. The ceiling was turned into a large grid giving latitude and longitude. The class was divided into eight cooperative groups. Each group was assigned a geographic location on which to do a report. The groups summarized the essential information about their location on a placard, located where on the ceiling it should be, and placed it there. The class then planned an itinerary for a trip to visit all eight places. Yarn was used to mark their journey. As they arrived at each spot, the appropriate group presented its report on the location, including its latitude and longitude.

Class meetings can be held as a forum for discussing how well the class is functioning and how the quality of classroom life may be improved. The class also processes how well students are using the social skills and civic values. Finally, a common identity creates interdependence, which may be created by such things as a class name, slogan, flag, or song.

Interclass Interdependence

Cross-class cooperation can occur in many ways. An interdisciplinary team of three to six teachers may organize their classes into a "neighborhood" or a "school within a school," in which classes work together and engage in joint projects for a number of years. Science and math or English literature and social studies, may be integrated and the classes combined. Students of different ages can be involved in cross-class "reading buddies" that meet weekly throughout the year so they can jointly share and explore literature. Several classes can do periodic projects on learning specific social skills and values so students from different classes can demonstrate the skills and values to each other and use them in the hallways, on the playground, and in the lunchroom. In these and many other ways, cross-class interdependence may be created.

School Interdependence

School-level positive interdependence is established in numerous ways (Johnson & Johnson, 1994). First, the school mission statement may articulate the mutual goals shared by all members of the school and may be displayed on the school's walls and printed at the top of the agenda of every meeting involving faculty and staff. This "keeps the dream" in front of the faculty and staff and is a constant reminder of their commitment.

Second, just as students work in cooperative learning groups, ideally teachers will work in a variety of cooperative teams (Johnson & Johnson, 1994). All faculty and staff can meet weekly in teaching teams or study groups. **Collegial teaching teams** are formed to increase teachers' instructional expertise and success. They consist of two to five teachers who meet weekly and discuss how better to implement cooperative learning within their classrooms. The teaching teams plan lessons together, orchestrate their use of integrated curriculum units, schedule the times they will teach together and apart, and explore how best to promote each other's instructional success for the following week. Regular teaming among faculty promotes collegial relationships, ongoing professional growth, and induction of new faculty. **Collegial study groups** are formed to read a book about an instructional method (such as cooperative learning, block scheduling, or creating an integrated curriculum) and discuss it at meetings. Teaching teams and study groups remind faculty and staff about the important instructional procedures, involve the faculty in a continuous improvement process, and provide a procedure for socializing new teachers into the faculty. At one of the schools we work with, for example, a teacher stated:

> *One challenge we face each year is bringing new faculty on board. We want them to become part of our school community as quickly as possible, and that means training them in the components of our program. Study groups help accomplish this. We have one study group, for example, on the **Nuts and Bolts of Cooperative Learning** for new faculty who have not been trained in cooperative learning, and another study group on **Teaching Students to be Peacemakers** for new faculty who have not been trained in conflict resolution. A trained, experienced teacher leads each study group. Each meeting, we take a chapter in the book and go over it in detail. Then we plan how to implement it in our classrooms. We make sure we have those programs in every classroom in the school. This is how we keep the climate the way it is.*

Third, in addition to the collegial teaching teams and study groups, teachers may be assigned to **task forces** to plan and implement solutions to schoolwide issues and problems such as curriculum adoptions and lunchroom behavior and **ad hoc decision-making groups** during faculty meetings to involve all staff members in important school decisions. The use of cooperative teams at the school level ensures that there is a congruent cooperative team-based organizational structure within both the classrooms and the school (Johnson & Johnson, 1994).

Finally, school interdependence may be highlighted in a variety of schoolwide activities, such as the weekly student-produced school news broadcast, special activities organized by the student council, all-school projects, and regular school assemblies.

School–Parent Interdependence

Cooperation is built between the school and the parents by involving parents in establishing mutual goals and the "strategic plan" to achieve the goals, participating in a division of labor, sharing resources to help the school achieve its goals, and developing an identity as members of the school. Parents can produce a weekly school newsletter. Parents, with the help of students, can publish the school yearbook. Parents can volunteer in their children's classes and help conduct special projects. Parents may serve on all school committees and the site council. They can organize and conduct a variety of school activities, including a school carnival, a school gift wrap sale, periodic parties in each classroom, and field trips. The Parent–Teacher Association (PTA) may raise money for additional supplies and technology. A faculty–parent task force may be formed to deal with serious discipline problems and ensure that parents are notified when a student misbehaves. The ideal goal is to have 100 percent of the parents participate in the school.

School–Neighborhood Interdependence

The school community may be extended into the neighborhood. The school mission can be supported by local merchants through such programs as giving a discount to students who have a card verifying that in the last grading period they achieved a "B" average or above. Members of the neighborhood could contribute resources to school activities such as playing in the school band. Classes could do neighborhood service projects, such as cleaning up a park or mowing the yards of elderly residents. There are many creative ways that the school and the neighborhood can join together to accomplish mutual goals.

The Second C: Constructive Conflict Resolution

In order for conflicts to be resolved constructively, a cooperative environment must be established. In a cooperative context there are mutual goals that all participants are committed to achieving (Deutsch, 1973; Johnson & Johnson, 1989). When conflict resolution and peer mediation programs are implemented in a competitive–individualistic context, their effectiveness is severely compromised.

Conflict is the moment of truth within any community. It is almost paradoxical that the more committed members are to the community's goals, and the more caring and committed the relationships among members, the more frequent and intense the conflicts. When the conflicts are resolved constructively, conflicts enrich and enhance the success of any learning community. When they are managed constructively, conflicts can (Johnson & Johnson, 1995a,b, 1996):

1. Be a source of excitement, energy, curiosity, and motivation.
2. Increase achievement, retention, insight, creativity, problem solving, and synthesis.
3. Increase the use of higher level cognitive and moral reasoning.

4. Increase healthy cognitive and social development.
5. Focus attention on problems and increase the energy dedicated to solving them.
6. Clarify own and others' identity, commitments, and values.
7. Release anger, anxiety, insecurity, and sadness that, if kept inside, makes individuals mentally sick.
8. Strengthen relationships by:

   a. increasing individuals' confidence that they can resolve their disagreements
   b. keeping the relationship clear of irritations and resentments so that positive feelings can be experienced fully
   c. renewing the support and caring.

9. Be fun.

If the conflicts are managed destructively, they destroy relationships and tear the cooperative system apart. A key to long-term school effectiveness, therefore, is how constructively conflicts are managed. Whether positive or negative outcomes result depends largely on (1) disputants having clear procedures for managing conflicts, (2) disputants being skilled in the use of the procedures and their value in using them, and (3) whether the norms and values of the school encourage and support the use of the procedures. If the answer to one or more of these questions is "no," then conflicts will tend to be managed destructively. Faculty and staff need to teach students (and to learn themselves) three procedures for managing conflicts: academic controversy, problem-solving negotiation, and peer mediation procedures (Table 7-4) (Johnson & Johnson, 1995a,b).

TABLE 7-4   Types of Conflict

Academic Controversy	Conflicts of Interest
One person's ideas, information, theories, conclusions, and opinions are incompatible with those of another, and the two seek to reach an agreement	The actions of one person attempting to maximize benefits prevents, blocks, or interferes with another person maximizing their benefits
Controversy Procedure	*Integrative (Problem-Solving) Negotiations*
Research and prepare positions	Describe wants
Present and advocate positions	Describe feelings
Refute opposing position and refute attacks on own position	Describe reasons for wants and feelings
Reverse perspectives	Take other's perspective
Synthesize and integrate best evidence and reasoning from all sides	Invent three optional agreements that maximize joint outcomes
	Choose one and formalize agreement

Academic Controversies

To ensure that intellectual conflict occurs frequently and skillfully, teachers need to structure academic controversies frequently and teach students how to resolve them (Johnson & Johnson, 1995c). A **controversy** exists when one person's ideas, opinions, information, theories, or conclusions are incompatible with those of another and the two seek to reach an agreement. Controversies are resolved by engaging in what Aristotle called "deliberate discourse (i.e., the discussion of the advantages and disadvantages of proposed actions) aimed at synthesizing novel solutions (i.e., creative problem solving)." Teaching students how to engage in the controversy process begins with assigning students randomly to heterogeneous cooperative learning groups of four members (Johnson & Johnson, 1979, 1989, 1995c). The groups are given an issue on which to write a report and pass a test. Each cooperative group is divided into two pairs. One pair is given the position against the issue and the other pair is given the position for the issue. Each pair is given the instructional materials needed to define their position and point them toward supporting information. The cooperative goal of reaching a consensus on the issue (by synthesizing the best reasoning from both sides) and writing a quality group report is highlighted. Students then use the following steps to reach a consensus:

1. **Research and prepare a position.** Each pair of students develops the position assigned, learns the relevant information, and plans how to present the best case possible to the other pair. Near the end of the period, pairs are encouraged to compare notes with pairs from other groups who represent the same position.

2. **Present and advocate their position.** Each pair makes their presentation to the opposing pair. Each member of the pair has to participate in the presentation. Students are to be as persuasive and convincing as possible. Members of the opposing pair are encouraged to take notes, listen carefully to learn the information being presented, and clarify anything they do not understand.

3. **Refute the opposing position and rebut attacks on their own.** Students argue forcefully and persuasively for their position, presenting as many facts as they can to support their point of view. Students analyze and critically evaluate the information, rationale, and inductive and deductive reasoning of the opposing pair, asking them for the facts that support their point of view. They refute the arguments of the opposing pair and rebut attacks on their position. They discuss the issue, following a set of rules to help them criticize ideas without criticizing people, differentiate the two positions, and assess the degree of evidence and logic supporting each position. They keep in mind that the issue is complex and they need to know both sides to write a good report.

4. **Reverse perspectives.** The pairs reverse perspectives and present each other's positions. In arguing for the opposing position, students are forceful and persuasive. They add any new information that the opposing pair did not think to present, striving to see the issue from both perspectives simultaneously.

5. **Synthesize and integrate the best evidence and reasoning into a joint position.** The four members of the group drop all advocacy, and synthesize and integrate what they know into a joint position to which all sides can agree. They (1) finalize

the report (the teacher evaluates reports on the quality of the writing, the logical presentation of evidence, and the oral presentation of the report to the class), (2) present their conclusions to the class (all four members of the group are required to participate orally in the presentation), (3) take the test individually covering both sides of the issue (if every member of the group achieves up to criterion, they all receive bonus points), and (4) process how well they worked together and how they could be even more effective next time.

As Thomas Jefferson noted, "Difference of opinion leads to inquiry, and inquiry to truth." Since the late 1960s, we have conducted more than twenty-five research studies on the impact of academic controversy, and numerous other researchers have conducted studies directly on controversy and in related areas (Johnson & Johnson, 1989, 1995c). The considerable research available indicates that intellectual "disputed passages" create higher achievement (characterized by higher achievement, longer retention, more frequent use of higher level reasoning and metacognitive thought, more critical thinking, greater creativity, and continuing motivation to learn), more positive interpersonal relationships, and greater psychological health when they (1) occur within cooperative learning groups and (2) are carefully structured to ensure that students manage them constructively (Johnson & Johnson, 1989, 1995c). Engaging in a controversy can also be fun and exciting. Two of the most important aspects for safe schools, however, are (1) the emphasis on viewing the issue from both perspectives and (2) learning that conflicts can have positive outcomes when people listen to each other and work cooperatively to reach solutions.

Conflict Resolution Training

Problem-Solving Negotiations

Intellectual conflicts are not the only conflicts that occur within a community and must be resolved constructively. There are conflicts based on individuals' differing interests within a situation. **Conflicts of interest** exist when the actions of one person attempting to maximize their wants and benefits prevents, blocks, or interferes with another person maximizing their wants and benefits. Ideally, they are resolved through problem-solving (integrative) negotiation. When negotiation does not work, then mediation is required.

All members of the school community need to know how to negotiate constructive resolutions to their conflicts. There are two types of negotiations: **distributive,** or "win–lose" (in which one person benefits only if the opponent agrees to make a concession); and **integrative,** or problem solving (in which disputants work together to create an agreement that benefits everyone involved). In ongoing relationships, only a problem-solving approach to negotiations is constructive. The steps in using problem solving negotiations are (Johnson & Johnson, 1995a,b):

1. Describing what you want. *"I want to use the book now."* This includes using good communication skills and defining the conflict as a small and specific mutual problem.

2. Describing how you feel. *"I'm frustrated."* Disputants must understand how they feel and communicate it openly and clearly.

3. Describing the reasons for your wants and feelings. *"You have been using the book for the past hour. If I don't get to use the book soon my report will not be done on time. It's frustrating to have to wait so long."* This includes expressing cooperative intentions, listening carefully, separating interests from positions, and differentiating before trying to integrate the two sets of interests.

4. Taking the other's perspective and summarizing your understanding of what the other person wants, how the other person feels, and the reasons underlying both. *"My understanding of you is..."* This includes understanding the perspective of the opposing disputant and being able to see the problem from both perspectives simultaneously.

5. Inventing three optional plans to resolve the conflict that maximize joint benefits. *"Plan A is..., Plan B is..., Plan C is..."* This includes inventing creative options to solve the problem.

6. Choosing one and formalizing the agreement with a hand shake. *"Let's agree on Plan B!"* A wise agreement is fair to all disputants and is based on principles. It maximizes joint benefits and strengthens disputants' ability to work together cooperatively and resolve conflicts constructively in the future. It specifies how each disputant should act in the future and how the agreement will be reviewed and renegotiated if it does not work.

Peer Mediation

Once the problem-solving negotiation procedure is learned, all members of the school community need to learn how to mediate conflicts of interest (Johnson & Johnson, 1995a,b). A **mediator** is a neutral person who helps two or more people resolve their conflict, usually by negotiating an integrative agreement. Mediation is not arbitration. **Arbitration** is the submission of a dispute to a disinterested third party (such as a teacher or principal) who makes a final and binding judgment as to how the conflict will be resolved. Mediation consists of four steps (Johnson & Johnson, 1995a,b) as follows:

1. Ending hostilities. Break up hostile encounters and let students cool off.

2. Ensuring disputants are committed to the mediation process. To ensure that disputants are committed to the mediation process and are ready to negotiate in good faith, the mediator introduces the process of mediation and sets the ground rules. The mediator first introduces him- or herself. The mediator asks students if they want to solve the problem and does not proceed until the students answer "yes." Then the mediator explains:

    a. "Mediation is voluntary. My role is to help you find a solution to your conflict that is acceptable to both of you."

    b. "I am neutral. I will not take sides or attempt to decide who is right or wrong. I will help you decide how to solve the conflict."

c. "Each person will have the chance to state his or her view of the conflict without interruption."

d. "The rules you must agree to are (1) agree to solve the problem; (2) no name calling; (3) do not interrupt; (4) be as honest as you can; (5) if you agree to a solution, you must abide by it (you must do what you have agreed to do); and (6) anything said in mediation is confidential" (you, the mediator, will not tell anyone what is said).

3. Helping disputants negotiate successfully with each other. The disputants are taken carefully through the negotiation sequence of:

a. jointly defining the conflict by both persons stating what they want and how they feel

b. exchanging reasons

c. reversing perspectives so that each person is able to present the other's position and feelings to the other's satisfaction

d. inventing at least three options for mutual benefit

e. reaching a wise agreement and shaking hands.

4. Formalizing the agreement. The agreement is solidified into a contract. Disputants must agree to abide by their final decision and, in many ways the mediator becomes "the keeper of the contract."

Once students understand how to negotiate and mediate, the peacemaker program is implemented. Each day, the teacher selects two class members to serve as official mediators. Any conflicts students cannot resolve themselves are referred to the mediators. The mediators wear official T-shirts, patrol the playground and lunchroom, and are available to mediate any conflicts that occur in the classroom or school. An example is as follows:

During lunch on the playground, a ball rolls out of bounds during a lively game of soccer. A cluster of students walking by laugh as one of them kicks the ball away from the player trying to retrieve it. An argument ensures. A pair of peer mediators with clipboards in hand quickly approach the two disputants. "Would you like some help resolving your conflict?" So begins the mediation process through which the disputants arrive at a mutually agreeable solution that makes both happy. They shake hands as friends and return to their activities while the peer mediators make a note of the resolution, then continue to be available for other schoolmates who may need help resolving conflicts.

The role of mediator is rotated so that all students in the class or school serve as mediators an equal amount of time. Initially, students mediate in pairs. This ensures that shy or nonverbal students get the same amount of experience as more extroverted and verbally fluent students. Mediating classmates' conflicts is perhaps the most effective way of teaching students the need for the skillful use of each step of the negotiation procedure.

If peer mediation fails, the teacher mediates the conflict. If teacher mediation fails, the teacher arbitrates by deciding who is right and who is wrong. If that fails, the principal mediates the conflict. If that fails, the principal arbitrates. Teaching all students to mediate properly results in a schoolwide discipline program in which students are empowered to regulate and control their own and their classmates' actions. Teachers and administrators are then free to spend more of their energies on instruction.

Continuing Lessons to Refine and Upgrade Students' Skills

Additional lessons are needed to refine and upgrade students' skills in using the negotiation and mediation procedures. Gaining real expertise in resolving conflicts constructively takes years of training and practice. A few hours of training is clearly insufficient. Negotiation and mediation training may become part of the fabric of school life by integrating them into academic lessons. Literature, history, and science units typically involve conflict. Almost any lesson in these subject areas can be modified to include role-playing situations in which the negotiation or mediation procedures are used. In our research, for example, we have focused on integrating the peacemaker training into history units and English literature units involving the studying of a novel. Each of the major conflicts in the novel was used to teach the negotiation or mediation procedures and students participated in role playing how to use the procedures to resolve the conflicts in the novel constructively.

Spiral Curriculum from the First Through the Twelfth Grades

The **Teaching Students to be Peacemakers Program** is a twelve-year spiral program that is retaught each year in an increasingly sophisticated and complex way. It takes years to become competent in resolving conflicts. Twelve years of training and practice result in a person with considerable expertise in resolving conflicts constructively.

Benefits of Conflict Resolution and Peer Mediation Programs

We have conducted fourteen studies on implementing the Peacemaker Program in schools involving students from kindergarten through the tenth grade, and several other researchers have conducted relevant studies (Johnson & Johnson, 1995a, 1996). The benefits of teaching students the problem-solving negotiation and the peer-mediation procedures are as follows.

First, learning the problem-solving negotiation and peer-mediation procedures not only resulted in a mutual understanding of how conflicts would be managed, but it also gave faculty and students a common vocabulary to discuss conflicts. As a result of training, students knew the negotiation and mediation procedures, retained their knowledge throughout the school year and into the following year, were able to apply the procedures to their and other people's conflicts, transferred the procedures to non-classroom settings such as the playground and lunchroom, transferred the procedures to nonschool settings such as the home, used the procedures similarly in family and school settings, and (when given the option) engaged in problem-solving rather than win–lose negotiations.

Second, the attitudes toward conflict became more positive. Students learned to view conflicts as potentially positive, and faculty and parents viewed the conflict training as constructive and helpful.

Third, students resolved their conflicts without the involvement of faculty and administrators. A teacher states:

> *It's so great to be able to say, "These people are having a conflict; is there someone who can help them resolve it?" Twenty hands go up and every-body wants to help them. And I choose someone and say, "All right, take these people back to the mediation table and solve the conflict and let me know how it goes." Sometimes it will take two minutes and sometimes it will take fifteen minutes. As a teacher, I respect so much and appreciate immensely that students can do that for themselves. It enables everybody in the class, including me, to focus on what we're learning.*

Fourth, the conflict resolution procedures enhance the basic values of the class-room and school. A teacher who emphasizes the value of "respect" states, "The pro-cedures are a very respectful way to resolve conflicts. There's a calmness in the classroom because the students know the negotiation and mediation procedures."

Fifth, students like to do it. A teacher states, "They never refuse to negotiate or mediate. When there's a conflict and you say it's time for conflict resolution, you never have either one say I won't do it. There are no refusals."

Sixth, classroom management problems are significantly reduced. The number of discipline problems teachers have to deal with decreases by about sixty percent and referrals to administrators drop about ninety percent. Faculty and administrators no longer have to arbitrate conflicts among students; instead, they spend their time maintaining and supporting the peer-mediation process. A teacher commented, "Classroom management problems are nil as far as I'm concerned. We don't do a lot of disciplining per se. A lot of times, when a conflict occurs on the playground, they resolve it there and do not bring it back to the classroom. So there is a lot less I have to deal with in the classroom."

Finally, when integrated into academic units, the conflict resolution training increases academic achievement and long-term retention of the academic material. Academic units, especially in subject areas such as literature and history, provide a setting to understand conflicts, practice how to resolve them, and use them to gain insight into the material being studied.

The Third C: Civic Values

> *Students are sitting in a circle on the carpet. A class meeting is in progress.*
> *Today the issue is respect. One of the students risked telling her classmates*

that she felt hurt during recess the day before because she was trying to tell kids the rules to a new game, but nobody would listen. So began a discussion on what it means to be respectful, why that is important, and the sharing of everyone's personal experiences of times they felt respected versus not respected.

Some historians claim that the decline and fall of Rome was set in motion by corruption from within rather than by conquest from without. Rome fell, it can be argued, because Romans lost their civic virtue. **Civic virtue** exists when individuals meet both the letter and spirit of their public obligations. For a community to exist and be sustained, members must share common goals and values aimed at increasing the quality of life within the community. No one should be surprised that in a community in which competitive and individualistic values are taught, people behave in accordance with such values. When that happens in a society, for example, people may stop obeying the law. Running stoplights may become a common occurrence as the individualist thinks it is rational to do so as he or she will arrive at the destination sooner. If someone is killed, it will be a pedestrian, not the driver. However, each of us is at some time a pedestrian. Community cannot be maintained unless members value others and the community as a whole, as well as themselves.

School and classroom management requires that all members of the school community adopt a set of civic values (Johnson & Johnson, 1996b). To create the common culture that defines a community, there must be common goals and shared values that help define appropriate behavior. Civic values underlie the cooperation and constructive conflict resolution that take place in the school. A learning community cannot exist in schools dominated by (1) competition where students are taught to value striving for their personal success at the expense of others or (2) individualistic efforts where students value only their own self-interests. There are many civic values necessary for a community to flourish. Some of them are commitment, responsibility, respect, integrity, caring, compassion, and appreciation of diversity.

Membership in a community requires the adoption of the community's values, which may be taught through direct instruction, modeling and identification, the enactment of assigned and voluntary roles, group influences, and the hidden curriculum existing in the pattern and flow of daily school life (Johnson & Johnson, 1997). First, the core values can be taught directly by placing them in the school's mission statement, posting them in every classroom, having lessons defining them and giving examples and how they may be expressed in interactions with other people, role playing how to put them into action, pointing out instances in which a student demonstrated the values, pointing out models to be imitated, and integrating them into the curriculum. Children's literature may be used to teach values. *The Great Gilly Hopkins* by Katherine Paterson may be used to focus attention on compassion, and *The River* by Gary Paulson may be used to help students focus on responsibility. Class meetings provide a safe forum for talking about the values and how they affect student and faculty lives. Being clear about what is valued enables aligned choice making throughout the curriculum—from instructional strategies, utilized to topics of study pursued, to instructional resources employed.

Second, faculty and administrators can teach students values through identification by (1) building positive, caring, supportive relationships with the students and (2) consistently modeling the values in interactions with the students. In its simplest form, **identification** occurs when a student tries to be like someone (an adult, older student, or mythical figure) that the student likes or admires; a person usually perceived as resourceful, powerful, or competent. A student can admire a teacher's scholarship, for example, and strive to become a scholar; or a student can see a teacher behaving honestly and decide to do likewise.

Third, values may be taught by assigning students social roles. A **social role** is a set of expectations (containing rights and responsibilities) aimed at structuring interactions within a reciprocal relationship. In school, students learn the roles of "student" as well as other roles such as "American," "citizen," "collaborator," and "mediator."

Fourth, individuals adopt the values of their **reference groups,** which are the groups to which individuals believe they belong or to which they aspire to belong (Johnson & Johnson, 1997). Individuals accept a system of values, attitudes, and behavioral patterns when they accept membership in a new group. The discussion and consensual validation that take place within a group result in personal commitments to adopt the values. Values are not inculcated by focusing on each individual separately, but rather by emphasizing membership in a group (or community) that holds the desired values. By adopting the school community as a reference group, students adopt its civic values.

Fifth, the value systems underlying competitive, individualistic, and cooperative situations are a hidden curriculum beneath the surface of school life. Whenever students engage in competition, for example, a set of values is taught inherently. The values inherently taught by competition are (1) commitment to getting more than others (there is a built-in concern that one is smarter, faster, stronger, more competent, and more successful than others so that one will win and others will lose); (2) success depends on beating, defeating, and getting more than other people (triumphing over others and being "Number One" are valued); (3) what is important is winning, not mastery or excellence; (4) opposing, obstructing, and sabotaging the success of others is a natural way of life (winning depends on a good offense—doing better than others—and a good defense—not letting anyone do better than you); (5) feeling joy and pride in one's wins and others' losses (the pleasure of winning is associated with others' disappointment with losing); (6) others are a threat to one's success; (7) a person's worth (own and others) is conditional and contingent on his or her "wins" (a person's worth is never fixed, it depends on the latest victory); (8) winning, not learning, is the goal of academic work; and (9) people who are different are to be either feared (if they have an advantage) or held in contempt (if they have a handicap).

The values inherently taught by individualistic experiences are (1) commitment to one's own self-interest (only personal success is viewed as important; others' success is irrelevant); (2) success depends on one's own efforts; (3) the pleasure of succeeding is personal and relevant to only oneself; (4) other people are irrelevant; (5) self-worth is based on a unidimensional view that the characteristics that help the person succeed are valued (in school that is primarily reading and math ability); (6) extrinsic motivation to gain rewards for achieving up to criteria is valued; and (7) similar people are liked and dissimilar people are disliked.

The values inherently taught by cooperative efforts are (1) commitment to own and others' success and well-being as well as to the common good; (2) success depends on joint efforts to achieve mutual goals; (3) facilitating, promoting, and encouraging the success of others is a natural way of life (a smart cooperator always finds ways to promote, facilitate, and encourage the efforts of others); (4) the pleasure of succeeding is associated with others' happiness in their success; (5) other people are potential contributors to one's success; (6) a person's own and other people's worth is unconditional (because there are so many diverse ways that a person may contribute to a joint effort, everyone has value all the time); (7) intrinsic motivation based on striving to learn, grow, develop, and succeed is valued (learning is the goal, not winning); (8) people who are different from oneself are to be valued as they can make unique contributions to the joint effort.

Sixth, the value systems underlying problem-solving negotiations and mediation situations are a hidden curriculum beneath the surface of school life. Constructive conflict resolution promotes the values of subjecting one's conclusions to intellectual challenge, viewing issues from all perspectives, reaching agreements that are satisfying to all disputants, and maintaining effective and caring long-term relationships. In other words, constructive conflict resolution inherently teaches a set of civic values aimed at ensuring the fruitful continuation of the community.

Benefits of a Civic Values Program

There are too many developmental and personal benefits from learning civic values to detail all of them here. At the school management level, teaching civic values takes the guesswork out of knowing what the school stands for. The values guide decision making about the curriculum, instruction, and resources. They provide a standard for making selections of curriculum materials. The values provide a structure for faculty and staff to talk to parents, students, visitors, and each other about what is important and why.

The Three Cs of Safe Schools

It is time to change from a classroom management paradigm based on selfishness and egocentrism to one based on community, personal commitment, and caring. It is time for classroom management systems to move beyond behaviorism, with its emphasis on self-interest and behaving in order to achieve extrinsic rewards and avoid punishments, to classroom management systems; which are based on a positive learning environment built on three interrelated programs: cooperative community, constructive conflict resolution, and civic values. To establish a learning community, cooperation must be carefully structured at all levels in the school. To maintain the learning community, constructive conflict resolution procedures must be taught to all members of the school. To guide and direct the cooperation and constructive conflict resolution, civic values must be inculcated in all school members. Although each of the Cs may be discussed and implemented separately, together they represent a gestalt in which each enhances and promotes the others.

Cooperation creates a structure within which faculty, students, and parents work together to educate the students. The more cooperative the structure, the more committed and dedicated faculty, students, and parents are to providing quality education. The greater the commitment to the school's goals, the more frequent and intense the conflicts around how best to achieve the goals and coordinate behavior. When the controversy and problem-solving negotiation procedures are used skillfully, the conflicts lead to higher level reasoning; the utilization of diverse perspectives, creative insights; synthesis of different positions; high quality and novel solutions; and trusting, supportive, and caring relationships. Civic values that highlight the need to work together toward the common good and maximize joint (not individual) benefits are the glue that holds the school together and defines how members should act towards each other.

The three Cs result in students being more autonomous individuals who can regulate and control their own actions by monitoring, modifying, refining, and changing how they behave in order to act appropriately and competently. Students who work effectively with others and resolve conflicts with skill and grace and who have internalized civic values have a developmental advantage that increases their future academic and career success; improves the quality of their relationships with friends, colleagues, and family; and generally enhances their life-long happiness.

Together, the three Cs are a complete management program for creating safe and nurturing schools in which few management problems occur and the well-being of students and other members of the learning community is promoted.

Acknowledgments

We wish to thank the Principal Peter Hodne and the teachers at Highlands Elementary School, Edina, Minnesota, for their implementation of the Three Cs Program. We also wish to thank Laurie Stevahn for conducting and analyzing the teacher and student interviews at Highlands that provided the examples used in this chapter.

References

Berk, I. (1994). *Child development* (3rd ed.). Needham Heights, MA: Allyn & Bacon.
Deutsch, M. (1949). A theory of cooperation and competition. *Human Relations, 2,* 129–152.
Deutsch, M. (1973). *The resolution of conflict.* New Haven, CT: Yale University Press.

Hertz-Lazarowitz, R., & Miller, N. (1992). *Interaction in cooperative groups.* New York: Cambridge University Press.

Johnson, D. W., & Johnson, F. (1997). *Joining together: Group theory and group skills* (6th ed.). Englewood Cliffs, NJ: Prentice-Hall.

Johnson, D. W., & Johnson, R. (1979). Conflict in the classroom: Controversy and learning. *Review of Educational Research, 49,* 51–61.

Johnson, D. W., & Johnson, R. (1989). *Cooperation and competition: Theory and research.* Edina, MN: Interaction Book Company.

Johnson, D. W., & Johnson, R. (1994). *Leading the cooperative school* (2nd ed.). Edina, MN: Interaction Book Company.

Johnson, D. W., & Johnson, R. (1995a). *Teaching students to be peacemakers.* Edina, MN: Interaction Book Company.

Johnson, D. W., & Johnson, R. (1995b). *My mediation notebook* (3rd ed.). Edina, MN: Interaction Book Company.

Johnson, D. W., & Johnson, R. (1995c). *Creative controversy: Intellectual challenge in the classroom.* Edina, MN: Interaction Book Company.

Johnson, D. W., & Johnson, R. (1995e). Teaching students to be peacemakers: Results of five years of research. *Peace and Conflict: Journal of Peace Psychology, 1*(4), 417–438.

Johnson, D. W., & Johnson, R. (1996a). Conflict resolution and peer mediation programs in elementary and secondary schools: A review of the research. *Review of Educational Research, 66*(4), 459–506.

Johnson, D. W., & Johnson, R. (1996b). Cooperative learning and traditional American values. *NASSP Bulletin, 80*(579), 11–18.

Johnson, D. W., & Johnson, R. (in press). Cooperative learning, values, and culturally plural classrooms. In M. Leicester, C. Modgill, & S. Modgil (Eds.), *Values, the classroom, and cultural diversity.* London: Cassell PLC.

Johnson, D. W., Johnson, R., & Holubec, E. (1998b). *Advanced cooperative learning* (3rd ed.). Edina, MN: Interaction Book Company.

Johnson, D. W., Johnson, R., & Holubec, E. (1998a). *Cooperation in the classroom* (6th ed.). Edina, MN: Interaction Book Company.

Johnson, D. W., Johnson, R., & Smith, K. (1998). *Active learning: Cooperation in the college classroom* (2nd ed.). Edina, MN: Interaction Book Company.

Snow, M. (1997, March 6). Mindworks: Disbehavior. *Minneapolis Tribune,* Section E, 1–2, 14.

Section III

The Evolution of Change

…a major change is occurring in our thinking about classroom management…. this change can be characterized as a shift from a paradigm that emphasizes the creation and application of rules to regulate student behavior to one that also attends to students' needs for nurturing relationships and opportunities of self-regulation.
(Carol Weinstein, p. 151)

In a world that requires flexibility, independence, and self-discipline, schools of the twentieth century have tended to model opposite. The models in Beyond Behaviorism provide concrete examples of alternatives to teacher as the sole source of discipline.
(H. Jerome Freiberg, p. 173)

8

Reflections on Best Practices and Promising Programs
Beyond Assertive Classroom Discipline

CAROL SIMON WEINSTEIN
Rutgers Graduate School of Education

Introduction

In 1988, my then seven-year old daughter came home from the first day of school bearing three important looking pieces of paper. She solemnly explained that we needed to read these together, that I needed to sign the papers, and that she had to return them to school the following day. On the first page, entitled "Classroom Behavior Rules," Laura had dutifully filled in the behaviors that were expected of all students in her second-grade class. They read as follows (with all of the original capitals, punctuation, and spelling intact):

1. follow diretions
2. respect their classmates.
3. Listen when someone is talking
4. bring books, pencils, Homework to class
5. Walk quitely through the halls.

On the second page was the teacher's "Discipline Plan." Here Laura had printed the consequences that students faced if they broke a rule:

1st Time: your name goes on the board as a warning
2nd Time: copy behavior rules in your homework Book and have a parent sing
3rd Time: you don't have recess
4th Time: a not is sent home
5th Time: you will call your parents a teacher–parent–student conference is set up

Finally, two jovial, smiling characters on the third page announced the rewards that "students who behave will earn." Laura had drawn a "smiley face" on the first line and had then listed two more items: "a certifeticate" and "a voucher for some thing you like."

As a teacher educator, I recognized the handouts as reproducible pages from the workbook accompanying Lee and Marlene Canter's *Assertive Discipline* (1976). It was clear that this "take-charge approach for today's educators," had gained adherents even in our tiny school district, one that prided itself on humanism, openness, and respect for students. I anticipated parental outcry, and I was right. The battle lines were soon drawn.

The debate that played out in my own community paralleled debates throughout the country. Published in 1976, *Assertive Discipline* was both fiercely loved and fiercely hated. The story of the program's widespread popularity, the criticism it received, and the way it has evolved since its publication is a metaphor for the field of classroom management as a whole—and for the new paradigm that seems to be emerging.

Growing out of the assertiveness training movement of the 1970s, *Assertive Discipline* emphasized the legitimacy and primacy of teachers' wants, needs, and rights. The first chapter, for example, was called "Power to the Teacher," and it began with this statement: "You, the teacher, must be able to get your needs met in the classroom" (p. 2). In order to do this, teachers needed to distinguish among three basic styles of interacting with students: *nonassertive* ("wishy-washy" or passive), *hostile* (abusive, aggressive, demeaning), and *assertive*. Teachers with an assertive style, according to the Canters, identified the specific behaviors they wanted and needed from students; communicated those behavioral expectations clearly; engaged in verbal "limit-setting"; decided on rewards for appropriate behavior and consequences for inappropriate behavior; and provided opportunities for students to *choose* whether the consequences would occur.

The *Assertive Discipline* program met with resounding success and enthusiastic approval among many teachers and administrators. Teacher educators and educational theorists, however, generally lambasted its stress on teacher control and the way it seemed to pit students and teachers against each other. Some critics (Render, Padilla, & Krank, 1989) observed that *Assertive Discipline* saw the classroom as "a battleground, with continual power struggles and therefore winners and losers" (p. 619). Others (Curwin & Mendler, 1989) argued that *Assertive Discipline* was

> *little more than an attractive, well-marketed behavior modification pro-*
> *gram in which one person (teacher or administrator) has all the power to*
> *define the rules while offering group and individual rewards for compliance*
> *and administering punishments through public disclosure. (p. 83)*

Critics also disputed the Canters' notion that the program provided children with the opportunity to make real choices, because *Assertive Discipline* offered only one choice to children—"Behave or else!" (Curwin & Mendler, 1989, p. 83).

Now fast forward to 1992, and the publication of a second edition of *Assertive Discipline*. Significantly, the new edition has dropped the original subtitle (*A Take-Charge Approach*), substituting *Positive Behavior Management for Today's Class-room*; it has also replaced the stark orange-and-black cover of the first edition with a much softer turquoise one, this time displaying a photograph of Lee Canter sur-rounded by smiling children.

The changes to the outside reflect changes to the inside. The first chapter is no longer entitled "Power to the Teacher," but "The Empowered Teacher." The differ-ence may seem minimal, but the tone of the two chapters is decidedly different. "You, the teacher, must be able to get your needs met in the classroom" has been replaced by "You have the right to teach and *your students have the right to learn* in a classroom free from disruptive behavior—a classroom that both reflects your own behavioral expectations *and* creates an atmosphere in which *student self-esteem can flourish*" (p. 5; italics added for emphasis). Chapters on verbal limit setting and follow-through are gone, and chapters on "teaching responsible behavior" have taken their place. There is a new emphasis on determining and teaching general norms for behavior and procedures for specific situations. There's a chapter on using positive recognition to motivate students to behave, and even a chapter on one-to-one problem-solving conferences.

To what may we attribute the changes in the Canters' ideas about classroom management? A large part of the answer lies in the "process–product" studies of the late 1970s, when federal funding enabled educational researchers to conduct large-scale observational studies of classrooms. Designed to identify teacher behaviors ("processes") related to various student outcomes ("products"), this ambitious pro-gram of research gave a prominent place to classroom organization and management (Doyle, 1986). One series of studies, conducted by Evertson, Emmer, and colleagues (Emmer, Evertson, & Anderson, 1980; Evertson & Emmer, 1982; Evertson, 1985, 1989a,b) at the R&D Center for Teacher Education at the University of Texas, Aus-tin, focused on how teachers establish a well-managed classroom at the beginning of the year. These studies indicated that teachers whose students demonstrated higher engagement rates, better academic performance, and less inappropriate behavior approached classroom management in a very systematic way. Specifically, these more effective managers spent considerable time at the beginning of the year planning and teaching general rules for conduct; instead of merely informing stu-dents of class rules, they provided rationales, generated examples, and checked for understanding. More effective managers also spent time planning and teaching procedures for specific activities, such as entering and leaving the classroom, distributing materials, and sharpening pencils.

Like many other texts on classroom management (e.g., Cangelosi, 1993; Jones & Jones, 1998; Weinstein & Mignano, 1997), the second edition of *Assertive Discipline* appears to have been substantially influenced by the research conducted by Evertson and Emmer (although, unlike these other texts, there are no references to this work anywhere in the book). In 1976, the Canters simply urged teachers to "communicate" the behaviors they wanted and needed from students; in 1992, they emphasize the importance of *teaching* the classroom discipline plan to students—by providing a rationale, explaining the rules, and checking for understanding. The 1992 edition also highlights the need for teachers to plan and teach procedures for specific situations (e.g., taking a test, entering the classroom, what to do when there is a fire drill), a topic not addressed in the earlier edition. Furthermore, the overall emphasis has shifted from *disciplinary intervention* to *prevention.*

Despite the fact that the 1992 edition of *Assertive Discipline* has abandoned much of the earlier emphasis on power and now reflects research-based knowledge of classroom organization and management, educators have been slow to recognize the substantial changes in the two editions. The reason, perhaps, is that the program still focuses on the development of an assertive teacher who sets and enforces firm and consistent limits. The Canters now suggest that teachers "consider involving students in choosing some of the rules" (p. 54), but the suggestion seems half-hearted at best. The 1992 *Assertive Discipline* has retained the emphasis on actions used by the teacher to bring about desired changes in student behavior, rather than presenting ways of helping students develop their own internal controls. Moreover, the program still takes a "cognitive" perspective toward classroom management (Shimahara & Sakai, 1995); in other words, it focuses on the creation and teaching of norms, rather than adopting a perspective that attends to students' affective needs.

Let us fast forward once more—this time to 1996. In "First, the Rapport—Then the Rules" (1996), Canter notes that changes in the students of the 1990s require teachers to alter their classroom management strategies:

> *To be successful, a discipline plan should be built on a foundation of mutual trust and respect. That's the fundamental change in the Assertive Discipline plan of the '90s. Before the rules, rewards, and consequences can be effective, you have to build relationships with students and earn their respect. Too many kids have been let down by the adults in their lives. You have to demonstrate that you're fair, that you stick by your word, that you care.*

If this statement had come from Thomas Gordon (1974) or Haim Ginott (1972), it would not have been so surprising; after all, these writers see establishing positive relationships between teachers and students as the *sine qua non* of classroom management. For the preeminent champion of teacher's rights to highlight caring, however, suggests that a major change is occurring in our thinking about classroom management. In general terms, this change can be characterized as *a shift from a paradigm that emphasizes the creation and application of rules to regulate student behavior to one that also attends to students' needs for nurturing relationships and opportunities for self-regulation.* The new paradigm integrates the "masculine" and "technicist" approach of the process–product research on teacher effectiveness (Bowers & Flinders, 1990) and the "feminine" responsive approach grounded in an ethic of caring (Noddings, 1986, 1992).

This shifting paradigm is well represented by the four programs described in this book—the Classroom Organization and Management Program (COMP), Consistency Management & Cooperative Discipline (CMCD), Judicious Discipline (JD), and the Three Cs (Cooperative Community, Constructive Conflict Resolution, and Civic Values). Not surprisingly, all of these programs also reflect an *earlier* paradigm shift that can be traced back to Kounin's classic 1970 study on the relationship between the characteristics of teachers' "desists" (i.e., their responses to inappropriate behavior) and their success in terminating "deviant" behavior. Unexpectedly, Kounin found that teachers' desists had little to do with students' behavior; rather, order was dependent on teachers' ability to *manage the activities of the group*—their ability to establish and maintain focus, to sustain momentum and pacing, and to implement smooth transitions from lesson to lesson. The publication of Kounin's research, combined with the early studies of Evertson, Emmer, and colleagues (1980, 1982, 1985) led educators to move from emphasizing disciplinary interventions to emphasizing the importance of prevention. "Discipline" *per se* became one topic within the larger field of classroom management, which now began to include topics such as the physical design of classrooms, managing instructional formats, pacing, motivation, and family–school relationships.

COMP, CMCD, JD, and the Three Cs all emphasize the prevention of inappropriate behavior. Indeed, Evertson and Harris (Chapter 4) write that one of the "four philosophical pillars" on which COMP is based is that "effective classroom management is preventing problems rather than handling them after the fact" (p. 82). Similarly, Freiberg (Chapter 5) observes that

> *classroom management is* problem prevention *rather than* problem solving, *thus reducing the need for intervention. Teachers can prevent or minimize future discipline problems by spending time before the start of the school year and during the first days and weeks establishing opportunities for students to achieve high standards for behavior as well as academics.* (p. 82)

In addition to this emphasis on prevention, however, the programs reflect more recent shifts in our thinking about classroom management. Indeed, I would argue that it is precisely these shifts that constitute the changing paradigm: (1) from management as a "bag of tricks" that can be acquired in a two-hour "in-service" to management as a body of knowledge and a set of practices that require thoughtful decision making and reflection; (2) from managerial practices designed to obtain compliance to practices that foster students' capacity for self-regulation; (3) from a purely cognitive perspective that emphasizes the importance of developing and teaching rules to a combined cognitive–affective perspective that also recognizes the need to establish caring, trusting relationships between students and teachers and among students; and (4) from management strategies that support a view of classrooms as places for routinized, teacher-directed work to management strategies that are consistent with a view of classrooms as places for active, student-centered learning (Table 8-1.) The next section of this chapter examines these shifting positions more closely.

Defining the New Paradigm

From Management as a "Bag of Tricks" to Management as Thoughtful Decision Making

For too many teachers, classroom management consists of "recipes" gleaned from two-hour in-service workshops where they are taught to put marbles in the jar, dispense stickers and stars, allow well-behaved students to pick from "the treasure chest," and not to smile until Christmas. Although these tips and tricks may prove helpful in achieving classroom order, they do not represent a coherent, systematic approach to classroom management. In contrast, the four programs described in this book view classroom management as a process that requires thoughtful decision making, informed by research and sensitive to contextual differences. Evertson and Harris (Chapter 4), for example, write that "each teacher must integrate research findings with his or her own experience and knowledge of academics and students, to develop, monitor, and continually refine effective classroom management" (p. 67). Similarly, Freiberg (Chapter 5) stresses that CMCD helps teachers create solutions that are unique to their own teaching context. He cites a beginning teacher who noted that CMCD did not give the students in her class a "model to teach like anyone else," but suggestions that allow them to teach like themselves, "only better" (p. 94). McEwan, Gathercoal, and Nimmo (Chapter 6) write that classroom management has moved beyond the question of how to bring about isolated student behaviors, to "a broad range of decision making and problem solving activities that are useful in maintaining safe and equitable learning environments" (p. 99).

Because classroom management is more than a "bag of tricks," these chapters also make it clear that becoming an effective classroom manager requires long-term study, reflection, and interaction among colleagues. Judicious Discipline, for example, introduces teachers to basic concepts and principles in September; from November through January, psychologists and counselors assist faculty and staff to learn more about JD, and faculty hold meetings to brainstorm democratic methods for dealing with problematic behavior. As McEwan, Gathercoal, and Nimmo (Chapter 6) write, it is not only critical to provide instruction for *students* about the concepts of JD; it is also critical to provide "opportunities for teachers and administrators to participate in some profes-

TABLE 8-1 Themes of the New Paradigm, as Reflected in the Four Programs

	COMP	CMCD	Three CS	JD
From management as a "bag of tricks," to management as a decision-making process that requires ongoing professional development, reflection, and collaboration	"The teacher's thoughtful decision-making is the basis of effective classroom management" (p. 65); provides teachers with an extended initial workshop; technical assistance is provided during the six to eighteen weeks in which teachers implement ideas they have learned	Helps teachers create solutions that are unique to their own teaching context; provides thirty-six hours of "just-in-time" professional development during the first year of implementation	Encourages teachers to meet weekly in colleagial teaching teams and study groups	Considers "a broad range of decision-making and problem-solving activities that are useful in maintaining safe and equitable learning environments" (p. 99)
From management for obedience to management for self-regulation	Guides teachers to develop a classroom environment in which students learn to take responsibility for their behavior; teachers are taught ways of involving students in developing rules as well as communication techniques to help students solve their own problems	Supports teachers in creating a prodemocratic environment for both decision making and the operations of the classroom; students are allowed to become real partners in the classroom	Explicit goal is developing self-regulation; teachers learn the steps involved in helping students learn how to regulate their own behavior and to be joint architects in matters that affect them; students must be trained to manage conflicts constructively, so that they are empowered to solve their own problems and to regulate their own and their classmates' behavior	Introduces students to the rights of freedom, justice, and equality; constitutional language is used to mediate problems between students and teachers so that the classroom can become a "participatory democratic community"
From management that emphasizes rules to management that also attends to caring and trusting relationships	Teachers learn ways of developing positive classroom climates and evaluating the climate of their own classrooms	Emphasizes caring, cooperation, and community; teachers are taught to honor the child while correcting the behavior; argues that trust underlies cooperation and self-discipline	Emphasizes that classroom management must be based on community, personal commitment, and caring	Promotes a language of equity and tolerance in order to build trusting and caring human relationships
From management for work-oriented classrooms to management for learning-oriented classrooms	Stresses that "students are an active part of the learning environment" (p. 67). Teachers are encouraged to examine different formats for student academic activities, including cooperative small group, student pairs, centers and stations, and individualized instruction	Helps teachers create a learning environment that allows for interaction in different group settings, student talk, and student self-governing behaviors; changes in instruction require parallel changes in the roles of students and teachers	One of the three Cs is cooperative learning—by its very nature, an instructional format that encourages students to be active and engaged	Does not explicitly address curriculum and instruction, but its approach is clearly consistent with a learner-centered classroom and a view of learners as active, competent decision makers.

153

sional development workshops during which they can share strategies, air concerns and discuss their successes in the area of classroom management" (p. 109).

The other programs are equally adamant about the importance of providing ongoing study opportunities. CMCD provides "just-in-time" staff development that is designed to mesh with the needs of teachers and students (p. 85). Initial workshops are held in the spring of the year "when the need for caring and peaceful learning environments are at a premium" (p. 85). During the first year of implementation, a full thirty-six contact hours are provided to each CMCD program school, and teacher interviews indicate that participants spend many hours on their own developing classroom materials, observing one another, engaging in self-assessment, and in planning the implementation of the program. The Three Cs encourages teachers to meet weekly in collegial teaching teams and study groups in order to increase instructional expertise, engage in continuous staff development, and provide a vehicle for the socialization of new teachers. COMP introduces teachers to its six topic areas in an initial workshop lasting two nine-hour days or three seven-hour ones. During the next six to eighteen weeks, teachers implement ideas—with technical assistance, if needed, from the workshop leader; they then meet in a follow-up session to reflect on what has occurred.

It is clear that these four management programs embody current thinking about professional development, a topic that has itself undergone substantial changes in the last several years. (In fact, the changes have been so dramatic that a book circulated by the Association for Supervision and Curriculum Development [Sparks & Hirsh, 1997] begins with a chapter entitled "A Paradigm Shift in Staff Development.") Essentially, the new professional development paradigm recognizes that significant educational reform can take place only if teachers are actively involved in sustained and collaborative study directed to their needs and concerns; if teacher research, joint planning, and study groups replace one-shot, one-size-fits-all in-service workshops conducted by outside experts; and if those responsible for staff development provide facilitation and consultation in addition to training. At the very basis of this paradigm shift is the belief that teachers need the very same opportunities for a wide array of learning experiences that students need. As Lieberman (1995) writes:

> [P]eople learn best through active involvement and through thinking about and becoming articulate about what they have learned. Processes, practices, and policies built on this view of learning are at the heart of a more expanded view of teacher development that encourages teachers to involve themselves as learners—in much the same way as they wish their students would. (p. 592)

From Obedience to Self-Regulation

In 1969, when the Gallup organization administered its first opinion poll about public education, "lack of discipline" was cited as the leading problem of the schools (Ravitch, 1983). Twenty-eight polls later, this public perception has not changed—"lack of discipline" still heads the list (Rose, Gallup, & Elam, 1997), followed by two related problems—use of drugs and fighting/violence/gangs. These three disciplinary problems (along with "lack of financial support") were the only ones to reach double digit figures (fifteen percent, fourteen percent, and twelve percent, respectively).

Concern about discipline is shared by teachers, many of whom report increasing problems. A study conducted for the Center for Education Statistics (1987), for example, found that forty-four percent of public school teachers reported more disruptive classroom behavior in their schools than five years earlier. Almost one-third of teachers stated that they had seriously considered leaving teaching because of student misbehavior. Similarly, in a study of 720 public schools conducted by the National School Boards Association (see Portner, 1994), eighty-two percent of the districts reported that school violence had increased in the past five years. Furthermore, the report indicated that violence is no longer confined to schools in inner cities, but affects rural and suburban districts as well.

Faced with the growing discipline problems, teachers and administrators have increasingly turned to approaches based on the principles of behavioral psychology; and rules, rewards, and penalties have been instituted as a means for bringing about obedience. (Witness the popularity of *Assertive Discipline.*) In reaction, other educators have proposed that the question should not be how to control students, but rather, how to prepare them to live ethical lives. Covaleskie (1993), for example, argues that a discipline program

> *that teaches children that they are simply expected to obey rules, even legitimate and duly established rules, fails the children and the larger society, even if it meets the needs of the adults in a school. A discipline program cannot be judged merely by asking whether it does a good job of keeping children out of trouble in school....Children must develop a framework within which they can make good choices about how to act, and we must help them do so. (p. 320)*

Covaleskie adds that teaching children that something is wrong *because there is a rule against it* is not the same as teaching them that there is a rule against it *because it is wrong,* and helping them understand why this is so.

Reflecting the changing paradigm, the four programs described in this book eschew behavioral approaches designed to bring about unthinking obedience in favor of approaches designed to develop moral responsibility. Judicious Discipline introduces students to the rights of freedom, justice, and equality. Constitutional language is used to mediate problems between students and teachers, so that the classroom can become a participatory democratic community. Students are taught a common language of civility, based on rights and responsibilities, that they can use to resolve conflicts peacefully and constructively. Similarly, the goal of CMCD is to create productive learning environments that build student self-discipline. The program supports teachers in creating a democratic environment for both decision-making and the operations of the classroom. By emphasizing Prevention, Caring, Cooperation,

Organization, and Community—the five themes of the program—students are allowed to become real partners in the classroom.

COMP (Chapter 4) also guides teachers to develop a classroom environment "where students learn to take responsibility for their decisions, actions, and learning" (p. 61). Although teachers are still viewed as authoritative leaders in the classroom, they are taught ways to involve students in both developing and teaching rules in order to promote student ownership and investment. When teachers consider "positive consequences" such as praise, the emphasis is on learning patterns that help students develop feelings of ability and competence ("Johnny, the way you are sitting facing front, looking, and listening will help you learn"), rather than those that foster dependence on adult approval ("I like the way Johnny is sitting in his seat"). When they reflect on ways of dealing with inappropriate behavior, they learn not only about *negative* consequences—penalties—but also about *corrective* consequences—strategies for helping students to monitor their own behavior (e.g., teaching students to set a goal and keep track of the times they meet the goal). In the follow up session, participants examine the topic of "Climate, Communication, and Student Self-Management Strategies." At this time, they practice one-on-one communication techniques to help students solve problems, and they consider ways of helping students assume even greater responsibility for managing their own behavior and learning.

The Three Cs is equally explicit about the goal of developing self-regulation. The program is designed to teach students the competencies and skills required to regulate their own and their schoolmates' behavior. As Johnson and Johnson (Chapter 7) point out: "Students are empowered to solve their own problems and regulate their own and their classmates' behavior when they are involved in cooperative efforts, manage conflicts constructively, and base their actions on civic values" (p. 121).

Given the emphasis on self-regulation, it is not surprising that the four programs are skeptical about the appropriateness or usefulness of external rewards. In the chapter on CMCD (Chapter 5), Freiberg states that "the need to reward students at every turn to get their cooperation is a shallow, short-term response to a long-term need of creating responsible citizens" (p. 77). COMP has teachers consider "possible counterproductive effects of tangible rewards" (p. 68). The Johnson and Johnson (Chapter 7) take an even stronger position: Because behavioral theory assumes that students are selfish and self-centered and that they seek to maximize their rewards and minimize their punishments, schools that adopt behavioral approaches may, in fact, create a self-fulfilling prophecy.

From Teaching Rules to Developing Trust and Caring

Nell Noddings (1984, 1986, 1992) has examined what it means to care and be cared for and how caring functions in an educational context. Contending that caring—not control—is central to the teacher–student relationship, Noddings recommends that we "relax the impulse to control" (1992, p. 174) and give students more responsibility to govern their own classrooms and schools. For Noddings, the job of schools is *to care for our children* and to produce "competent, caring, loving, and lovable people" (1992, p. 174).

The importance of developing trust and establishing positive relationships with students has been the hallmark of humanist approaches to classroom management represented by Gordon's (1974) *Teacher Effectiveness Training,* Dreikurs, Grunwald, and Pepper's (1982) *Maintaining Sanity in the Classroom,* Rogers and Freiberg's (1994) *Freedom to Learn,* and Glasser's (1965) *Reality Therapy, Schools without Failure* (1969), *Control Theory in the Classroom* (1985), and *The Quality School* (1990). More dominant approaches to classroom management, however, have been "cognitive" in orientation. In *Learning to Teach in Two Cultures,* Shimahara and Sakai (1995) compare American strategies of classroom management with those that predominate in Japan. In America, they write, management strategies emphasize "the creation and application of rules to regulate student behavior":

> *Successful classroom management is predicated upon students' ability to develop cognitive linkages between the rules created for them and the goals to be achieved…We are struck by the fact that there are so many rules stipulated in the handbooks for students, teachers, and parents. What is enunciated here is the codification of acceptable behavior. (p. 79)*

America's cognitive approach contrasts vividly with that of Japan, where the approach is more interpersonal. Instead of codifying acceptable behavior, the Japanese approach to classroom management emphasizes

> *emotional ties, interpersonal relations, character development, and moral sentiments. Its success does not depend on many rules, but on a sense of trust and interdependency between the classroom teacher and his or her students and among the students. (p. 79)*

Despite (or *because of*) the predominance of the cognitive approach, caring emerges as a recurring theme in both public and professional perspectives of teaching. Films like *To sir with love* and *Stand and deliver* portray teachers who are able to transform disaffected, failing, and unruly classes through caring and dedication (and certainly no courses in classroom management). However, the importance of caring also emerges in research on students' and teachers' attitudes toward school (e.g., Cohln & Kottkamp, 1993; Phelan, Davidson, & Cao, 1992; Weinstein, 1989).

The development of caring relationships is also a major theme in the programs described in this book. In Chapter 5, on CMCD, for example, Freiberg writes: "Students want to know how much you care, not how much you know" (p. 83). Stressing the need for teachers to honor the child while correcting the behavior, CMCD stresses that trust underlies cooperation and self-discipline. Similarly, the goal of the Three Cs program is to "change from a classroom management paradigm based on selfishness and egocentrism to one based on community, personal commitment, and caring" (p. 142). The means for achieving this goal are cooperative learning and conflict resolution. During cooperative learning, students can contribute to each other's "well-being and quality of life" (p. 129), while conflict resolution ensures that conflicts do not "destroy relationships and tear the cooperative system apart" (p. 133). Underlying both cooperative learning and conflict resolution are the civic values necessary for a community to flourish—"commitment, responsibility, respect, integrity, caring, compassion, and appreciation of diversity" (p. 140).

Although caring is not as explicit a theme in the chapters by Evertson and Harris (Chapter 4) or by McEwan, Gathercoal, and Nimmo (Chapter 6), it is clear that both COMP and JD seek to build positive relationships between teachers and students. COMP's final module, "Climate, Communication, and Student Self-Management Strategies," has teachers consider ways of developing positive classroom climate, evaluate the climate of their own classrooms, and explore ways to involve their students in evaluating that climate. Judicious Discipline has teachers use a language of equity and tolerance to build learning environments that are safe, respectful, and productive. To teachers concerned about the amount of time required by JD, McEwan, Gathercoal, and Nimmo respond: "There is no quick path to the establishment of trusting, caring human relationships" (p. 116).

From Work-Oriented Classrooms to Learning-Oriented Classrooms

The four programs described here reflect classroom management approaches that are consistent with a view of the classroom as a place for *learning* rather than as a place for *work* (Marshall, 1992). In "work-oriented classrooms," students engage in routinized activities; they focus on learning discrete facts, answering questions with right answers, and completing specific products to the teacher's specifications. Work-oriented classrooms are quiet and smoothly functioning—like a "well-oiled machine" (Evertson & Randolph, 1995). In contrast, "learning-oriented classrooms" are often noisy, with the potential for conflict or disagreement—"a bee-hive of activity" (Evertson & Randolph, 1995). Here, students not only listen and follow directions, they also challenge answers, generate questions, discuss with peers, and share ideas.

COMP, CMCD, JD, and the Three Cs are all consistent with the academic tasks and activities characteristic of learning-oriented classrooms—collaborative learning, problem-centered instructional activities, peer-tutoring, opportunities for choice, and "hands-on" activities. In these programs, good classroom management is not achieved at the *expense* of good instruction; rather it supports and facilitates good instruction. The authors of these chapters recognize that problem solving does not take place in a setting that values silence. In Chapter 5, Freiberg, for example, notes that traditional inner-city classrooms are often characterized by lack of interaction among students. Rather than applauding the silence, however, Freiberg urges teachers to create a learning environment that allows "interaction in different group settings, student talk, and student self-governing behaviors" (p. 95), and to encourage higher level learning activities.

Similarly, Evertson and Harris (Chapter 4) stress that "students are an active part of the learning environment, and classroom management must take into account student differences" in attention spans and learning modalities (p. 67). COMP encourages teachers to examine seven possible formats for student academic activities: whole group, teacher-led small group, cooperative small group, noncompetitive small group, student pairs, centers and stations, and individualized instruction.

The Shifting Paradigm: Antecedents and Implications

It is interesting to speculate about the reasons for this change in our thinking—from a paradigm of rules, rewards, and penalties to a paradigm of self-regulation and caring. One possible (and somewhat cynical) explanation is that we are witnessing nothing more than the customary swing of the educational pendulum. From this perspective, it is only to be expected that enthusiasm for stars, stickers, popcorn, and pizza parties would eventually wane while approaches that shun external rewards and emphasize self-discipline gather strength. Movement away from behavioral approaches is especially understandable given the value of individualism and the suspicion of control that are so deeply rooted in American society. Consider Render, Padilla, and Krank's (1989) contention that "the goal of education in a democracy should be to produce self-disciplined, responsible persons who never blindly comply with the demands of an authority figure" (p. 627). Boostrom (1991) puts it more bluntly: "Living as we do in a society that values freedom, individuality, and personal responsibility, we are conditioned to think of following directions as a mindless, toadying approach to life." (p. 199).

Even if we accept the cynic's interpretation of the paradigm shift as an inevitable swing of the pendulum, we still need to ask why the oscillation is occurring at this time. At least two factors appear to be involved. The first is our dismay with contemporary societal trends. Increasing concern about violence, for example, has led educators to emphasize the importance of teaching students to solve conflicts constructively and peacefully. Concern about poverty, family instability, and substance abuse has resulted in efforts to make schools "safe havens" (see *Educational Leadership,* October 1997)—orderly, caring communities in which students can develop trust and security. Concern about irresponsibility, crime, and greed has propelled attempts to foster self-discipline, respect, and understanding of democratic principles.

A second factor is our growing recognition that behavioral approaches to management do not mesh with current thinking about curriculum and instruction. McCaslin and Good (1992) write:

> *To the extent that progressive school districts have responded to articulate calls for curriculum reform (e.g., documents like* Everybody Counts *and* Becoming a Nation of Readers*), educators have created an oxymoron: a curriculum that urges problem solving and critical thinking and a management system that requires compliance and narrow obedience. The management*

system at least dilutes, if not obstructs, the potential power of the curriculum for many of our students. Students are asked to think and understand, but in too many classrooms they are asked to think noiselessly, without peer communication or social exchange." (p. 12)

Jones (1996) notes this same disparity between curriculum and management: "Despite student-centered additions to curriculum and instruction such as whole-language, self-regulated learning, and cooperative learning, student discipline is still viewed largely as providing rewards and consequences to students" (p. 504).

It seems apparent that the paradigm shift reflects growing awareness of the need to create a better match between instruction and management. Indeed, aligning instruction and management may even bolster the impact of the reform curriculum in schools. A study by Freiberg, Connell, and Lorentz (1997), for example, demonstrated that mathematics achievement in seven elementary schools was greater when a constructivist mathematics program was combined with CMCD than when the same mathematics program was implemented alone.

If approaches to management are to be consistent with curriculum and instruction, the two will have to be better integrated in professional development and teacher education programs. Both preservice and in-service teachers must not only study learner-centered instruction (e.g., "hands-on" inquiry activities in mathematics, cooperative learning, the use of centers and stations, problem-based instruction), they must also examine strategies for avoiding or minimizing the managerial "hazards" (Carter, 1985) that such instruction presents. *Complex, nonroutinized instruction has far greater potential for disorder than instruction that is teacher directed and predictable.* If concerns about noise, disorder, and lack of control are not addressed, it is unlikely that teachers will work to create learning-oriented classrooms.

Final Comments

The chapters on COMP, CMCD, JD, and the Three Cs generate both optimism and concern. The optimism derives from the fact that serious evaluation efforts have accompanied the development and implementation of these programs. Experimental studies conducted during the years since 1982 have repeatedly demonstrated the ability of COMP to change both teacher and student behavior. Research on CMCD reveals increased student and teacher attendance, increased student achievement, and reduced discipline referrals. The Mankato Action Research Project suggests that JD can facilitate the development of student autonomy and responsibility. Studies of the Three Cs program indicate that training enables students to engage in problem solving rather than win–lose negotiations; moreover, training results in a decrease in discipline problems and an increase in achievement. Evaluation efforts like these demonstrate the efficacy of these programs across a wide spectrum of school settings. Because these are not untested models of classroom management, developed far from the reality of classrooms, we can be more confident that they will survive and thrive.

Nonetheless, there is still cause for concern. In many ways, the chapters in this volume echo an earlier reform movement that also stressed active learning, self-regulation, and collaboration. In the late 1960s, advocates of what came to be called "open education" criticized American schools for their "preoccupation with order and control," "obsession with routine *qua* routine," "absence of noise and movement," "joylessness and repression," and demands for "docility and conformity" (Silberman, 1970). Like the progressive education movement that preceded it, open education eschewed extrinsic reward and teacher direction, assuming instead that "given the opportunity, children will choose to engage in activities which will be of high interest to them" (Barth, 1972, p. 26).

Unfortunately, reality did not always validate these assumptions. In *Open Education and the American School,* Barth (1972) describes an inner-city school in which children were encouraged to make decisions and to take responsibility for their own behavior. With honesty and sensitivity, Barth describes the pattern that emerged all too frequently:

> *A teacher would introduce choice into a classroom situation. The children would exercise choice, take advantage of the situation, and disrupt the classroom. The teacher would then withdraw the choice, often punishing the child as well. Everyone concerned would then feel frustrated and resentful. (p. 138)*

Unfortunately, situations like this were not uncommon. By 1974, enthusiasm had diminished, and open education was accused of lowering academic standards and undermining discipline (Ravitch, 1983). "Back to basics" became the new rallying cry.

Reflecting on the rise and fall of open education, I am apprehensive that the learning-oriented classrooms and the new classroom management paradigm will also fall victim to distortion and excess. As increasing numbers of enthusiasts adopt the language of self-regulation and caring, it is imperative that the authoritarian teacher, whose goal is obedience, not be replaced by the *laissez-faire* teacher, who abdicates responsibility in the name of freedom. Rather, teachers in the new paradigm must be like Baumrind's (1971) "authoritative parent" (McCaslin & Good, 1992). They promote self-discipline, but know how to set limits; they are responsive, yet firm; they explain their standards for behavior and teach students how to meet them.

The new paradigm must not become an excuse for permissiveness. If it does, disruption and disharmony will characterize our classrooms, and the pendulum will swing back rapidly to a paradigm of external control.

References

Barth, R. S. (1972). *Open education and the American school.* New York: Agathon Press, Inc.
Baumrind, D. (1971). Current patterns of parental authority. *Developmental Psychology Monographs, 4*(1, Pt. 2).

Boostrom, R. (1991). The nature and function of classroom rules. *Curriculum Inquiry, 21*(2), 193–216.

Bowers, C. A., & Flinders, D. J. (1990). *Responsive teaching: An ecological approach to classroom patterns of language, culture, and thought.* New York: Teachers College Press.

Cangelosi, J. S. (1993). *Classroom management strategies: Gaining and maintaining students' cooperation* (2nd ed.). New York: Longman.

Canter, L. (1996). First, the rapport—then, the rules. *Learning, 24*(15), 12–13.

Canter, L., & Canter, M. (1976). *Assertive discipline: A take-charge approach for today's educator.* Santa Monica, CA: Canter & Associates, Inc.

Canter, L., & Canter, M. (1992). *Assertive discipline: Positive behavior management for today's classroom.* Santa Monica, CA: Lee Canter & Associates.

Carter, K. (1985, March–April). Teacher comprehension of classroom processes: An emerging direction in classroom management research. Paper presented at the annual meeting of the American Educational Research Association, Chicago, IL.

Center for Educational Statistics. (1987). *Public school teacher perspectives on school discipline.* Washington, DC: OERI Bulletin, Center for Educational Statistics.

Cohln, M. M., & Kottkamp, R. B. (1993). *Teachers: The missing voice in education.* Albany, NJ: State University of New York Press.

Covaleskie, J. F. (1993). Discipline and morality: Beyond rules and consequences. In J. W. Noll (Ed.), *Taking sides: Clashing views on controversial educational issues* (pp. 319–326). Guilford, CT: The Dushkin Publishing Group, Inc. [Reprinted from *The Educational Forum,* Winter 1992, *56* (2)].

Curwin, R. L., & Mendler, A. N. (1989). We repeat, let the buyer beware: A response to Canter. *Educational Leadership, 46*(6), 83.

Doyle, W. (1986). Classroom organization and management. In M. C. Wittrock (Ed.), *Handbook of research on teaching.* (pp. 392–431). New York: Macmillan.

Dreikurs, R., Grunwald, B., & Pepper, F. (1982). *Maintaining sanity in the classroom: Classroom management techniques* (2nd ed.). New York: Harper & Row.

Emmer, E. T., Evertson, C. M., & Anderson, L. M. (1980). Effective classroom management at the beginning of the school year. *The Elementary School Journal, 80*(5), 219–231.

Evertson, C. M., & Emmer, E. T. (1982). Effective management at the beginning of the school year in junior high classes. *Journal of Educational Psychology, 74*(4), 485–498.

Evertson, C. M. (1985). Training teachers in classroom management: An experimental study in secondary school classrooms. *Journal of Educational Research, 79*(1), 51–58.

Evertson, C. M. (1989a). Improving elementary classroom management: A school-based training program for beginning the year. *Journal of Educational Research, 83*(2), 82–90.

Evertson, C. M. (1989b). Classroom organization and management. In M. Reynolds (Ed.), *Knowledge base for the beginning teacher* (pp. 59–70). Pergamon: Oxford.

Evertson, C. M., & Randolph, C. H. (1995). Classroom management in the learning-centered classroom. In A. C. Ornstein (Ed.), *Teaching: Theory and practice* (pp. 118–131). Boston: Allyn & Bacon.

Freiberg, H. J., Connell, M., & Lorentz, J. (March 1997). *The effects of socially constructed classroom management on mathematics achievement.* Paper presented at the annual conference of the American Educational Research Association, Chicago, IL.

Ginott, H. G. (1972). *Teacher and child.* New York: Macmillan.

Glasser, W. (1965). *Reality therapy: A new approach to psychiatry.* New York: Harper & Row.

Glasser, W. (1969). *Schools without failure.* New York: Harper & Row.

Glasser, W. (1985). *Control theory in the classroom.* New York: Harper & Row.

Glasser, W. (1990). *The quality school: Managing students without coercion.* New York: Harper & Row.

Gordon, T. (1974). *T.E.T.: Teacher effectiveness training.* New York: Peter H. Wyden.

Jones, V. F. (1996). Classroom management. In J. Sikula, T. Buttery, & E. Guyton (Eds.), *Handbook of research on teacher education* (Vol. 2, pp. 503–521). New York: Macmillan, 503–521.

Jones, V. F., & Jones, L. S. (1998). *Comprehensive classroom management: Creating communities of support and solving problems* (5th ed.). Boston: Allyn & Bacon.

Kounin, J. S. (1970). *Discipline and group management in classrooms.* New York: Holt, Rinehart & Winston.

Lieberman, A. (1995). Practices that support teacher development. *Phi Delta Kappan, 76*(8), 591–596.

Marshall, H. H. (1992). *Redefining student learning: Roots of educational change.* Norwood, NJ: Ablex Publishing Corporation.

McCaslin, M., & Good, T. L. (1992). Compliant cognition: The misalliance of management and instructional goals in current school reform. *Educational Researcher, 21*(3), 4–17.

Noddings, N. (1984). *Caring: A feminine approach to ethics and moral education.* Berkeley, CA: University of California Press.

Noddings, N. (1986). Fidelity in teaching, teacher education, and research for teaching. *Harvard Educational Review, 56,* 496–510.

Noddings, N. (1992). *The challenge to care in schools: An alternative approach to education.* New York: Teachers College Press.

Phelan, A., Davidson, A., & Cao, H. (1992). Speaking up: Students' perspectives on school. *Phi Delta Kappan, 73*(9), 695–704.

Portner, J. (1994, January 12). School violence up over past 5 years, 82% in survey say. *Educational Week,* 9.

Ravitch, D. (1983). *The troubled crusade: American education 1945–1980.* New York: Basic Books.

Render, G. F., Padilla, J. N. M., & Krank, H. M. (1989). Assertive discipline: A critical review and analysis. *Teachers College Record, 90*(4), 607–630.

Rogers, C. R., & Freiberg, H. J. (1994). *Freedom to learn* (3rd ed.). Columbus: Merrill.

Rose, L. C., Gallup, A. M., Elam, S. M. (1997). The 29th annual Phi Delta Kappa/Gallup Poll of the public's attitudes toward the public schools. *Phi Delta Kappan, 79*(1), 41–56.

Shimahara, N. K., & Sakai, A. (1995). *Learning to teach in two cultures.* New York: Garland Publishing, Inc.

Silberman, C. E. (1970). *Crisis in the classroom.* New York: Random House.

Sparks, D., & Hirsh, S. (1997). *A new vision for staff development.* Alexandria, VA: Association for Supervision and Curriculum Development.

Weinstein, C. S. (1989). Teacher education students' preconceptions of teaching. *Journal of Teacher Education, 40*(2), 53–60.

Weinstein, C. S., & Mignano, A. J. (1997). *Elementary classroom management: Lessons from research and practice* (2nd ed.). New York: McGraw-Hill.

Sustaining
the Paradigm

H. JEROME FREIBERG
University of Houston

The Forest from the Trees

There once was a woodcutter who was the best in the village. He could cut ten cords of wood a day. Every day he would sharpen his ax to a shiny fine point. At first he would only sharpen his ax every week, but he saw a woodcutter from another village sharpen his ax every day and increase the number of cords of wood he could cut, so the first woodcutter decided to make the change. He cut more wood than any other woodcutter and was paid very well. Over time, however, the number of cords of wood he cut decreased to nine, then to eight, and, in a short while, to three. But he was working as hard cutting the three cords of wood a day as he had when he was cutting ten cords a day. Although he knew sharpening the ax every day was important, he bought many new things with his new money, and this took time away from his sharpening the ax each evening. He thought it would matter little if he skipped a night or two from sharpening his ax. He also bought many new things on credit, knowing that the money would be there after he cut the wood. He was a very miserable person because he was paid by the number of cords of wood he cut, not how hard he worked. Now he was working to pay for the items he bought on credit. Because the number of cords was much lower, many of the people began to buy their wood from another woodcutter. He told his plight to his friend, a farmer. His friend listened patiently to the woodcutter's story and smiled. He looked over by the tree and saw the woodcutter's ax and picked it up and examined the blade. The farmer exclaimed, "You are cutting fewer cords of wood because your ax is dull; the blade must be sharpened." "I know that," said the woodcutter. "But I don't have time to sharpen my ax, I have all this wood to cut."

This parable reflects the inability of the woodcutter to sustain the paradigm shift that allowed him to become more productive and be a leader. He lost his focus (the need to cut more wood—the trees) without seeing the larger picture (continuing to sharpen his ax—the forest). Sustaining the new classroom management paradigm presented in this book requires an understanding of the broader picture. Each of the five models (COMP, Consistency Management & Cooperative Discipline, Judicial Discipline, and three Cs) place the learner at the center of their classroom management models. The paradigm of student-centeredness is not new. It has been a topic of discussion, and school reform efforts for most of the twentieth century. From John Dewey (*Democracy in Education*) to Carl Rogers (*Freedom to Learn*) to John Goodlad (*A Place Called School*), the student has alternately been the center of attention or the object to be shaped by the teacher. Arthur Perry, who wrote a book for school principals in 1908, reflects on the same issues: Within these necessary limitations, pupils should have a maximal amount of freedom (p. 167). Regarding departmentalization at the elementary school and its impact on the student, Perry (1908) states:

> *The subjects are taught instead of the pupils. There is a danger the child is lost sight of, and the subject becomes the center of the teacher's interest. She becomes the teacher of "arithmetic" instead of the teacher of "Seven A Boys." (p. 187)*

Cuban (1990) studied the pendulum swing from teacher-centered to student-centered instruction and learning, which he reports in an article entitled. *Reforming Again, Again and Again.* He sees school reform efforts as a swinging of the pendulum from teacher-centered to student-centered reflecting the social, and political patterns in American society. He concludes that: "Reforms do return again, again and again. Not exactly as before or under the same conditions, but they persist. It is of even greater importance that few reforms aimed at the classroom make it past the door permanently" (p. 11). Cuban proposes that, "We can do better by gathering data on particular reforms and tracing their life history in particular classrooms, schools, districts and regions" (p. 12).

Learning from the Past or Repeating It

There are three significant differences that distinguish current models for changing the classroom management paradigm presented in *Beyond Behaviorism* to past efforts to change both discipline and instruction:

1. Several of the programs described in this text have moved beyond theory to models that have university and school-based organizations behind them, highly refined staff development components, materials that have been classroom tested, and support systems with multiple sites linked together by common programmatic experiences. They also bring a broad base of experience to future sites.

2. Some of the models presented in *Beyond Behaviorism* already meet this criteria for longitudinal data. For example, Fashola and Slavin (1998), in their follow-up review in *Phi Delta Kappan* article entitled: "Schoolwide Reform Models: What Works?" reviewed 13 national school reform models. The Consistency Management & Cooperative Discipline Model was one of only four school reform models to meet their criteria for gains in student achievement. In addition to the CMCD model, COMP and 3 C's have multiyear or multisite data that could be utilized for school district personnel to compare program effectiveness.

3. There is a body of knowledge that has been developed since the late 1960s that was not available to the innovators of educational reform efforts during most of the twentieth century. Other professions—medicine, law, or accounting, for example—have slowly changed their paradigms as knowledge has been built based on sustainable and verifiable research. The education profession has been slower in developing its knowledge base. However, this limitation seems to be improving with the development of research centers, laboratories, the focus on student learning, and with the elevation of education to the national public agenda.

Lessons from the History of Medicine

In the short term, it is easier to keep the status quo than to change. The history of reform in education has been more a pendulum than an upward spiral. The pendulum moves forward, then back to its original state. Whereas reform efforts in other professions, for example medicine, have spiraled from primitive and ineffective to sophisticated and highly effective, education seems to have followed a path that leads it back and forth rather than forward and upward.

The advent of antibiotics, especially penicillin, gave physicians tools to actually cure people from disease. The profession, however, was preparing for this change long before the invention of antibiotics. According to Lewis Thomas (1979), a medical historian, in the 1830s the medical profession discovered that the "greater part of medicine was nonsense" (p. 159). In most cases people went to hospitals to die, not to get well. Almost all of medicine was based on trial and error, and even the methods that were highly ineffective "lasted decades even centuries before being given up" (p. 159). The medical profession was in such disrepute at the turn of the twentieth century that physicians looked for ways to give themselves greater prestige and credibility. They borrowed the term *doctor* from the universities and bestowed a "doctor of medicine" on themselves. The art of medicine only became the science of medicine with the "meticulous, objective, even cool observations of sick people" (p. 159). It is hard to imagine in today's high-tech world of medicine that as late as 1930, most physicians did not believe they could treat disease and actually cure patients. Joseph Lister, who is credited with correlating the unsanitary conditions of hospitals with postsurgery infection, had to bear the ridicule of his fellow physicians who refused to understand that the fatal hospital infections were caused by tiny organisms that could not be seen. The changing paradigm in medicine occurred when professional knowledge was built and disseminated widely to both physicians and the public. Medicine is again going through another paradigm shift, with the realization that technology alone is not enough to take humankind to a healthier life.

The New Paradigm: Looking In Classrooms

What would the new classroom management paradigm look like if you walked into a classroom or school? There would be classroom climate as well as organizational differences. We send messages to students about how we wish to interact, messages that are delivered personally through our nonverbal communication, eye contact, and body language; and verbally through the tone of our voice. We communicate visually in terms of how the classroom is organized. For example, a classroom with bare walls, or walls with teacher work alone sends a message to the students that, "this is the teacher's classroom." Selecting the work of a few students for display also sends a message that "only the best need apply." The older the students, the more ingrained the message becomes.

Student Work

An eleventh-grade high school mathematics teacher in a school located in a low income neighborhood of Chicago's west side changed the way she displayed student work. She told the students that they would be asked to select their best work and she would place it on the walls of the classroom. Three students handed in what amounted to scribble. The teacher placed it up along with the other students' work. The next class, they asked if they could have their work returned. When asked why, they indicated they wanted to re-do it and then have it placed on the "wall of fame." The teacher explained that the quality of student mathematics accomplishments has improved significantly as students took greater responsibility for their work and have shown a sense of pride in their efforts. Many of the papers were not "A" but were "B" or "C" work; however, for many students this was a dramatic improvement. Allowing students to select their work for display rather than the teacher making the determination allowed students to reflect on their efforts and see other models of student work.

Whose Rules?

There are necessary but not sufficient conditions for learning. Having an orderly rather than a chaotic environment is a necessary condition for learning for most students, but this is only the beginning. How that order is achieved is the difference between a teacher-centered and person-centered learning environment. There would be rules for the classroom or school, but the rules would be established by the students and the teacher in the classroom and by the larger community within the school. The development of rules could be in the form of a Classroom Constitution or a Magna Carta. Changes could be made in a constitutional convention perhaps midway through the school year. Several of the classroom management models presented in Section II discuss how rules can be developed with, rather than to, students. Student self-discipline will not be achieved if it occurs only when someone in authority is watching. The involvement by the students is the thread that links the four classroom management models and brings about a much more productive and enjoyable learning experience.

What's My Role?

Clearly, your role will change—from that of a director or perhaps dictator to that of a coordinator or facilitator. You will not be giving up power or control, you will be sharing the responsibilities that have been on your shoulders with your students. In the long run, you will actually gain much more than you will lose. This is the response I have received in years of interviews with teachers who have changed their paradigm of thinking and their paradigm of actions. They express relief at not having to be "in control at all times" and not being exhausted at the end of the school day or numb by the end of the school year. Providing greater freedom for students does not mean providing licence to do what ever they want. Freedom has responsibility; licence does not. You are *not* abrogating your responsibilities as an adult and teacher, but rather sharing those responsibilities with your students. Carl Rogers, the first author of *Freedom to Learn* (Rogers & Freiberg, 1994) and developer of the concept of person-centered education, had some important advice about granting freedom:

> *Don't grab freedom if you are uneasy about it. Better to [have] a little freedom that you can be easy with than to try to go all the way in giving your students responsibility for their learning and then getting cold feet and trying to pull it back to yourself. That can be disastrous. It's better to take small steps...that you really mean and can stand by than to take it [freedom] all at once....Giving students freedom means that they are going to make some mistakes in the handling of that responsibility. And that means a complete rethinking of the ordinary classroom procedure...mistakes are the most valuable way of learning, provided the students are encouraged to examine what they did. (C. Rogers, personal communication, 1984)*

The notion of starting small is good advice. There is some degree of the unknown in change and the process will be somewhat new for both students and teacher. A secondary teacher, for example, may want to begin with one or two classes and expand from there. Secondary teachers who have started changing their paradigm about classroom management have reported excellent responses from students. They also report being much more relaxed and effective as professionals. The following example should provide some context for changing the classroom management paradigm.

A 7th grade middle school English teacher: I began with my first-period class. We started slowly, with my asking them about what it would take for the class to work for them. I then told them what it would take for the class to work for me. I was amazed at the overlap. They wanted to know up front what I expected in terms of tests, quantity and quality of work, late assignments, talking in class, and amount and how often they would have homework, where they could sit, grading and whether classroom participation counted. We talked about the best classes and the worst classes. We talked about respect and the need to respect ideas and each other, to listen to and be willing to be an active participant without [verbally] running over other people in the class or being run over. I talked about "my teacher time" and their "student time." Well, this was five months ago and I am amazed at the level of cooperation. I am well ahead of last year in the curriculum; we have class meetings once a week to see how things are going and adjust as needed. We created a classroom constitution and had a constitutional convention when we felt it needed to be changed. I didn't believe it would make a difference, the students really surprised me with their level of maturity and responsibility and I surprised my self with my own willingness to change. This has been a great year and I am sorry to see it end and my students leave to another grade level. I am considering asking my principal to move me to eighth grade so I could have the same students again. I have been teaching for fourteen years and this has been my best year. I feel supported by my students and my students told me they feel supported by me.

The notion that everything works with every student or class is not realistic. In working with one class, the seventh-grade teacher was a able to test her own ideas without being overwhelmed. The idea that students and teachers can work together to support learning is not novel, but it takes some practice and moving beyond what is to what could be.

Pillars of Support

Years ago, the education of students was sustained by five pillars of support: families and the home, culture, religion, community, and the school (Figure 9.1). The high rate of divorce, combined with the economic need for both parents to work outside the home, has shattered the ability of the family to focus on and support the education of their children. Divorce, job changes, and housing mobility resulting from poverty have also destabilized the community. As we move into the twenty-first century it is

FIGURE 9-1   Pillars of Support.

Consistency Management and Cooperative Discipline. © 1998 Consistency Management Associates.

the school that is becoming the primary pillar of support for the child. According to researchers (Pallas, Natriella, & McDill, 1989), if current trends remain the same, by the year 2020, nearly fifty percent of all students will be educationally disadvantaged. Although adult crime and violence has been declining throughout the 1990s, youth violence has grown dramatically and is projected to increase still further through to the year 2020. Although society is asking more of schools and particularly teachers, the older the learner, the less responsibility the student seems to be given in school.

The climate of the classroom is set by the teacher but enhanced and developed by the students. Students look to the teacher for leadership, and there are many different types of leaders, from democratic to *laissez-faire* to autocratic. Read the following poem from the Chinese philosopher Lao Tzu and think about how his view of leadership relates to changing the classroom management paradigm.

A leader is best
When people barely know that he exists,
Not so good when people obey and acclaim him,
Worst when they despise him.
"Fail to honor people
They fail to honor you;"
But a good leader, who talks little,
When his work is done, his aim fulfilled,
They will all say, "We did this ourselves."

Lao Tzu

The doubling of teen suicides from the early 1980s to the late 1990s, growing student alienation, drug abuse, and apathy are symptoms of a greater problem—the lack of freedom for human interaction in schools and classrooms. The sharing of time in the classroom with students, providing the opportunity for students to learn from each other, and creating a level of shared decision making and choice are necessary if students are to become fully functioning individuals.

Granting freedom is not a method, it's a philosophy; and unless you really believe that students can be trusted with responsibility, you won't be successful. Now, you can't build that philosophy out of thin air; you have to build it out of experience. (C. Rogers, personal communication, 1984)

Administrator Role

The field of medicine changed at the turn of the twentieth century as a result of the leadership in the field, with administrators, researchers, and practitioners joining together to improve practice. The teaching profession has the same need. The school principal and district superintendent and other administrators need to be able to change along with the classroom teacher. Two elementary teachers from different schools shared their reaction to a state-mandated formal principal observation of their class-rooms, which are required about the same time of the year across the state of Texas.

Teacher 1: My principal sat in an empty seat and watched as my students handed out materials, organized themselves in groups, discussed assignments and worked with a partner in reading and writing for the time period the principal was in the room. She was very pleased at the level of interaction and cooperation in class. The students were on-task for the entire time period and I spent my time working with small groups. There was a low buzz in the room but it was the productive sound of people working together. The students explained to her what they were doing now and what they had planned to do next, based on their assignment charts they had developed earlier that morning. My classes of "average" students always score very high on the state-mandated tests and I feel its because they have the chance to really learn what they are doing.

Teacher 2: I began changing my classroom management philosophy and approach after attending a series of management workshops. I was amazed at how the students from my challenging inner-city elementary school took to the jobs and responsibil-ities in the classroom. These one-minute managers had to complete job applications and I interviewed all the students for their positions. I realized that not only would they help the class and me in their new roles but they would learn important skills for after high school when they go for job interviews. However, during my princi-pal's observations I noticed she was frowning when my students left their seats near the end of the lesson and began their jobs. She explained to me after the lesson that it was *my job* to hand out papers, take care of materials for students who were absent, and organize the books and folders. I was very deflated by the feedback. I realized that I had changed my way of thinking and was really seeing a change in the behav-ior and motivation levels of my students, but I had not done a very good job of explaining these changes to the principal. I will be looking for a new school this next year because I am not prepared to go back to the way I managed the classroom for the last eighteen years.

The principal can be a source of support and resilience for the faculty and staff or another barrier to improvement. The lack of communication between teacher and principal is evident in the second account. There was little dialog about what was happening with the students and why from the principal's perspective. Very often when teachers attend staff development meetings, the administrators from the school to the district level are absent, drawn to the piles of papers and other administrative work. If change is to occur, however, it must occur at all levels. Changing the para-digm will need everyone's effort.

Conclusions

Behaviorism has a strong history in the American classroom during the twentieth century. It will not be easy to change, and, once changed, it will be harder to sustain. Much like the woodcutter, in the short term, behaviorism seems to solve the question of controlling student behavior; but in the long term it requires teachers to exert greater and greater levels of control and more and more incentives for fewer results. Children begin to expect to receive rewards to comply with what should come naturally. External control applied by the teacher provides few opportunities for children to see models of behavior that come from within and even fewer opportunities to experience self-discipline.

In a world that requires flexibility, independence, and self-discipline, schools of the twentieth century have tended to model the opposite. The models in *Beyond Behaviorism* provide concrete examples of alternatives to teacher as the sole source of discipline. How well this paradigm is sustained during the twenty-first century and for a new millennium may rest with the ability of its developers to create databases that reflect real results, over time, in real classroom and school settings. The sustaining paradigm will also need models that respond to the social and political changes of the society while maintaining fidelity to their fundamental principals and philosophies.

References

Cuban, L. (1990). Reforming Again, Again and Again. *Educational Researcher, 19*(1), 3–13.

Fashola, O., & Slavin, R. (1998). Schoolwide Reform Models: What Works? *Phi Delta Kappan, X*(X), 370–379.

Pallas, A., Natriella, & McDill, E. (1989). The changing nature of the disadvantaged population: Current dimensions and future trends. *Educational Researcher, 8*(5), 16–22.

Rogers, C. R., & Freiberg, H. J. (1994). *Freedom to learn* (3rd ed.). Columbus: Merrill.

Perry, A. (1908). *The management of a city school.* New York: Macmillan.

Thomas, L. (1979). *The medusa and the snail: More notes of a biology watcher.* New York: Viking Press.

Tzu, L. (1962). *The way of life according to Lao Tzu* (W. Bynner, trans.). New York: Capricorn Books.

Index